mana

BUSIN

SUPP

SERVI

or befor

D0533314

managing
BUSINESS
SUPPORT
SERVICES

STRATEGIES FOR OUTSOURCING & FACILITIES MANAGEMENT

JONATHAN REUVID & JOHN HINKS

RECOMMENDED BY
INSTITUTE OF DIRECTORS

Catering and Support Services

CAP GEMINI
ERNST & YOUNG

KOGAN
PAGE

First published in 2001.
This second edition published in 2002.

Kogan Page Ltd
120 Pentonville Road
London N1 9JN
www.kogan-page.co.uk

© Kogan Page and Contributors 2002

British Library Cataloguing in Publication Data
A CIP record for this book is available from the British Library
ISBN 0 7494 3900 9

Typeset by Saxon Graphics Ltd, Derby
Printed and bound in Great Britain by Bell & Bain Ltd, Glasgow

Contents

fmx

The magazine for workplace management

Each issue explores a cross section of subjects relating to buildings, human resources, technology and legislation. Case studies illustrate key topics. Workplace guides act as an introduction to essential topics for both new and experienced buyers. News is covered in a special section. News analysis pages put the latest developments into context. Our product pages offer an up-to-the minute, objective guide to the latest products and services.

To subscribe or enquire about FMX please contact us on **01245 491717** or email us on **fmxsales@wilmington.co.uk**

List of Contributors

Robin Baron is a partner in the IT and e-commerce Department at Fox Williams, a City of London law firm. He has a practice in information systems and technology law, computer law, internet and intranet law, intellectual property law and data protection law. Robin has extensive experience in advising clients on legal issues associated with technology including outsourcing and facilities management. He sees the role of the commercial lawyer as being manager of risk for the client. Clients include: software companies, outsourcing companies, on-line businesses, dotcoms, technology users and purchasers including businesses to outsource services.

Peter Cardwell is Managing Director of FirstPerson Consulting, which specialises in understanding employees as consumers in the workplace. To do this, First Person conducts one of the largest benchmark surveys of its kind in the UK, a rich source of insight into employee motivation and quality of life at work.

Claire Coleman is a solicitor in the Technology Media and Telecoms Department at Denton Wilde Sapte in London. She is part of a 25-strong team within the department, specialising in IT, internet and e-commerce transactions. She has advised both suppliers and users on several major IT Services and outsourcing deals and is qualified as a solicitor both in the UK and Ireland.

Peter Cordy BSc (Hons) MRTPI, MBIFM, FFB Head of Property Services, London Borough of Hillingdon joined the London Borough of Hillingdon in March 2000 as Head of the newly formed Property Services Department, combining the in-house Strategic Property Management, Estates & Valuation, Property Consultancy (Design & Maintenance); Facilities Management (Uxbridge Civic Centre) and Direct Contracts (Security/CCTV, Catering and Cleaning) Groups within one organisational grouping. He has since undertaken a thorough review of property services within Hillingdon and has completed a cross-cutting Best Value Review of the management and use of Hillingdon L.B's Property assets. He is currently engaged in implementing the resulting action plan. He joined Hillingdon L.B from Hertfordshire Constabulary, where he held the position of Head of Estates and Administration. He developed the Constabulary's first Estate Strategy, working closely with the Chief Constable and his 'top team'. As Chairman of the National Police Property Services Managers' Group, he contributed to the development of the Audit Commission's asset management guidance contained in the report 'Action Stations' and has developed an extensive network of contacts within both the public and private sectors as a result. His varied career has embraced a number of local government appointments with Devon, Bedfordshire and Hampshire County Councils, Slough Borough Council and Portsmouth City Council focusing upon Strategic Property Management, Property Review, Facilities Management and planning aspects of land development. He is a member of the British Institute of Facilities Management, and takes an active interest in its affairs, representing the interests of Corporate members on the Council and National Executive Committee. He is currently Chairman of the Institute's Research Committee and has responsibility for the organisation of the research input to the Institute's Annual Conference. He is also a Chartered Town Planner, being a Member of the Royal Town Planning Institute, and has recently been elected a Fellow of the Faculty of Building.

Gerald Davis is President, and **Francoise Szigeti** is Vice President, of the International Centre for facilities (Canada), a non-profit organisation whose mission is to improve the quality and functionality of the places where people work and live.

Professor John Hinks B.Sc. (Hons), M.A., Ph.D., is Professor of Facilities Management at Glasgow Caledonian University. John was the inaugural Director of CABER, the Centre for Advanced Built Environment Research. CABER is the virtual research organisation involving the Building Research Establishment, Glasgow Caledonian University, and The University of Strathclyde. John sits on the editorial boards of the international journals *Facilities* and *Journal of Facilities Management*, and has been Guest Editor for both publications. John also co-authored the RICS Report *Facilities Management and The Chartered Surveyor: Members' Perceptions and Strategic Priorities* with John Kelly and Gavin McDougall.

John's interest in FM originated in the technology of building performance, subsequently expanding to analysing the interaction between facilities management and the business process. John's concern is how to tailor Facilities Management Services to most effectively support changing business priorities. John speaks internationally on strategically aligning FM with business needs, and has advised major organisations including Standard Life Assurance on the strategic assessment of their facilities management services and facilities.

John Kelly is a Chartered Surveyor with the industrial and academic experience. His quantity surveying career began with a national contractor moving to a small architects practice specialising in commercial development and later to an international surveying practice. His academic career began at the University of Reading as a research fellow, moving to Heriot-Watt University as a lecturer and later senior lecturer. His research into value management began in 1983 and continues with the significant support of grants from several research agencies. His numerous publications include the first UK textbook on value management (written with Professor Steven Male of the University of Leeds). Professor Kelly is a firm believer in the principle of putting research into practice and has undertaken value management studies as research consultancy on a variety of construction projects.

Weng Lee is Partner and Head of Global FM at EC Harris. His expertise has been acquired through learning and experience. Weng has developed a strategic view of FM as a business support service and is leading the strategic development in this area at EC Harris, a leading International Capital Projects and facilities Consultancy.

Alexi Marmot and **Joanna Eley** are Directors of AMA Alexi Marmot Associates, specialists in creating new workstyles and new workspace. Many large organisations, blue chip companies and government departments are AMA clients who have been helped to introduce change in their working patterns and radically improved work environments. Alexi and Joanna have co-authored two authoritative books on office design: *Understanding Offices: What Every Manager Needs to Know About Office Buildings* (London: Penguin 1995) and *Office Space Planning: Designing for Tomorrow's Workplace* (New York: McGraw-Hill, 2000).

Elias Mazzawi is a consultant in Cap Gemini Ernst & Young's outsourcing business. The **Cap Gemini Ernst & Young Group** is one of the largest management and IT consulting organisations in the world. The company offers management and IT consulting services, systems integration, and technology development, design and outsourcing capabilities on a global scale to help businesses continue to implement growth strategies and leverage technology in the new economy. In early 2002, the organisation employed more than 56,500 people worldwide and reported 2001 global revenues of more than 8.4 billion euros. Its offers include a comprehensive consulting service around outsourcing which helps clients to develop their strategic thinking on outsourcing – encompassing developing strategic clarity on what to outsource and what to keep in house; quantifying the potential scale of value creation by clarifying the as-is service delivery and highlighting scope for improvement; thinking through how outsourcing could act as an enabler of change; and envisioning fit-for-purpose and innovative deal structures. For more information on this service, please contact Elias Mazzawi on 0870 905 3260. More information about individual service lines, offices and research is available at www.cgey.com

Trevor Payne is the Head of Facilities at the Oxford Radcliffe Hospital NHS Trust (one of the largest acute teaching hospitals in the UK) which has an international reputation as a centre of excellence. He has a professional engineering background, having trained in both Electrical and Plant Engineering, and subsequently took an MSc in FM at the Centre for Facilities Management (CFM), Strathclyde Management Business School, graduating in 1998. He is a member of the British Institute of Facilities Management (BIFM) and a number of national UK learning sets and benchmarking clubs. Trevor is also an active member of HEFMA (Healthcare Estates and Facilities Management Association) and is a member of the national training and development sub-group; he has also submitted papers for their yearbooks. Trevor is responsible for a wide range of facilities services covering four diverse hospital sites within a mixed economy of in-house and outsourced providers. He has particular interest in performance monitoring, benchmarking and facilities strategy and is currently working on best value and a healthcare PFI project. He has recently managed a project for NHS Estates (an executive agency of the Department of Health) entitled 'FM Futures' which will attempt to predict future trends, training/development requirements and service delivery models for healthcare FM as part of the Developing Capacity project. He regularly presents papers at seminars and conferences on matters relating to FM and is a member of the editorial board of the journal Facilities Management (www.irseclipse.co.uk). His first book *'Facilities Management – A Strategy for Success'* was published in May 2000. Early in 2000 Trevor worked on an international healthcare project that took him to Morocco and Bulgaria and in October 2000 presented a paper at the 16th Congress of the International Federation of Hospital Engineering in Sydney, Australia.

Dr. Marie-Cécile Puybaraud PhD, PG Cert, BSc(Hons), ACIOB, ABIFM, ILTM is a Senior Research Fellow at the University of West of England, Bristol, where she works as a Facilities Innovation Director in partnership with Johnson Controls. Prior to this, she was the Course Director of the MSc in Facilities Management and led the Facilities Management Research Group at Heriot-Watt University, Edinburgh. Her expertise is in Fire Safety Management & Business Continuity Planning in facilities. She is also specialised on the aspects of the Legislation for the construction industry in the EU; Contractual Law & Administration of UK and International construction contracts, and Strategic Procurement. Marie-Cécile's research interests focused on the role of management in fire safety scenarios and fire safety management in facilities. Her groundbreaking and unique research in the field of fire safety on construction sites lead to the creation of a *Fire Safety Management Model* for the Construction Industry through an interactive CD-Rom. She obtained her PhD in July 2001 and was awarded the MacFarlane Medal for best doctorate of the year, excellence in research and major contribution to research. She is currently extending her expertise by collaborating with fire safety experts in the UK, France, Australia and China.

Marie-Cécile is an associate member of the Chartered Institute of Building (CIOB) and the British Institute of Facilities Management (BIFM) and a member of the Institute of Learning and Teaching.

Jonathan Reuvid graduated in economics at Oxford and was employed as an economist by the French national oil company, Total, at the time of its UK market entry. From there he moved into investment banking, financial consultancy and marketing strategy. After seven years working for a US multinational engineering group with European general management responsibility, he engaged in the development of joint ventures and technology transfers in Northern China, where he remains involved. In 1989 Jonathan embarked on a new career in business publishing, editing and writing a series of international business books with Kogan Page. He has a developing interest in the delivery of adult learning on the Internet.

Phil Roberts is Head of Strategic Facilities Management for one of the largest UK Local Government organisations. He is a past Chairman of the Research Committee of the British Institute of Facilities Management and also a member of the Board of the International Facility Management Association. He is a regular speaker and author on the practice and development of Facilities Management.

Ken Robertson is Principal of KLR Consulting Inc., Vancouver, British Columbia, Canada. KLR provides consulting in alternative officing, project management and general management. Mr Robertson has an MBA degree from Simon Fraser University, holds the Information Processing Systems Professional certification through the Canadian Information Processing Society and is a member of the Project Management Institute. For the past ten years Ken has been working with organisations to help them gain greater business value for their corporate service functions. In the past few years, he has specialised in work transformation and often acts as the 'glue' that brings together human resources, information technology and facilities management functions. For more information on work transformation, read Ken Robertson's book 'Work Transformation: Planning and Implementing the New Workplace' published by HNB Publishing in New York.

Sodexho Alliance is the largest and most progressive catering and support services provider in the world, with a turnover approaching 11 billion euros, and more than 314,000 employees in 70 countries. Gardner Merchant became part of the Alliance in 1995 and adopted the Sodexho name for its operations early in the year 2000. In the UK and Ireland, they provide catering, education, healthcare, leisure and defence sectors. More than 53,000 staff serve 3500 client locations.

Paul Aitchison, a Chartered Engineer, BSc (Hons), MBA (London Business School), has been involved with Sodexho's PFI activity since its commencement in 1994, bringing a wealth of NHS Estates and General Management experience which he gained prior to joining the company in 1994. As Director PFI, Sodexho Limited, Paul now has the responsibility of leading the company's PFI development, reporting directly to the board. As the senior company representative, Paul was instrumental in assisting with the financial closure of South Manchester University Hospital PFI Project in August 1998, Hereford Hospital in April 1999, King's College Hospital in August 2000 and Fife Schools, which reached financial close in September 2001. He is a Director of the Special Purpose Vehicle companies for each project.

John Dyson is Managing Director of Safegard, provider of Food Safety, Health and Safety and Environmental Management Services to Sodexho in the UK and Ireland as well as a wide range of clients external to Sodexho. John is a Corporate Member of the Chartered Institute of Environmental Health and a Fellow of the Royal Institute of Public Health.

Martin Gash is HR Director for Sodexho, covering personnel and training activities for business and industry. Previously he has covered health, education and leisure sectors. Before joining Sodexho, Martin was employed by Granada and General Motors in their human resources department. He gained a BSc in psychology from the University of London.

Toby Hirst is the PFI Projects Director for Sodexho Defence Services. In the early Nineties he was responsible for establishing the market testing and competing for quality programme for the Army's United Kingdom Land Forces. He represents the Business Services Association on the joint Industry / MoD Commercial Policy Group and on the CBI's Defence Procurement Panel.

Chris Piper is UK Sales Director – Support Services for Sodexho, the world's leading catering and support services provider. He spent the first 8 years of his career with Trusthouse Forte Hotels before transferring to Gardner Merchant(a subsidiary company) in 1989. Since this period Chris has been involved in both operations and new business development. He has wide experience of all aspects of people and business services within the corporate market place. Chris has spent the last two years delivering a strategy of multi-service provision within Sodexho's existing client base.

Peter Roberts has worked in the catering industry for over 30 years. He first worked in the industry in 1966, obtained a HND in Catering Administration and joined the Gardner Merchant Executive Training scheme of Gardner Merchant in 1972. After nearly 20 years in various operational roles he became Research & Development Director in 1989 for Gardner Merchant's Food Services team responsible for the development of a variety of systems and equipment and involved in bidding for some significant contracts both in the UK and Europe. In 1991 he was promoted to his current role as Research Director in support of the central marketing function.

Today his role includes responsibility for the commissioning and organisation of research projects using internal and external resources. The Customer Feedback mechanism was developed with Peter as one of the principal architects. From initial development it has been expanded and applied into other major business segments and versions are being evolved to cover every type of service offered by the company. Other responsibilities include supporting marketing and communications departments as a data clearing house to all businesses, conducting segment-specific research to aid market positioning, eg school meals and lifestyle survey, developing support research techniques for operations and sales with an emphasis on CRM, organising customer and client research, designing and developing sales and marketing database systems and data, innovating and supporting effective use of marketing data across segments, supporting strategic planning activities, and liaising with external associations and bodies.

Danny Shiem-Shin Then is Associate Professor in Strategic Asset Management and Facilities Management at the School of Construction Management and Property, Queensland University of Technology (QUT). Danny joined QUT in 1997 from Heriot-Watt University, Edinburgh. He is Course Director of the Graduate Programmes in Facilities Management and the current co-ordinator of CIB Working Commission W70 on Facilities Management and Maintenance. Danny has published widely and co-authored with Wes McGregor the book *'Facilities Management and the Business of Space'* (Arnold, UK, 1999). He has also consulted Asset and Facilities Management in the UK, Singapore and Brisbane. He is a member of the Editorial Board of the Journal of Facilities Management published by Henry Stewart Publications UK.

Foreword

A year ago we published the first edition of *Managing Business Support Services* reflecting the way outsourcing has changed in nature, expanded in scope and grown in importance in recent years.

It proved extremely valuable to many members. Today we publish an updated and expanded version, reflecting further insights and giving additional guidance as this whole field moves forward.

What becomes ever clearer is that the opportunities are greater and the benefits wider than recognised in the past – slimming the fixed cost base, giving access to wider skills, enabling management to concentrate on the genuine 'core' functions and giving much greater flexibility. However, what is also increasingly apparent is that turning to external services does not mean getting shot of a function and forgetting about it. Success requires insight into what the whole process entails. It needs careful thought about what to contract out, how to select the most appropriate provider, how to structure and negotiate the contract, and how to manage the relationship.

This book sets out to explore these issues and give the latest guidance on best practice.

George Cox
Director General – IOD

Acknowledgements

Like the original book, and as its subtitle indicates, this second edition of *Managing Business Support Services* sets out to provide guidance to decision-makers on developing strategies for outsourcing and facilities management. It provides an analysis of support service experience that will aid a better understanding of best practice in outsourcing, and of how long-term outsourcing relationships can add value to core businesses.

As before, the book is arranged in five parts and a number of chapters from the original edition have been retained or updated. Part one identifies the key principles of outsourcing and facilities management and now includes a chapter by Elias Mazzawi of Cap Gemini on *Transformational Outsourcing*, the challenging new approach to strategic development. Part two revisits outsourcing practice and application with new chapters on *Tendering Best Practice* and *Outsourcing Health and Safety Management*. The *Private Finance Initiatives* chapter has been extensively revised.

Part three focuses on commercial and management considerations in outsourcing with new chapters on *Defining the Need, Managing the Decision, Living with TUPE* and *Multi-site Management Issues*. In Part four, the process of building on experience is extended by chapters on the *Role of FM in Business Continuity Planning and Management* and the use of two analytical techniques which Sodexho has adapted and refined: *Monitoring Client/Consumer Feedback* and *Customer Profiling*. In Part five the case studies of the first edition are revisited and supplemented with an account of the Shell/Sodexho North Sea Alliance business partnership.

My sincere thanks are offered to each of the distinguished authors who have contributed to the book. Many of them also wrote for the first edition and I am particularly grateful to Professor John Hinks, my co-editor of the original book, who has provided additional material and continued to write for this edition. A number of senior Sodexho managers have contributed chapters this time for Parts two, three and four relating to the disciplines in which they are expert; their time and personal interest in the book are much appreciated.

Our thanks are due to George Cox, Director General of the Institute of Directors who provided the Foreword, and to the Institute for its endorsement. Finally, we gratefully acknowledge the sponsorship of Sodexho Alliance, the world's largest catering and support services provider, joined this time by Cap Gemini, the leading international management consultancy firm. Their participation has helped to ensure the continuing success of this project.

Jonathan Reuvid
London, September 2002

Part 1

The Principles of Outsourcing and Facilities Management

The Business Context for Outsourcing Non-core Service Functions

Professor John Hinks,
*The Centre for Advanced Built
Environment Research (CABER)*
Jonathan Reuvid

The evolution of outsourcing

Outsourcing emerged as a distinct term primarily as a response to a number of coincident pressures on organisations. These pressures included the need to reduce overheads in a recessionary climate; the eruption of the business process re-engineering phenomenon; and the prospect of heavy investment and training requirements associated with the emergence of a range of specialist business processes and information technologies. The net effect of this coincidence of investment burdens and financial constraints was to threaten core business innovation and competitiveness in a time of change. Faced with a dilemma over which aspects of the business process to invest in, the matter of prioritising and removing or reducing non-core costs and risks became pivotal to prosperity or even survival and for many businesses a shrinkage in work and a shortening of time horizons and innovation cycles, plus a need to re-engineer their main (core) activities in order to maintain competitiveness.

The trend which emerged focused around the distinction between investment in the core and the non-core elements of the business, and 'outsourcing' blossomed as a procurement tactic. For some organisations it was to grow in status from an expediency to a strategy. For others, it remained a way of disengaging financially and managerially the 'non-core' from the 'core'. This was especially so in the case of IT, where the cost of investment and people training was disproportionate to the perceived relevance of the business or the pace of change and the cost of adaptation. Plus, the risk of getting it wrong simply threatened to overwhelm organisations. For many, of course, outsourcing was never the preferred procurement solution.

For many of those that did turn to outsourcing, it was in response to a feeling that operating their business support service issues in-house was distracting the organisation from its core business specialism and placing demands of secondary-level importance on limited resources. Outsourcing allowed them to devolve the financial responsibility and risk to outside specialists. For many, this extended to devolving the managerial responsibility, too. As some have discovered, devolving the management of risk outside the core can actually rebound as vulnerability in business-critical areas.

With this development, the non-core soon became viewed generally as being profoundly operational, predominated by reactive business support service functions, and strategically earthbound. Managing the non-core management came to be seen predominantly as a cost-efficiency task – with the route to core competitiveness being widely regarded to be through least-cost outsourcing. This was compounded by outsourcing business support services on a function-by-function basis and, to a large extent, the view of it being non-strategic became self-fulfilling.

For many organisations, outsourcing transfers – which provided the scope to displace cost and other associated employment burdens outward by transferring staff to external providers, thereby displacing the exposure to volatility in the markets and the burdens of training and equipment investment – worked well. For many specialised business support services, the providers have advanced to levels of capability that their client business could not realistically match – financially or functionally. However, potential problems do arise; for instance, a lack of common goals and agendas can mean that there is a divergence between core and non-core in terms of priorities, technical advancement and training. The non-core organisation may not be able (or willing) to respond to the changing needs of the core organisation, and if this should occur within the period of a contract it could impair the agility of the core organisation. The effect could be to stagnate innovation in their business.

Cultural distinctions can become important as well, and the scope to make year-on-year savings whilst remaining at the cutting edge of technology and training can prove to be impracticable for the out-source provider when driven beneath that which is financially sustain-able by a myopically cost-oriented core organisation. Ultimately, both stand to lose out, more so where the outsourced function is critical to the core business operations or organisational agility. In each case, the investment gap that would have to be bridged in order to bring the function back inside the core organisation can leave the core client business vulnerable to a dependency upon the continued successful-ness of the outsource provider.

At the other end of the spectrum, as client organisations become remote from the detail of providing and integrating business support services with their core processes, their understanding of these roles in strategically important core capabilities can become limited – espe-cially those which are pivotal to organisational and structural change within the business. There is also the chance of the client becoming vulnerable to the less scrupulous business support service provider who chooses to take advantage of their eroded expertise in the area. In each of the above instances, there is clearly the potential for dysfunc-tionality and other ineffectiveness in the linkage between core needs and business support service provision. Ultimately, this is an issue for the directors of the core business.

As organisations increasingly focused their investment strategies on the core process, so they tended to displace their non-core func-tions on a task-by-task *ad hoc* basis as business strategists sought economies of scale in the outsource provider market. In the short term, this development served to reduce core headcount, displace technological and other training burdens and uncertainty, and trans-fer the management of risks associated with the non-core outside of the core organisation. At a stroke, this made the companies appear lean and able to focus their various investments on the core. The longer-term impact was to cap the viewpoint about these elements of the organisational system with a functional, task-oriented perspec-tive. Moreover, the relevance of co-ordinating and managing the strategic dimensions of these operationally categorised functions as part of the evolving core business processes was generally under-appreciated.

Even for those organisations that did not outsource in order to achieve competitiveness, new pressure for cost efficiencies in these non-core services/functions led to the emergence of new management roles. Amongst these was that of the IS manager, which was consolidated by the leverage that high spend and an increasingly pivotal role in business continuity bring. IT was also a 'supertanker' development that could not be resisted or turned, only responded to. There was also the rise of the HR manager, as skill shortages and the value of the individual in the corporate intelligence and the learning organisation became ever more clearly business enablers or inhibitors, according to how well the personnel resource was matched to the business need. Few would deny the value of quality HR to the core business competitiveness. Then there was the emergence of facilities management (FM). Yet here lies an important distinction. Of the three, FM remains recognised only occasionally for its potential strategic value to the core business.

Broadly speaking, FM appears to retain the status in many business directors' minds of an operational command-and-control function; and a function concerned with the collective management of all the non-core issues outside the IS and HR remits. The emergence of FM became associated with the visibly operational nature of the outsourced subtasks which it was charged with managing: safety management, security, cleaning, transport, postal services, property maintenance, and other miscellaneous business support service functions all tended to fall under the catch-all heading of FM.

For many directors, FM became synonymous with outsourcing (or, in the case of in-house operations, functions that would otherwise be eligible for outsourcing). As FM consolidated into a visible, professional role, ready to contribute to the strategic planning and management of the core organisation, it appears to have remained largely associated by directors with the operationally-oriented and facility-oriented dimensions of the business.

Being born of a climate of financial constraint and the displacement of risk, outsourced FM has been unable to entirely shrug off these narrow terms of reference by the core business. In-house FM has not fared much better either. Whilst directors may recognise the operationally pivotal reliance on FM issues – such as the availability and reliability of their buildings, the provision of the necessary management and operation of their corporate property portfolios, the handling of environmental issues and compliance with health and safety legislation – other dimensions of functional significance seem to have been removed from the outsourcing equation. There has been an overall tendency for organisations to 'fit and strategically forget' outsourced functions. This may be because the act of outsourcing contracts tends to limit the linkage between the function and the core business. It could simply be that directors have not recognised the value to the core business of incorporating the support they will need to enable changes in the operation of the business process to their strategic planning process.

The importance of outsourcing for contemporary business

First, with the maturation of FM into a more widely recognised and consistently defined professional role, and the emergence of change as a lever for business competitiveness, the competitive value to the business from simple spend reductions has been reduced.

Second, the emergence of new technologies and the mixed experience of the new economy have generated another phase of business adjustment. For many organisations, their approach to business support service issues has become the difference between them using functions like FM as an enabling component in their overall organisational agility, or simply viewing the support function as a reactive resource. In contrast to the pressures of the first cycle of outsourcing, it is now the better integration of business support services that is the key to competitiveness. Thus, value replaces cost.

Multinational outsourcing contracts for soft services represent a new dimension in the drive to add value from the coordinated management of non-core functions internationally. Large multinational corporations are trying to develop closer relationships with suppliers and terms such as 'strategic supplier', 'partner' and 'stakeholder' are common currency in the vocabulary of purchasing and facilities managers. Although tendering documents are invariably different and carry different interpretations from one country to another, the common language of international outsourcing is English and UK purchasing executives are in the forefront of multinational procurement which is generally managed by teams drawn from each region or country concerned. The use of e-Auctions in the competitive tendering process is a further innovation which is being driven by US procurement organisations such as Covisint (created and owned by most of the major automotive manufacturers acting in concert).

Meanwhile, the potential impact on the organisation of dysfunctionality in the links between core and non-core is now approaching the status of competitive differentiator. Continuity and reliability of supply, plus attunement of the business support services to fit closely with increasingly interdependent core process needs, and a realisation that this interlacing is strategically central to competitiveness, may spearhead a revolution in the outsourcing market – perhaps via strategic partnerships, mergers or integrated supply chains.

For some organisations, the solution to this need for greater integration is to consider insourcing; others never outsourced, or only outsourced particular tasks and coordinated them through a remaining in-house service (examples of this mixed economy approach include the use of external outsourcer providers to top up for fluctuations in workload for the in-house department). For many, the outsourced solution is still to be preferred – if they can effectively link the core and the non-core (perhaps by out-placing a manager with the outsource provider to maintain the link). There will be many organisations which have not yet made a positive decision on this; others will be at or approaching the renewal point for contracts and will have to reconsider their options based on a balance of experiences and anticipated future requirements. There are no universal right answers. The appropriate decision depends on the needs of the core business.

So a new pressure emerges. Leadership and vision in a business world where it is recognised that maximum effectiveness depends on maximising the value of the outsourced function to the needs of the core business, not simply minimising the cost. Threat or opportunity? It depends on the director's response and understanding of the options. A properly integrated and well-thought-out outsourcing solution can provide value for money, and for many organisations this will work well. The wrong outsourcing solution can arise from the demand or supply side, or from the combination of the two, and could be disastrous. To achieve the best value of outsourcing business support services for the organisation is going to require a thorough understanding of the relationship between the service and the core need. The business director is likely to have a good overview of this, but cannot resolve the strategic conundrum alone. Nor can the FM either, and the initiative lies with the director.

The key challenge of this book is whether you consider outsourcing as simply a procurement technique for your business support services or whether you see strategic dimensions. So the book discusses issues that you have to consider when using outsourcing as a procurement method. The first edition focused on FM, since for many directors this remained the unexplored territory. The potential leverage FM offers for the core/client organisation appeared to be poorly understood. This second edition broadens the range of issues that you should consider for your organisation when making or reviewing decisions about outsourcing. Overall, it presents a variety of perspectives to illustrate that ignoring the strategic facets of outsourcing business support services generally, and FM in particular, can have opportunity costs for your business.

Further consideration is given this time to managing outsourcing decisions including health and safety management, multi-site delivery issues and the implications of employment transfers under TUPE regulations. Under the heading of 'Building on Experience' the book examines the role of FM in business continuity planning and management and the use of consumer feedback and customer profiling as tools for the measurement of user satisfaction with delivered services.

Ultimately though, to get the competitive value of FM and business support services as a whole, the director has to make outsourcing decisions on a strategic as well as tactical procurement level, and design these to suit the needs and nature of their organisation, perhaps in the context of business partnership development. Hence, the subtitle of this work. We invite you again to read on and to revisit your thinking about outsourcing.

2

Transformational Outsourcing: from Controlling Cost to Achieving a Step Change in Performance and Agility

Elias Mazzawi
Cap Gemini Ernst & Young

Change and volatility have become inescapable and permanent features of the business world and companies are increasingly alive to the need to become adaptive enterprises – fast, flexible and agile. The prize is competitive success.

The transformation to an 'adaptive' state to meet this relentless change and volatility is a major and inescapable challenge for every enterprise, impacting on its structure, its processes, its technology – even its culture. It is no use having your finger on the pulse of the market if you cannot act responsively because your business processes are hard-wired to the past. Especially if, given the all-pervasive nature of IT in today's world, your systems architecture and management approach are too inflexible to cope with change on all fronts and at every level.

Consequently, transformation is perhaps the CEO's biggest challenge and dilemma: finding an economically attractive way to simultaneously improve both short-term performance and to deliver longer-term change.

Traditionally, outsourcing has been seen as a relatively straightforward cost reduction tool with a clearly defined and limited scope – something to be used to reduce the cost of non-core activities.

However, the picture is set to change. Transformation to the adaptive state (fast, flexible, agile) demands new styles of external services which no longer separate process re-engineering from technology management from advice. Outsourcing is still about accessing the best skills and capabilities at each stage of the value chain – but it is now about more. Transformational outsourcing – combining consulting, technology and outsourcing to stimulate and facilitate business change – helps to create and sustain the adaptive enterprise.

Transformational outsourcing is a powerful tool to enable an organisation to proactively manage change and volatility – and to enable it to win quick and sustained benefit from new market opportunity. It links the benefits of sound high-level vision to a realistic road-map for strategic change – either through one major leap or a series of progressive steps. It focuses on core activities and business issues rather than non-core. It helps to create the organisational flexibility to achieve change, and delivers the systems and process flexibility to support it and make it work. It uses outsourcing as a core element of the wider strategic agenda rather than as a standalone.

From traditional to transformational: a potted history of the evolution of outsourcing

There are now two key types of outsourcing – traditional and transformational – and a range of options within each key category. Each of these two approaches targets different objectives, involves different levels of integration into the business and consequently adds different levels of value.

Traditional outsourcing focuses on 'sweating assets harder'.
Transformational outsourcing focuses on changing the paradigm: targeting the adaptive enterprise. Traditional outsourcing will no longer be a competitive differentiator.

Traditional outsourcing: 'sweating assets harder'

Traditional outsourcing is about shedding non-core services: adding value by accessing best-practice and economies of scale in non-complex and non-core areas. It is about leveraging economies of scale, skills and technology access to cut costs and deliver enhanced, properly managed service levels. It is about focusing on avoiding doing internally what others could do more efficiently and effectively externally.

Under traditional outsourcing, performance improvement is operational in nature rather than strategic: doing the same things a bit better, a bit faster or a bit cheaper. To some extent, a shift from fixed to variable costs is both practical and achievable; but typically there is little or no scope for significant and fundamental business change. Traditional outsourcing is principally about 'sweating' assets.

The earliest conventional wisdom was that only well-run operations should be outsourced: problems should first be fixed in-house. That logic was based on the perceived complexity of using third parties to fix-and-run problems. The situation has changed: outsourcers have substantial experience in operational performance improvement and clients are increasingly eager to access that expertise to fix issues more rapidly. Traditional outsourcing evolved into something which could be termed 'traditional plus' or 'problem solving' outsourcing, focused on achieving all the benefits of basic traditional outsourcing, but adding some operating performance improvement.

However, the value that traditional outsourcing can add is capped: it is tactical rather than strategic in its nature.

Transformational outsourcing: changing the paradigm

Transformational outsourcing is fundamentally different. It targets and enables paradigm shift. Where traditional outsourcing was about doing the same things but doing them better, faster and cheaper, transformational outsourcing is about helping to create a new business model and a new management approach. Where traditional was about sweating assets, transformational is about changing the paradigm to something smarter, more flexible and more streamlined. Where traditional was contracted on the basis of long-term stability, transformational outsourcing is predicated on perpetual volatility and change. It is about changing the business paradigm in a joined-up way. The characteristics of traditional and transformational outsourcing are summarised in Figure 2.1.

Traditional outsourcing	Transformational outsourcing
Operational focus	Business focus
All about cutting costs	All about creating value
Helps impose control	Helps manage uncertainty
Aligns with fundamentally unchanged business processes	Aligns with the business processes that change in line with strategic goals
Based on external IT specialists achieving higher performance than a non-specialist company	Based on the creation of a network of partnerships in the new connected economy
Removes non-core functions from the business to provide a one-time release of capital	Business change and cost re-engineering enable sustained value creation

Figure 2.1 Achieving cost re-engineering and sustained business value growth through creative partnerships

Using transformational outsourcing to become adaptive

Moving a business to an adaptive state is a very significant task and it requires substantial skills. The four key elements needed to achieve this transformation through outsourcing are illustrated in Figure 2.2.

Commercial leverage is about helping companies to manage the costs and risks of major change while preventing serious adverse impacts on either the balance sheet or the P&L. It typically involves:

- Leveraging existing assets (perhaps through transfer to the outsourcer);

- Turning fixed into variable costs through pay as you go/transaction based contracts;

- Smoothing of the investment curve thereby flattening out front-end loaded investments;

- Focusing on generating near term returns to create the self-funding investment 'snowball'.

It also involves more commercially innovative reward, payment and financing structures. Commercial leverage is both an enabler – freeing up and generating funds for investment in the overall transformation – and a major contributor to flexibility in its own right.

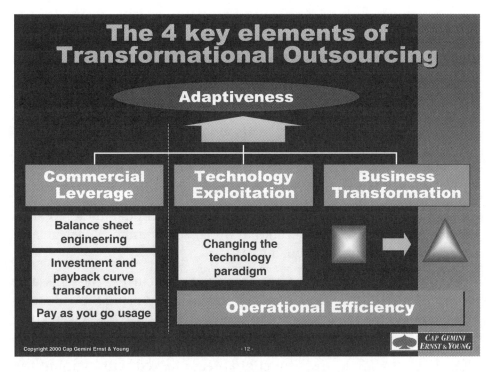

Figure 2.2 The four key elements of transformational outsourcing

Technology exploitation is about changing the technology paradigm for an organisation – not about wholesale technology replacement. In practical terms this means:

- Focusing on the economic enterprise web, not just the enterprise;
- Deploying standards based services, not proprietary platforms;
- Valuing high service levels, not fire-fighting heroes;
- Allowing organisations to broker resources, not build them;
- It creates the platform upon which business capabilities can be dynamically reconfigured.

Business transformation is about changing the way the business operates and is structured. It is about moving beyond the traditional approach to business process re-engineering – which for so long has focused on establishing end-to-end enterprise-wide processes – and into the establishment of business networks and business webs; adaptive structures aligned to a clear and compelling corporate structure.

Operational efficiency is about ensuring that hour-to-hour, day-to-day, year-to-year customers are supported by robust, effective and efficient processes and systems. It provides both the stable platform for change and the controlled environment into which change is managed.

The power of transformational outsourcing is in the way these four elements are deployed together and in a long-term aligned partnership: harnessing best practice transformation skills, best practice operation skills and economies of scale. Benefits include:

- Using the cost savings and release of invested capital made possible by the outsourcing of operational processes to finance change and development across the business;

- Setting to work from day one to migrate all current systems and processes in the direction of maximum flexibility, using the full range of the outsourcer's experience to achieve a responsive serviced environment, with pervasive IT support on tap whatever the need;

- Deploying a single cross-functional team tasked with helping the client simultaneously to achieve strategic transformation and improved operational effectiveness.

Transformational outsourcing is a powerful, effective and joined-up tool to help businesses to achieve the rapid operational improvement and paradigm-change needed to meet increasingly demanding goals. It allows a business to change the way it pays for and invests in services, the way it operates and the way the services are delivered. Management's degrees of freedom to transform its businesses can be significantly increased.

Successful outsourcing

Outsourcing decisions and transactions are typically large and complex, strategically and operationally important, and involve significant organisational strain. In many ways, they are like merger/acquisition transactions – and, like mergers/acquisitions, outsourcing can deliver paradigm-changing benefits.

In our experience, there are three key ingredients to 'setting up for success'.

Be clear about what you want to achieve

The goals for a traditional outsource are very different from the goals for a transformational outsource. Clear aspirations and expectations need to be set and shared upfront – and the vision needs to be embedded in both companies' top-down strategic goals.

Make it an enduring, mutually advantageous relationship

Traditional outsourcing tends to be self-contained, potentially ring-fenced, and governed by tight service performance indicators; whereas transformational outsourcing tends to be more integrated into the organisation, more fluid and of longer duration.

Traditional outsourcing is about contracting for efficiency; whereas transformational outsourcing is about contracting for competitive advantage out of uncertainty.

Commercially, transformational outsourcing contracts are geared around guaranteed outcomes and the sharing of risks and rewards. They start from the perspective of aligning the business objectives of both partners through appropriate incentive mechanisms that encourage flexibility, not intransigence, in the face of unpredictable change.

Align the key elements of change

Experience has shown that the combination of a business change team working in close harmony, continuously and simultaneously, with a new technology team and a service delivery team can achieve far greater results, far more quickly – and above all with greatly reduced risk – than when these three vital areas are tackled in isolation and sequentially. The single point of accountability offered by such an approach can make the transformation programme much easier to manage and control for the CEO and his/her team.

Our experience of implementing and fine-tuning outsourcing arrangements over a 30-year history tells us that success is driven by the quality of relationships rather than the fine details of the contract. Top-down, aligned, mutually beneficial relationships deliver results and build-in the 'room for manoeuvre' which allows both partners to ensure that their partnership is as appropriate to their circumstances and business imperatives at the end of year five as it was on day one.

In conclusion

Outsourcing is growing rapidly. It is still about getting hold of the best skills and capabilities at each stage of the value chain, but there is increasing choice around which type to use and when.

Traditional outsourcing has delivered significant short-term cost reduction for many companies, typically in their support – rather than core – activities. But there is a clear ceiling to the level and nature of value that this 'traditional' version of outsourcing can deliver.

Transformational outsourcing can help accelerate and finance transformation, making outsourcing perhaps the most effective way of facilitating change, rather than merely being an approach to containing and cutting costs.

It is still valid to use outsourcing to do the same things cheaper, but it is no longer going to be enough competitively to rely on an outsourcer to 'sweat assets' – it is difficult to find areas of the market in which this is not routine. Increasingly, outsourcing is becoming a means of achieving a step change in performance and agility.

Different companies have different strategic imperatives, but whatever the challenges they face, one thing is a safe bet – meeting them will depend crucially on bringing the right capabilities together rapidly and effectively. The speed at which companies can respond to their challenges will depend on how they organise to address them as well as the degree of flexibility and adaptability built into their supporting IT systems and infrastructure. Transformational outsourcing is a powerful enabler for organisations targeting speed, flexibility and agility.

Unlike traditional outsourcing, transformational outsourcing focuses on core activities and business issues rather than non-core activities, and uses outsourcing as a core element of the wider strategic agenda rather than as a stand-alone. For companies considering outsourcing some activities (or indeed, even for those which are not), transformational outsourcing offers a different approach to transforming businesses and a different way to think about outsourcing. It is a new paradigm. The choice for management is the extent to which it chooses to embrace outsourcing as a means of facilitating change rather than simply as a means of reducing cost.

3

The Identification of Core Business Processes and their HR and IT Implications

Ken Robertson, MBA
KLR Consulting Inc.

Managing business support services entails managing facilities. This includes dealing with all of the real estate related transactions and processes for all facilities owned or leased by the organisation. Interior planning and outfitting is another key process for the facilities group. This involves working with designers to deliver a workable space plan and selecting and installing appropriate office furniture.

Real estate, space planning and outfitting tend to be intensive project-based activities in an organisation. The day-to-day aspects of facilities management (FM) include operating and maintaining the facilities and dealing with the constant moves and changes (churn) which are common in every organisation today. These activities are ongoing and require a mix of proactive planning as well as the ability to react quickly to immediate requirements.

Without a doubt, business depends on FM. Organisations clearly need to have space from which to work – but is FM merely an operational function or is it strategic? This question is being asked at the executive table of many organisations. If FM is merely operational, then a simple outsourcing arrangement may be a very effective solution. However, if it has a strategic element then perhaps FM, or some portion of it, should be a core competency of the organisation and kept in-house.

To determine if FM is strategic, the executives must consider how it can impact the business strategy. At first glance, executives might consider it to be only providing basic real estate services and, as such, consider it important but not core to the business. However, upon more thorough consideration, executives may start to realise that FM can indeed impact business strategy. In fact, when combined with other corporate services functions, such as human resources and information technology, the facilities group can be a critical element in delivering the 'environment' within which the organisation can flourish as it continually changes to keep pace with the new economy.

The linkages between FM, HR and IT may seem surprising to some executives. After all, these three groups are often renowned for working in isolation and perceived as not being particularly effective. Many organisations view these functions as necessary components of the business, while at the same time they are seen as being unresponsive, expensive and focused on their own agendas.

The real strategic opportunity is to get all of these three corporate service functions to work collectively to deliver greater business value to the organisation. This value is both in operational effectiveness terms and in longer-term strategic positioning. However, the strategic benefit of collaboration can only be achieved if *all* of these groups work together.

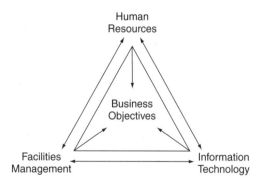

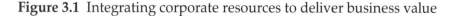

Figure 3.1 Integrating corporate resources to deliver business value

Figure 3.1 illustrates the collaboration of the key corporate service groups in terms of a triangle (Robertson, 1999). Their consolidated effectiveness is based on their ability to work together. As with a three-legged stool, the delivery of business value will be maximised when they work together. If an organisation can only get two of these groups to collaborate then the strategic value will be greatly reduced. The middle of the triangle shows the common focus on business objectives. The collaboration of these groups means that they will no longer have their own specific agenda to push but rather a consolidated strategic direction that will collectively support the organisation's business objectives. This may seem like an obvious point, but unfortunately it is one that is often missed. If this collaboration does not deliver the business objectives then little has been accomplished.

Information technology

In the past few years the IT function has moved up the corporate ladder to the position of now significantly impacting corporate strategy. The advent of the Internet, wireless technologies and the ease by which communications can take place around the world, has driven many organisations to much greater operational and strategic reliance on IT.

Today, more and more organisations are moving into new lines of business and new ways of delivering products and services based on emerging technologies. Even traditional 'blue chip' companies are finding that technology is levelling the field and new competitors are coming out of nowhere to take away market share. The move to e-business and e-commerce, or e-anything for that matter, confirms the strategic importance organisations are now placing on their technology groups.

IT is clearly changing the way we work, as well as where we work. High-speed telecommunications is now allowing employees to work from home, where appropriate. Wireless technologies that were once so expensive that they were only for a chosen few are now available to everyone. The technology has also become much more portable and affordable with notebook computers and personal digital assistants (PDAs) growing in popularity.

So how does this really impact FM? Dramatically! Facilities must now be flexible enough to handle the scenario of working from any place at any time. This means not only focusing on traditional corporate real estate but having to deal with facilities-related issues in many distributed office locations, employees' homes, customers' offices, hotels, vehicles, etc. The technology now permits the employee to work from anywhere that makes sense for the work they are performing.

Employees will in the near future be even more portable as the proliferation of personal appliances continues. Imagine employees who are able to carry their computing requirements easily to any location within the facility and perform their work. A finance employee may be in the marketing department and want to print a spreadsheet for a meeting. With their bluetooth-enabled technology they will be able to take their portable computing appliance (notebook, PDA or whatever) and via radio signals have it printed on the nearest printer. They will not have to borrow someone else's personal computer or plug into a network jack.

In essence, the technology can now be attached to the individual and not just to a physical place. This dramatically changes the dynamics of how offices are structured. Employees can now work from anywhere in the office; so, it is critical to structure the office to be flexible enough to handle any type of situation. Offices today are typically structured to accommodate fixed groups of people working in fixed locations. The near future will have some of the same but a growing number of people who work from multiple locations; locations which they may not be able to predict ahead of time.

Most organisations have realised that their employees are more effective when working in teams. Organisations that put an emphasis on collaborative work find today's work environment of separate cubicles and offices not overly conducive to collaboration. These organisations are looking for spaces where they can have this type of collaboration on an *ad hoc*, when required, basis. These organisations are looking for open team areas that allow for easy collaboration along with quiet places where employees can go to for heads-down work (in some cases this may be at home). The Gartner Group predicts that by 2002, 25 per cent of all workers will be mobile (Greiner, 2000).

Teamwork is not limited to the corporate office. Today's technology is also making great strides in bringing geographically dispersed people together for collaborative work. The growth in electronically mediated team environments is seen in desktop video conferencing, electronic whiteboards, corporate 'chat rooms', etc. The facilities group needs to structure the office with areas where these types of facilities can be shared, where electronic whiteboards can be rolled into a team space and where larger communal monitors can be used to facilitate these high-tech meetings.

The FM group is faced with the struggle of managing a workplace that is both 'virtual' and 'real'. The 'virtual' workplace is, in most organisations, the sole domain of the information technology group. The 'real' workplace is the sole domain of the FM group. However, to be effective, an organisation needs to marry these two environments to ensure that they complement each other. An organisation that works on strictly a virtual basis may find that it is not as effective as one that leverages off of the benefits of the 'virtual' workplace complimented by a 'real' workplace where these virtual workers can come together for face-to-face human interactions. The most successful organisations in the next decade will be those that can marry these two divergent ways of working.

Human resources

The number one issue for most organisations today is attracting and retaining knowledge workers. This issue is a worldwide phenomenon as the adoption of new technologies to compete in the new economy is dramatically increasing the demand for knowledge workers. Retaining knowledge workers is also critical, as the cost of turnover is significant. A recent Watson-Wyatt study showed that the average cost of turnover of a knowledge worker was equal to 1.5 times their annual salary (Schellenbarger, 2000).

While organisations are struggling with attracting and retaining employees, employees are struggling with balancing their work and personal lives. The demands on both sides of this equation are growing every day.

HR groups are now looking at ways to solve their attraction/retention issue with a focus on helping employees with their own balancing issues. This has led to the implementation of alternative work arrangements in many organisations. Arrangements such as regular part-time, phased-retirement, job sharing and teleworking (working from home two to three days per week) have become more popular.

These new work arrangements start to impact dramatically the dynamics of how the office is designed and utilised. Consider this scenario – five employees in the engineering department are teleworking three days per week. They currently have five permanent workstations assigned to them. These workstations sit idle more than 50 per cent of the time. Is this the best utilisation of space? No, these employees would be prime candidates to share space. Further analysis would probably find that they do their heads-down work at home and do their collaborative work back in the office. In this scenario, the type of shared space provided back in the 'regular' office would be different to that provided to similar employees who are in the office five days a week. This scenario clearly shows the need for human resources and facilities management to work together to provide the best working environment for these valuable employees.

The telework concept is also growing quickly. This work option started to gain popularity in the early 1990s and is predicted by the Gartner Group to include more than 108 million employees worldwide by 2002 (Greiner, 2000). If employees are to do their heads-down work at home then they will be spending the majority of their days at their home workstations. If the FM group believes in ergonomics in the office and providing a safe work environment, then some of these concepts need to be applied to the teleworker's home office. This expands the scope of work from the traditional on-premises environment to include off-premises environments.

There is also a direct connection between the design of the workplace and the ability of the organisation to attract and retain employees. In essence we are making the office more like our homes (and conversely with telework our homes are becoming more like our offices). Employees are under a lot of stress to perform; therefore, their environment should be more comfortable – a place where they want to be, a place they are proud to talk about and show to others. A recent survey sponsored by the American Society of Interior Designers showed that 'the physical workplace was one of the top three factors employees said top-of-mind [without prompting] have influence on their decisions to accept or leave jobs' (ASID,1999). So to help retain and attract these valuable knowledge workers, the facilities must be appealing and represent the corporate culture that is being espoused.

The importance of office design is further driven home by *Fortune Magazine*'s research into the top 100 companies to work for in the United States. This research concluded that the 'workplace must be a place to live not just a place to work' (Useem, 2000). This is obviously another element in attracting and retaining employees. The research revealed that 26 per cent of these top 100 companies offered personal concierge services for employees while 46 per cent offered high quality meals to take home. These types of offerings help employees to create a better balance between their work and personal lives.

Most organisations are now utilising a far greater number of contingent workers than ever before. These workers provide specific services for a specific period of time to help an organisation overcome peaks in workload, ensuring that the organisation is not reducing permanent staff levels during the valleys. In some cases, these contingent workers also bring specialised skills to the organisation which can be passed on to the organisation's employees. Of course, these contingent workers need to be accommodated in an environment designed to optimise their performance. Today, these contingent workers are often accommodated in spaces that make it difficult to be productive under the premise that they are not 'real' (i.e. permanent) employees. However, the cost per hour to the organisation of having these contingent workers is likely to be significantly higher than the permanent employees; so, whatever can be done to make them more productive would be beneficial to the organisation.

Some organisations are taking the contingent worker approach a step further and creating integrated teams of specialised resources to deliver on a specific project. This approach is referred to in North America as the 'Hollywood' model. The idea being that, like a Hollywood film, you bring together the director, producer, actors, support people, etc, for a specific job and then release them at the end. This way the organisation is getting the 'best' people available in the market place for the duration of the specific initiative. Again, these people need appropriate space – space that may be specifically leased for the duration of a project.

Business

IT and HR clearly have a direct impact on FM. To be successful, the collaboration of these three key corporate service functions must be focused on delivering business value to the organisation.

Business is changing rapidly and it is essential that organisations continue to improve and evolve. IT is allowing more flexibility and is changing at an exponential rate. HR is providing flexibility in work arrangements and is beginning to pick up speed in terms of adjusting people practices to the changing market place. FM has, in many organisations, been inflexible and slow to change.

In order to succeed, the FM group must dramatically improve the degree of flexibility of the work environment and adapt to the 'internet' pace of change that is driving business today. Jim Keane (Vice President, Corporate Strategy, Research and Development for Steelcase, Inc.) makes the analogy between corporate real estate and live theatre. Keane suggests that organisations should think of their base building like a stage – it should have wide open spaces, flexible services and natural light. Like a stage it should be ready to accommodate any production. The interior design and furniture are like the props in a play – again, flexibility is the key for rapid scene changes or new productions. Keane's best words of wisdom are to 'never design a stage for today's props' (Keane, 1999). This statement speaks volumes about the need to be strategically focused, to be flexible enough to accommodate today's needs and to be able to adapt easily to tomorrow's requirements.

It is interesting to note that Keane's analogy to the theatre matches with the 'Hollywood' staffing model being used by some organisations. Again, the theme is flexibility, change, fast pace and, while you're at it, provision of the best environment to get the job done.

The pace of business change is forcing many organisations to make major changes to their corporate culture. Executives are asking employees to be more flexible, to work faster and to be innovative in delivering quality solutions to the market place. FM has a wonderful opportunity to support cultural change by being innovative in designing the office space. Nothing speaks louder to the employees about cultural change than the style and layout of the office. What kind of message is it if the CEO is preaching fast-paced change, collaboration and innovation while the space is in a traditional style with 'enclosed offices' on the windows and open cubicles lined up in rows in the interior?

The space provided must be very flexible. It should be possible for team members to easily reconfigure their work areas to meet their immediate needs. It should provide areas outside of the open team area that will support quiet heads-down work and casual areas for exchange of ideas between teams. Basically, the facilities group has to provide a solution that can be customised to meet the user's specific needs – very much in the same way that companies today are moving to mass customisation of the products and services they are providing.

The concept of the office being a Monday to Friday 8 a.m. to 5 p.m. environment is starting to disappear. Many organisations have employees working extended hours to deliver on tight deadlines or to service customers who are expecting extended hours of service. The Internet is available 24 hours a day, 7 days a week. Customers are now beginning to expect 24/7 service from everyone. This shift will have a major impact on the operations of the building and will drive the need to make the office a more comfortable place for employees to work from during these 'non-traditional' hours and days.

Organisations are realising that knowledge workers are critical to their success. The challenge is not only finding and keeping them, but also creating situations in which workers can share knowledge to expand the overall knowledge level of the organisation. Laurence Prusak, Executive Director of the IBM Institute of Knowledge Management in Cambridge Massachusetts, one of the leading experts on knowledge management, suggests that there is a link between knowledge management and the physical space in the office (Prusak, 1998). Prusak suggests that it is important to create places for people to have effective face-to-face interactions, where ideas can be cultivated and knowledge propagated.

Changes required to traditional views

HR, IT and FM are all struggling to deliver enhanced business value to the organisation. The global market place and the electronic-based economy are driving changes at an unprecedented pace.

In many organisations, FM is handled in isolation. Consideration for flexibility, speed and innovation are often stuck within the 'walls' of the FM group. In this traditional context, FM looks like the ideal candidate for outsourcing. In essence, it appears to be primarily an operational group with limited strategic value.

To be successful, FM must be prepared to change some of its traditional views of the office and move forward in collaboration with HR and IT to support the constantly changing business climate. This means taking a more strategic focus on how people, space and technology can be brought together to help the organisation gain competitive advantage (or enhance service delivery in public sector organisations). When these three groups are working collectively it will deliver more strategic value to the organisation.

FM needs to be prepared to make major changes. The group must consider their mandate to branch out to all areas in which people work, to deliver flexible space that can be constantly customised by teams and to provide facilities that support the HR and IT strategies.

One of the most challenging changes will be the ability to function in both 'real' and 'virtual' worlds. The virtual world is comprised of the electronically mediated meeting places for workers who are spread over a broad geographic region (this could include the entire world). Michael Bell of the Gartner Group, whose research focuses on workplace transformation and the virtual enterprise, suggests that:

> *Place is more important now than ever before. Face time is critical. There's a deep-seated social need in all of us for maintaining relationships, and that requires physical proximity to read the cues and to build and maintain trust and rapport. And there are practical reasons. That's where business is transacted, where you have access to customers, suppliers and employers. So you need real portals, just as you need Web portals. Place is the ultimate portal in terms of having access to those resources. (Bell, 2000)*

Bell reminds us that virtual offices will not totally replace real offices; rather that the future holds a combination of the two. The real office needs to be structured so that it actively supports this kind of interaction. Significant changes will be required to today's traditional office which is geared more to individual work than it is to human interaction.

Leadership role

Change is required to move FM from a low-level supplier and operator of space to being a key strategic partner in the organisation's business. To do this, it must partner with IT and HR. It is easy to say they must work together, but harder to make it happen in reality.

IT groups are running hard to operate existing systems, bringing forward innovative new technologies and handling the incredible growth in computing requirements across the organisation. HR is focused on trying to find knowledge workers, keeping them and creating opportunities for these employees to share their knowledge with each other. FM is equally busy but probably the best positioned to bring together this collaboration.

FM has, on an operational level, the ear of senior management due to the very large financial value associated with real estate and fit-up transactions. They are better positioned than HR, who are often perceived by senior management as being passive. They are better positioned than IT, who are revered for the innovative new technologies that could catapult the organisation into their next product or service while at the same time being maligned for their ability to deliver.

Indeed, now is the time for FM to take a leadership role in bringing together corporate service functions to deliver real business value to the organisation. Facilities should do whatever is necessary to help all three groups understand each other and work towards a strategic plan that will better support the strategic direction of the organisation. Again, this is easy to write about but it is no small undertaking for the facilities group.

New work environment – breaking the rules

The new work environment will be the result of a collaborative effort with the other corporate service groups and the actual users of the space (operational divisions/departments). The key to the new work environment will be to throw away some of the old rules and consider more creative ways of delivering space and adding value to the organisation.

One of the primary rules that should be broken immediately is the concept of assigning space on the basis of status or rank. A much better approach is to assign space based on need – give people, at any level, the space they need to do their job. This not only applies to the amount of space but also to the furnishings. Don't just put soft seating and couches in reception areas and executive offices; make them available for anyone to use throughout the space. This will create casual interaction spaces that will support the *ad hoc* face-to-face interaction we need.

Do not get stuck in the 'one-size-fits-all' approach. Many companies come up with a standard cubicle and a standard office and then replicate this throughout their space. The better strategy is to provide an appropriate mix of open and enclosed spaces that meet the needs of the business. The design is to support the business, not to be the easiest for FM to deliver and support.

Another common rule is 'one person gets one dedicated workstation'. This was fine when the technology was fixed to the location and the number of mobile workers was minimal. Today the technology is portable and people are working from multiple locations. So be prepared to have shared workstations and to support people working from multiple external and/or internal locations.

Design the office so that employees can easily adjust parts of the layout to meet their changing needs. This should be something that teams can do on their own without having to bring in a crew of maintenance staff. The best strategy is to design the basic floor plate with enough flexibility in the primary delivery systems (power, HVAC, telecommunications) combined with a 'kit of parts' approach to furniture that can be easily customised to meet individual or team needs.

Be prepared to make the office more livable – add some soft seating, café spaces, high quality food, workout areas, outdoor spaces, decompression areas (quiet places to lay down or relax), games areas, etc. These places will be magnets for people and will help in *ad hoc* interactions and knowledge exchange.

Probably the most import aspect of the new work environment is to 'make it legal'. Today, if someone is sitting in the cafeteria too long the perception is that they are 'slacking off' or if you see someone sitting on a soft couch they must be 'on a break'. To make the new environment work, the organisation has to make it clear that it is perfectly 'legal' to be anywhere in the office. The goal is to get the work done and to recognise that sitting at a single workstation is not the way that work can be performed.

On the real estate side of the equation, be prepared to support a broad range of office facilities. This will include the traditional office real estate but will also include distributed telework centres (drop-in offices that are closer to the employees' homes), customer offices, partner/alliance offices, offices in vehicles, etc. The facilities group should also work closely with the IT group to ensure that appropriate arrangements are made for virtual offices.

Determining core/non-core processes

In looking at a traditional FM group one might be able to pick out easily the core and non-core processes and then determine what should be outsourced and what is better to be left in-house. The material presented in this chapter suggests that before making the outsourcing decision the organisation needs to consider the strategic business value that could be derived by getting FM, HR and IT to work collectively to deliver enhanced business value to the organisation. This type of collaboration will change the definition of what is core and non-core. It will likely change the view of FM from primarily a low-level operational function to one that has a more important strategic focus.

When bringing the three key corporate services together there is no single expected outcome that can be applied to all organisations. It is, therefore, difficult to determine what processes under this arrangement would be core and what would be non-core. Areas that are deemed to be non-core must be clearly defined and the relationship/impact with HR and IT must be documented. If these linkages are not documented it is unlikely that they will become an integral part of the outsourcing agreement. Inevitably the organisation will lose out on the business benefits of this collaboration.

There is no right or wrong about what is core or non-core – the answers are found in the collaboration with other internal service providers to determine where facilities provides the greatest strategic impact. For instance, if the organisation is embarking on major cultural changes and transformations in the way products and services are delivered, then outsourcing the space planning might be inappropriate. In this case, the design of the space would be a reflection of the new culture and would be core to the new direction of the organisation. Although facilities will want to engage leading industry designers to create the new space, it should continue to drive the strategic objectives and direction of the plan internally.

On the other hand, outsourcing the building operation/maintenance might be a perfectly good decision so that the FM group can put more emphasis on the strategic aspects of their role.

Summary

FM can no longer be managed in isolation. It needs to be considered within the context of IT and HR. If collaboration does not occur, FM will continue to be merely a low-level operational function that provides limited strategic value to the overall business. Organisations that move from managing in isolation directly to outsourcing will likely find themselves with a facilities function that delivers even less strategic value.

FM needs to partner with IT and HR to collectively deliver greater business value to the organisation. FM needs to work with these other groups to determine where facilities can support and enhance other corporate support initiatives. They need to break out of traditional ways of thinking to see the many opportunities that could be of greater strategic value to the organisation.

Facilities must work carefully with their partners and users to determine the core/non-core processes – the processes that are considered strategic and operational. Those processes that are considered strategic to the business should be kept in-house, those that are operational should be considered for outsourcing. Remember that it is easier to outsource an operational process than it is to outsource strategic innovation and creativity.

In conclusion, there is no simple answer to outsourcing FM. The key is understand the role of FM within this new partnership with the other corporate service functions. Only then can it maximise the core business effectiveness of the organisation.

References

1. American Society of Interior Designers – ASID (1999) *Recruiting and Retaining Qualified Employees by Design* Washington, D.C.
2. Bell, Michael (2000) 'Web-ify or Die: How Cyberspace is Remaking Corporate Real Estate', *Site Selection Magazine* (September 2000)
3. Greiner, Lynn (2000) 'The Ubiquity of Mobility', *Computing Canada* (July 7, 2000)
4. Keane, Jim (1999) 'Technology and the Future of the Workplace' presentation at the International Development Research Council (IDRC) conference in Nashville, Tennessee (October 19, 1999)
5. Prusak, Laurence, Davenport, Thomas H. (1998) *Working Knowledge: How Organizations Manage What They Know* Harvard Business School Press, Boston, MA
6. Robertson, Ken (1999) *Work Transformation: Planning and Implementing the New Workplace* HNB Publishing, New York
7. Shellenbarger, Sue (2000) 'Work & Family, To Win the Loyalty of Your Employees, Try a Softer Touch', *Wall Street Journal* (January 26, 2000)
8. Useem, Jerry (2000) 'Welcome to the New Company Town', *Fortune Magazine* (January 10, 2000)

4

The Role of Support Services and FM in the Introduction of Change Management

Weng Lee
EC Harris

Change management is a strategic function that equips the business to perform to its objectives. These will change as the market circumstances shift. 'Management of change is not simply a behavioural issue. It consists of behavioural, economic, historical, decision-making, political, and social aspects' (D C Wilson 1992). Change creates new cultures and permeates throughout an organisation irrespective of whether it relates to core or non-core activities. FM has a key role to play in supporting change management and in many instances it may be the driver. Non-core functions often feel the greatest impact and in many cases, irreparable damage is done. This is particularly the case where there is no clear strategy to the non-core support (FM) functions.

Too frequently the problem lies in the perception that change management in a business can be viewed in isolation from the support activities and FM. 'You cannot change the culture without physical change' (Sir Peter Davies, Chairman of Sainsbury 2000). In this instance, it is the move of Sainsbury's HQ from a number of buildings to a single building. Many organisations implement change in the core competencies and the non-core elements of support services and FM is ignored or considered when problems arise. The result is business support infrastructure 'failure' as it falls short of the expectation.

This chapter attempts to identify the role of support services and FM, in a change management process. It will identify the direct and indirect relationships of FM and the business through the application of a 'value tree' approach. It will put the case for FM to be the catalyst for change in organisations.

Some background may assist in understanding support services and FM often referred to as the non-core activities of the business. These could include property, workspace management, corporate office services and those that are often associated with the 'bog roll and spanner brigade'. Historically, these tasks are delivered by in-house middle management, administrative and operational staff (many untrained), in response to senior management who views them as a cost to the business. More recently in the UK, some of these are out-tasked or outsourced to external suppliers whose core businesses are FM services. This trend in the UK in the last ten years is underpinned by the Government outsourcing its property ownership and support services to their DSS (PRIME) and Inland Revenue (STEPS) Estates under a Private Finance Initiative or Public Private Partnership arrangement. In the private sector, the shareholder demands concentration on share portfolios and pressure to concentrate on core businesses, hence the increasing activity of rationalising property and support services.

A survey undertaken by one of the top six UK consultancies, reported that up to 40 per cent of value of the top UK100 companies is tied up in capital assets. This is a fixed cost, which is fairly inflexible, particularly when it brings with it other fixed costs in FM. Consider these questions in the context of this finding:

- Do the organisations need them on their balance sheets?

- Are these properties fully and best utilised? Reducing revenue costs adds directly to bottom line.

- Are there alternative uses and opportunities to create income or release the capital for the core business?

- If they are needed, are they in the correct location and do they need to be where they are?

- Will a review of the workspace accommodation allow the business to dispose of some of these properties?

- Do these organisations know they have these assets with the inherent value and related costs?

Businesses that can recognise the ability to use FM as a source of competitive advantage are managing their environments more proactively.

Leading private sector organisations like BT, BBC, Abbey National and ICL are beginning to recognise FM as a process that can help to meet changing business needs.

Businesses can begin by adopting FM as an integral part of the business and therefore part of the strategic management. This is particularly relevant in rapidly changing markets, where businesses are focusing on customer needs, people retention, cost reduction and a 'service economy'. Fundamentally, business executives need to understand how FM brings value to its business and conversely, FM practitioners need to understand core business needs and the source of competitive advantage or value. They need also to have the ability to communicate to the business.

FM is a common denominator (Fig.4.1) active as the enabler for the key elements of the business, the people, place and product/service to integrate and perform to optimum efficiency.

If FM plays its role, the support infrastructure will be more efficient and flexible to respond to changes in the core business. Executives do not have to focus time on their non-core competencies but only to account for them in their strategic planning. It may be that as part of planning, executives consider the options provided for FM provision, for example one option could be to outsource all non-core activities to external suppliers and act as the intelligent client. If so, how does an executive ensure that the service provided is of the quality expected. Another option would be to review the workspace and the need for fixed assets in buildings.

The role in establishing what is required by the business is essential. Setting up the correct quality systems and procuring the appropriate supplier/s to deliver the support to the core business activity will fundamentally effect performance. Cisco, like some of the motorcar

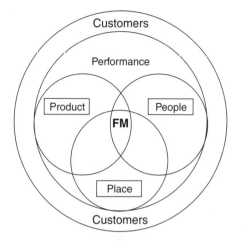

Figure 4.1

companies, have taken facilities outsourcing further and outsourced their core production and supply chain to external 'partners'. They retain expert systems to control quality and programme. Key questions for FM are:

- How far can FM go?
- Are there developed systems to control external suppliers?
- Can suppliers meet the challenge?

Drivers for change

Let us start from the premise that businesses (with less exception) exist for the purpose of contributing value to shareholders. For most this means making a profit at an acceptable risk. Business managers, in response, formulate strategies to set the direction (mission and business definition) and set their use of scarce resources, maintain consistency and retain flexibility. Drucker identified three aspects to business management:

- making the existing business effective;
- identifying and exploiting the potential;
- changing the business to exploit a changed future.

Executives have a hard enough task to address each of these but to integrate them is the reality of business management, particularly in a fast changing external environment. It is the business environment within which a business operates that forces change. Economic cycles, cultural change, levels of education and expectation all act as drivers for business and for FM. The challenge for FM is to:

- develop in the same direction and speed as the business (Figure 4.2),
- focus resources in the correct areas (matching people skills to functions rather than 'he has always been there and done it that way') to support the business;
- provide a consistent service (defining central policy, control systems and applying service levels locally), sometimes globally; and
- retain flexibility to respond to changing needs of the business.

In recent years further influences have arisen:

- technology revolution;
- globalisation;
- financial pressure.

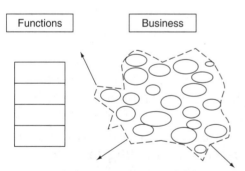
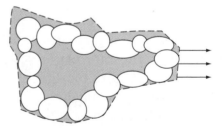

Support Functions Isolated from Business   Support Functions Integral with Business

Figure 4.2

Technology

Technology is a driver for change as it impacts on the product/service and through web technology whole markets. The take up of new technology is more rapid than we have ever experienced before, for example the adoption of the Internet in three years as compared to the widespread use of television which took nearly 20 years.

Many have observed the influence of technology and some predict:

- continued move from a manufacturing base (migrated to the emerging economies) to a service-based economy in the UK;

- processes will be streamlined in all aspects of business;

- increased transparency and improved communication;

- improved information and management systems, with real time information;

- speed of change will increase;

- reorganisation of whole supply chains;

- greater flexibility to the way we work, therefore workspace design, place of work from the fixed office and desk, to the home/serviced/hotel office and touchdown stations/hot desking;

- existing buildings may become redundant unless they can provide the infrastructure to accommodate the new technology and user needs. Organisations tied to the risks of long-term leases or property ownership may struggle to compete unless they can manage their assets better than the market and to match FM to business user needs.

Technology also creates a different type of customer. Customers buy through the Internet (Tesco), bank over the telephone and Internet (Virgin), obtain a mortgage, loan, insurance (Direct Line) without leaving home. Management and staff can communicate through the Internet. Intranets and video conferencing is falling in price to the point where it could now become commonplace. This has a direct impact on the property needs of suppliers of those services, the type and configuration of properties, the need for HQs, and the need for call centres.

Shopping centres will need to reflect the fact that shopping is more of a leisure experience than a chore, distribution will replace manufacturing, and even manufacturing with new technology will require different building configurations with more clean areas and IT control rooms.

In the late 1990s and into early years of the new Millennium, technology, or more specifically, e-commerce brings uncertainty, challenging how in reality we need to undertake business. This may become clearer as the industries consolidate and the dotcoms demonstrate sustainability. In the meantime, the uncertainty requires businesses to be flexible to respond to the potential changes.

Globalisation

Globalisation is the breaking down of market barriers, and is directly linked to technology. On the supply side technology enables cross border alliances and migration of the supply chains to emerging economies and on the demand side customers are influenced by other cultures and purchase/consumer patterns change. Organisations either become bigger to compete in the global market or shrink to be a niche player in smaller geographical regions.

Business across time zones will require 24-hour services. These have to provide usable, secure, clean and fresh environments for the different shifts. Maintenance has to be carried out at times where it does not disrupt the business. This has major implications for the FM and support services team. It is essential that FM is a core component of the planning in order that last minute decisions are avoided.

Finance

Increased pressure on the effective use of capital and the maximisation of return against risk is forcing property owners to examine the logic of ownership. Ownership brings opportunity for capital gain subject to market conditions and time of sale. Subject to the funding of the asset, it also provides a capacity for raising short-term capital. However, the demands of shareholders are increasingly focused on being the best at the core business. Property ownership may be a revenue eater and distraction. Few companies have achieved the 'Holy Grail' of turning the cost of property ownership into a sustainable source of competitive advantage.

There is clear pressure on managers to squeeze more out of their property investments. The normal rental income and service charge arrangements between landlords and tenants are under pressure. Land Securities' purchase of Trillium clearly confirms this view. Landlords will also seek greater return and there is a move to create more business from their portfolio, through servicing the support needs of their tenants.

For some businesses, with 40 per cent of value tied in fixed capital assets, this must be an obvious place to start. Businesses should review their property portfolios and establish what is core to their business needs and what is flexible and surplus. This may need some creative thinking. Their performance in terms of the return on investment could improve with a rationalisation of their portfolio. This includes:

- establishing the future space needs of the business;

- configuration of space and design;

- establishing the degree of flexibility required for space;

- reviewing of the locations;

- reviewing of the match between current and future needs;

- establishing the base cost for occupying the space;

- considering the options for change.

One must also remember that rent reviews in lease agreements eat directly into profits. A move from freehold to leasing is not necessarily an ideal solution or a panacea.

There is also the increased pressure on margins due to more intense competition. On the revenue expenditure, a common claim is that efficiencies of up to 30 per cent can be achieved through outsourcing FM and support services. This will contribute directly to the bottom line of organisations.

Consider for a moment this simple scenario:

Company A

Revenue Expenditure:	£100,000,000
FM &Support Services accounts for:	£5,000,000 (5%)
Net Profit	£4,000,000 (4%)

By streamlining the FM & support service through outsourcing, Company achieves 20 per cent efficiencies.

FM & Support Services is reduced by £1,000,000 which will directly contribute to Net Profit. Revenue Expenditure reduces by 1 per cent.

Result: Profit increases by 25 per cent and the value to shareholders could be significant, depending on the PE Ratio.

Executives should be aware however, that cost savings in FM have to be considered against service standards and staff expectations and other business drivers. It is not 'doing it cheaper' but 'doing it better, simpler and cheaper' that needs consideration. FM practitioners can contribute by proactively reviewing their FM and support services to develop a strategy, which balances these factors, and demonstrates the potential options for their boards to make decisions with full knowledge of the implications of each decision. From the author's experience with numerous organisations, it is necessary to start with the strategy, otherwise the solution will not be correct for the organisation.

Given these pressures and changes to organisations, it is even more important for today's executives to focus their attention on the core activities of their businesses to formulate strategies to deliver the profit and returns to shareholders. There is more uncertainty in this environment and no longer can one predict the economic cycles. Organisations need flexibility to adapt to change. Druckers third aspect of business management, 'The need to be flexible and responsive to market changes' is more vital than ever before. Drucker's advice in 1993 was 'every organisation has to prepare for the abandonment of everything it does'. This does not come easily with successful structures and strategies that are embedded into the culture of an organisation where there is a resistance to change.

Similarly for managers within the FM world, practices have not changed or been subject to innovation. Ironically it is the Government that is leading the way in maximising value and forcing innovation. FM and support services are coming of age and playing a part in strategic planning processes.

The days of large in-house FM operational departments are numbered. A mass of low wage work in the FM operational delivery sectors is transferring to the FM supplier sector through outsourcing, providing retraining opportunities and skills improvement for individual companies. This has to be part of an overall change programme and not done in isolation to the core business.

But how are these FM and support services relevant to the core business?

In-house FM and support services in general are still entrenched in the old culture of organisations. They are rigid and static, with little flexibility to change. FM run on this basis will always be a cost to the organisation, either fixed or variable. The potential is for executives to consider outsourcing non-core functions to provide greater flexibility for change. Common excuses for the status quo are that we have always done it this way and it has always worked and by outsourcing we will loose control and damage the corporate culture. Complete outsourcing may not be the answer but it needs to be considered in the light of your business need and branding. The solution will be different for each organisation but it has to be integral to the business.

A sure path to oblivion is to stay where you are.

Bernard Fauber, CEO of Kmart 1986

Any leadership position is transitory and likely to be short lived and what exists is getting old.

Drucker 1966

The transfer of complete property portfolios, an inflexible and fixed cost to an organisation, as undertaken by Abbey National, the DSS and HM Inland Revenue and Customs and Excise, has allowed these entities to concentrate on their core businesses using their winning competencies. For example, Abbey National is not in the business of property ownership but in providing financial services to customers. They have, as a result of the transfer of property and outsourcing of elements of their FM, achieved flexibility to change their business to meet future market needs. They have transferred their fixed cost to variable and released capital value tied up in assets into the core business.

They have also improved FM team performance and through TUPE reduced overall headcount. In conjunction with these fundamental changes to property management and ownership, Abbey National has also begun to look at franchising their operations in some areas. Ownership and maintenance of their business delivery environment is then wholly transferred.

To quote Robin Priest, the chief executive of Mapeley who took on the property portfolio of HM Inland Revenue and Abbey National, 'Companies are starting to ask themselves, 'Why do we own all these assets?' By relinquishing its property portfolio, a company can free up capital, take away risks and uncertainty of the property market and focus on its core business.'

The two Public Sectors organisations have taken it further by buying their FM and support services from the Companies who took over their properties. These models guarantee the provision of a serviced workspace environment for their core business, that is:

- appropriate and fit for the purpose;
- adaptable and flexible to changing needs;
- affordable;
- available;
- accessible;

The risk of this provision is also transferred to the companies, who in many ways provide a fully serviced office space. This model of the PFI/PPP requires clear definition of needs of the businesses, strategy for change and clarity of FM service levels required from suppliers.

Outsourcing is not a passing fad. It is here to stay in one way or another. Businesses are focusing more on their core business activity. Outsourcing will have an impact on business success in changing markets.

Value tree principles and change strategy

Facilities Management exists to support the core business.

(Simpson 1996)

The value tree principles are used as a simple indicator to establish the linkage of the core business objectives of organisations to some specific FM and support services and in some cases how an activity may contribute to the strategy of your business.

It will not however provide a definitive measure of the actual impact on the core competencies, for example a measurable improvement on productivity or customer satisfaction.

The diagram of a value tree tracks an organisation's objectives to business drivers and the enablers. I hope that it gives managers a view of the impact it has on their core business activity. Whilst only three objectives are stated, there are others which could include:

- profit;
- brand;
- competitive advantage;

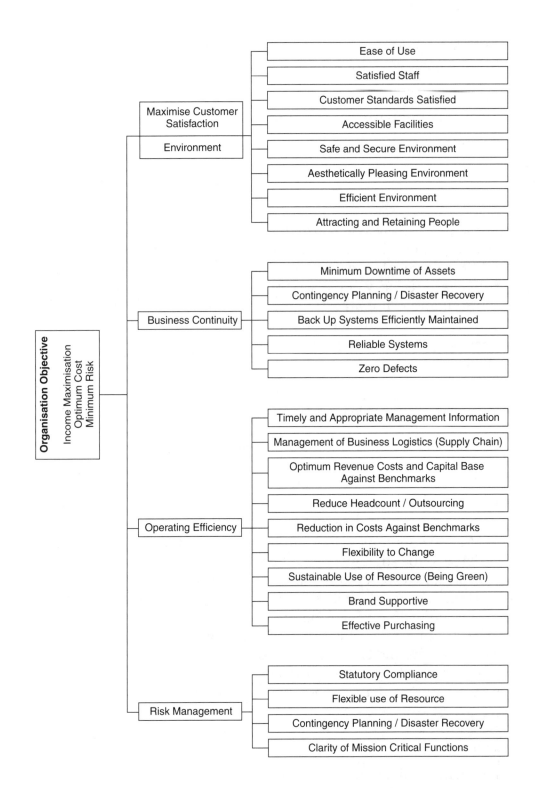

- flexibility;

- staff retention;

- customer retention.

Organisational objectives will also be different for every organisation; even those in the same sector, and likely to vary for the same organisation at different periods of its business cycle and external environment.

Take the example of income maximisation, which results from maximising customer satisfaction. To achieve this you need matured staff not disgruntled ones. Research suggests that if staff are paid and rewarded well, the environment they work in becomes more important. This relates to Maslow's hierarchy of needs and other psychological models of human drivers. Higher order drivers tend to manifest themselves in higher staff retention and greater productivity. An UK Investment Bank in Singapore noticed significant difference in staff attitudes and physical productivity when they relocated to a better environment. In such a highly charged business, the environment plays an important part in success. Employers also have obligations to meet the need to satisfy Health & Safety and Environment regulations.

Shopping Centres provide a good example of linkage between business objectives and FM activity. A shopping centre aiming to maximise income will have all the elements in the value tree linked to it, in particular customer satisfaction. If one were to explore each of the elements, they relate to the people (staff) and the environment:

- Ease of use – well designed with the correct signage, user friendly, adequate information and helpful staff.

- Accessible – located in the correct place, good transport facilities, and adequate access for all users.

- Safe and secure – having visible security, CCTV, and clear signage of escape routes.

- Aesthetically pleasing – adequate lighting levels, a clean appearance, using design effectively.

- Efficient – available for use and working services at all times, for example, escalators, lifts, revolving doors, lighting, heating or cooling, etc.

These require well-trained FM staff, maintenance, cleaning and security specialists all having input into the design. The application of these operational issues when changing an old concept shopping centre to a new 'leisure experience' centre is essential. Similarly, one could apply these to the upgrades of rail/tube stations, cinemas and most properties in public use.

A further example is a supermarket where the focus of the business or core competencies are buying, logistics, stock control, marketing sales (including customer surveys) and branding. Refrigeration is a support activity. Yet if the refrigeration fails, an increasing part of stock and the ability of stores to operate are compromised. Twenty-four hour opening will challenge the provision and maintenance of the refrigeration. In practice this has always been carried out in a closed period and costs of failure may have built into the overall costs, but is this acceptable?

Mechanical and electrical services, whilst not considered as core could impact on business continuity. It is a matter of degree and what is critical to an organisation. It may not be as critical in an office building as in an operating theatre or a controlled environment room. To take this further, one could argue that the back up and contingency systems are even more important as they kick in when normal systems fail.

The point is identification of what is critical to the business and to devise a plan to manage the FM.

From the value tree analysis, executives could get a grasp on how the FM and support services can impact on their core business objectives. Conversely, FM practitioners should understand the link and formulate plans for their management to consider as part of the overall business change strategy.

Conclusion: FM enabling change management

This is easier said than done in practice.

Having established the link of FM to the core business, we can consider how it can achieve a proactive role in helping an organisation change in the way it operates to meet a changing environment.

If we accept that the business environment is changing and to retain market position and be world class, executives have to continually review and establish new strategies to adapt and change their business focus into core areas and get better. FM has a major role to play in two key aspects:

One of the key areas for FM in change management is in the workspace environment which in turn determines property needs. To do this effectively, FM has to establish the current and future business needs in terms of people, the place and the processes of production, the way the business uses its accommodation, and how adaptable it is to new technology with the necessary options for the business to make decisions. Business in continuous improvement with innovation in the core business has to be matched by its FM support. There is so much written and there are so many ideas tested in workspace solutions. Internal FMs should be exploring the opportunities and proposing the appropriate ones to their executives to initiate change. This will bring together all the issues discussed earlier in having a clear idea of your property needs to outsourcing part if not all your properties in order to concentrate on your core business.

The second key aspect is that of clarity in the requirements for their FM and support service, in order that they are built into the agreements with the suppliers or if not outsourced, the in-house staff. Executives need to challenge the status quo and question if it is working elsewhere, what will work for my organisation and what benefits will be realised. Executives should support and encourage their FMs to have more exposure to the best practices in the market and to participate in a 'learning' environment. New working methods appropriate to your specific needs but based on FM best practice utilising efficient management systems as well as processes to meet the customer (occupiers and visitors) needs can then be adopted to support your business. They need to identify what is critical to the business and its brand, and have the ability to demonstrate the value to the business. If a solution is to adopt outsourcing, it has to be done in a way that gives a 'win-win' situation to the business, the staff and suppliers. This needs planning and a clear direction from the business. This 'outsourcing' initiative will create change in the organisation, as occupiers will be paying for a service with expectations managed to agreed service levels.

Conditional to this happening is:

• business executives to understand the role that FM can play in their business. The author sees that there are great opportunities for businesses to review their property needs and how FM is delivered to them;

- FM to understand the business (objectives, product/service, processes to achieve them, and future growth plans) – knowing where you are and where you want to get to;

- executives to expect FM to be proactive and construct plans for supporting their businesses in the right areas and demonstrate how it interacts with the core functions of place, people and business processes. Identify areas where non-core functions can be externalised and managed with minimum risk to the business;

- willingness to challenge and change from the historical ways of working to best practice, partnering suppliers, buying better and creating a 'continuous improvement' environment.

Significant shifts in the market are being observed from:

- property ownership to provider of space;

- fixed costs to variable costs;

- client to customer;

- landlord/tenant to provider/customer;

- projects to services;

- core and non-core to core;

- capital to revenue (occupancy cost);

- cost to value.

All these aspects involve FM and support services and bringing them into strategic change management earlier will reap significant benefits to businesses.

Part 2

Outsourcing Practice and Applications

make your hospital smile

By offering a range of services from catering and portering to domestic services, Sodexho is improving the daily quality of life in healthcare. This can increase productivity, improve patient turnaround and enhance your reputation – which means not only more contented staff and patients but a happier, healthier look to your finances. **Call 0800 169 49 59.**

sodexho.co.uk

Sodex'ho
Catering and Support Services

turning a cost into a value

5
Support Services Outsourcing for the Private Sector

Jonathan Reuvid

Support services today are generally classified as 'hard' or 'soft'. The former are those related to the management of physical facilities: the renovation, repair and maintenance of buildings, vehicles and equipment (otherwise described as FM and engineering services). Soft services comprise, broadly, of those which are 'people-based', where complete departments and staff functions of an organisation are subcontracted out.

The mechanics of public sector contract tendering are described in Chapter 6. Frequently, the public sector prefers to offer a single contract for both hard and soft services together and tenders are submitted by consortia of service providers which combine their specialist capabilities to cover the full range of requirements. In the private sector, by contrast, the engagement of external service providers is often a more evolutionary process with the provider extending the range of its service offering to match the client's growing or changing needs.

Sodexho and the market for soft services

For the major soft service providers the broadening of its people-based service capability is a logical sequence in strategic development.

The evolution of the product range that Sodexho's Business and Industry Division now offers to its private sector clients mirrors the development of the market and the diversity of clients' growing demands.

Historically, catering has been the driver of Sodexho's people-based service development. Founded in 1886, the original organisation, then trading as Gardner Merchant, undertook catering assignments for outside and major hospitality events; this tradition was maintained throughout the period of the company's ownership by the Trust House Forte group from the 1970s and the subsequent management buyout in 1993 until it was acquired two years later by Sodexho. Over the preceding 35 to 40 years, the original catering business had evolved into a comprehensive range of conference management services for corporate clients and, in parallel for the same client base, into the provision of cost-effective catering at all staff and workforce levels.

Providing corporate clients with hospitality catering and staff restaurants has led on to additional people-based services including reception, switchboard, help desks, mailrooms, retail facilities for staff, cleaning, reprographics and ground maintenance.

The advantages to the client of outsourcing soft services to a single, multi-service supplier and, for larger companies, of delegating provision of the same services at all its facilities to one multi-site contractor are readily apparent. In management terms, there are efficiencies to be gained from the more effective use of executive time in negotiating, monitoring and working to achieve continuous improvement with a single contractor. The realisation of uniformly high quality standards in outsourced services within each facility and across a network of facilities is similarly advanced.

The same reasoning applies to multinational corporate clients to whom Sodexho offers the same range of high quality services internationally in 70 countries worldwide.

Sodexho's clients now include three out of every four FTSE 100 companies. In the UK alone, including public sector contracts, Sodexho operates in 3,500 client permanent locations. It also manages, caters and provides hospitality for sporting events at venues including Ascot, Kempton Park and Kew Gardens.

An underlying driver for the development of soft service outsourcing was the recession of the early 1980s which compelled private sector companies to undertake downsizing programmes and corporate restructures with the primary objective of eliminating fixed costs (industry's euphemisms for planned redundancies). These painful experiences bred a determination to avoid remanning for non-core activities and to recruit only staff who would add direct value during periods of economic buoyancy and expansion. The focus on maintaining a lean organisation, reinforced by the IT revolution of the 1990s, has stimulated the market for outsourced soft services. Any reversal in strategic thinking is unlikely.

Naturally, the change in organisation culture has been adopted by the 'new economy'. High technology companies have no place in house for non-core activities or support services. A virtual organisation is the logical extreme.

The process of contracting

In the private sector, the pursuit of soft service contract opportunities is less formalised than the sealed envelope tendering routines of the public sector, described in Chapter 6.

Service providers maintain their own market intelligence databases from which they identify upcoming contract renewal opportunities and potential new clients within their chosen industry sectors.

On the client side, the majority of companies employ external consultants, who tend to be catering-orientated or former healthcare managers, to advise and help prepare contract specifications, develop tender templates and recommend shortlists of pre-qualified suppliers who are invited to submit proposals. External consultants also participate in the further selection processes and may be engaged in the auditing of awarded contracts.

Unlike much of the public sector, although the construction of tender templates is procurement driven, receivers of the services to be contracted are involved in the design and specification processes. In the private sector, there is also considerable flexibility for the service provider to adjust the contract specification when preparing and submitting a proposal. Indeed, contractors are expected to adjust service provision to the over-use and under-use of clients' facilities, both at the tendering stage and during the course of the contract. Such projects sometimes demand the refurbishment or refreshment of existing facilities involving substantial investment in which the contractor is expected to participate.

As well as corporates, the private sector includes independent schools and colleges and, in healthcare, privately-owned specialist or general care hospitals, nursing and retirement homes, residential homes and housing associations for the elderly and not-for-profit or charity-funded hospices and special care units.

Just as the receivers of services on the client side are involved in the procurement and contract negotiation processes, so too should the service providers operating management be engaged. In Sodexho's case, operations (often in the person of the manager designated for the contract under offer) is a part of the sales team; sales development and contract management are a joined up process. Conversely, when a contract is gained, the Sodexho sales manager participates in the initial review meetings with the client and is on call to re-engage in the discussion of major extensions to the contract and subsequent contract renewals.

Contracts in the private sector tend to be of three to five years duration with provision for extension up to two years. The period of contract development is quite short; typically three months from the issue of a tender to the contract award.

Key elements in the management of support services contracts

Most private sector contracts include service level clauses specifying the acceptable levels of performance in the delivery of each element of the contract against indicators.

Usually, the contract provides for incentives in terms of rewards when prescribed service levels are exceeded, and penalties when performance falls short.

The contractor identifies the Code of Practice and the benchmarks against which best practice is determined. The contract should specify monitoring, review and audit procedures, sometimes with provision for self-monitoring and audit against the mutually agreed performance indicators.

In Sodexho's case, each service division maintains its own training unit which instructs staff in craft-based skills, quality assurance and the technical and legal requirements to be satisfied in providing each type of service. Staff who are engaged under Transfer of Undertaking (Protection of Employment) – TUPE arrangements – and were formerly employed by the client or the previous contractor, are subjected individually to a skills audit and are trained internally to Sodexho standards or redeployed. Appropriately for an organisation delivering people-based services, the emphasis is on skills and HR.

Human Resources (HR)

Human resources are, indeed, the essential ingredient of soft service provision and Sodexho's declared mission to improve the quality of life for its customers (see Chapter 19) is a reflection of the company's environment in which its people are stimulated to flourish over the long-term.

Recruitment

Sodexho divisions recruit locally the staff for specific contracts at the skill and experience levels necessary to fill positions not covered by the employees acquired through TUPE arrangements under private and public sector contracts; they also provide supplementary craft skills training. The group HR function concentrates on the recruitment of experienced management personnel and management trainees.

The company uses media advertising and employment agencies to recruit into functional and operational areas. For its management trainee and graduate development programmes, Sodexho liases with schools, colleges and universities to generate applications.

The recruitment profile throughout the company is for high energy, busy and extrovert people who are adaptable, flexible and, above all, confident with the ability to work successfully as part of a team and present themselves well. A high proportion of staff are women, and about 60 per cent of the group's middle management is female.

A key recruitment criterion for middle management is the ability to manage change in order to match the pace of clients in a fast-moving marketplace. To a great extent, the continuing organic growth of Sodexho is dependent on the ability of its management to extend the range of services provided to each client through entrepreneurial flair and innovation.

Employee relations

Sodexho cherishes its Investors in People (IIP) accreditation in the UK and Ireland, gained for the whole business. Personal performance and achievement are recognised through fora organised at local and national levels, including long service awards presented annually in London by the group's UK and Ireland CEO.

Internal communication mechanisms are deployed widely within the organisation including the use of a company intranet and management and staff magazines.

Career opportunity and development

As a direct result of the sea-change in organisation culture described earlier, most company management structures in both manufacturing and service industries have been delayered and opportunities for vertical career development by promotion are limited in the newer 'flat' organisations.

Relatively few companies can provide continuing opportunities for horizontal career development and job enlargement, but major service providers can. Joining a group the size of Sodexho can present a challenge to new employees transferring from a smaller organisation, because a wider understanding of both people and product is demanded. However, the size, growth and diversity of the business and its developmental culture opens doors to career progression. In contract management, for example, jobs get bigger with increased responsibility as the services provided are extended, or a single location contract is expanded into a multi-site operation.

As a basis for career and succession planning, the company conducts a management audit and review in each division following annual staff appraisals in the last quarter of each year. In addition to the training and developmental activity which takes place at divisional level, more than 3000 employees pass through the company's resident management training and development centre at Kenley each year.

Graduate and management trainees embark on a structured development programme from entry, and graduate trainees are encouraged to study for MBA level qualifications.

At senior management levels, techniques such as interactive project work, one-to-one mentoring by senior executives and training in generic subject areas such as leadership skills and strategic management are used widely.

Internal job vacancies are advertised on the group's intranet system and also via divisional bulletins; people are encouraged to apply or nominate others for different roles within the organisation. Many senior employees have 10 or 20 years work experience within the group including time spent within a range of operational and functional areas.

For employees in mid to senior management levels, pay is quite tightly linked to individual and divisional performance. Typically, between 10 per cent and 30 per cent of a middle manager's income may be linked to a performance-related bonus. Managerial performance is measured against Specific Measurable Achievable Relevant Trackable (SMART) objectives which link directly to the plans and objectives of the division or department in which a manager operates.

The Sodexho approach to human resources represents best international practice in the field of outsourced service provision and the attention to training and career development are crucial to the group's success. The policy has also proved cost and quality efficient in terms of operational management. In an industry where high employee 'churn' rates are legendary, Sodexho's staff turnover is significantly lower than normal.

Acknowledgements

Paul Daly, UK Sales Director, Business & Industry, Sodexho Catering and Support Services, and Chris Piper, Business Development Director – Support Services for their provision of content and contributions to this chapter and related case studies.

6

Professional Services Outsourcing for the Public Sector

Jonathan Reuvid

When the contracting out of services first became a widespread practice in the 1980s, outsourcing was perceived by some as a severe threat to the existence of the public sector. Privatisation, it was said, would lead to loss of control of social and other public services for central government, local authorities and the civil service. A more immediate threat was the implied risk to jobs which inevitably generated whole-hearted Trade Union opposition.

Government policy of the day was focused upon the doctrine of Compulsory Competitive Tendering (CCT). However, the policy failed to survive in its original form, not because of Trade Union and Civil Service opposition but because it carried the seeds of its own destruction. On the one hand, an avoidance culture was developed to ward off private sector predators; on the other hand, private contractors were reluctant to bid for contracts against in-house teams, if there was a likelihood that the playing field might not be level. Moreover, the statutory timetable, inevitably tied to the public sector Budget Year, ensured that hundreds of spending authorities went to tender at the same time so that competent bidders could not tender for all contracts within such narrow timeframes. In the white collar areas rather few voluntary private contractors were let in and CCT did not deliver the volume of outsourced contracts expected.

However, CCT in its original, and subsequently less stringent 'market testing' form, was a necessary first step towards the current concept of 'Best Value' introduced by the New Labour government in 1997 as a relaxation of a regime which caused contracts to be awarded on the most competitive price from registered bidders with little regard to other consideratons.

The Best Value environment

Best Value allows purchasing authorities to take into consideration the quality of service as well as the price in tender evaluation. Within recent years measures have been introduced by successive governments to raise accountability and the exposure of local authorities to their electorates. Best Value is entirely consistent with a declared commitment to accountability and providing a stronger and more transparent public service to taxpayers.

The Best Value concept is still in its pilot phase; when it was introduced in 1997 it attracted a number of authorities, previously opposed to outsourcing, to engage in pilot projects – in some cases, perhaps, as a means of early escape from the rigours of CCT.

As yet, there is no Best Value legislation. Pilot projects are being monitored and evaluated continuously. When it comes, legislation and the accompanying definition of Best Value is likely to be based on precedents from practical experience. Mindful of the hostile reactions to CCT, the Government is taking care not to introduce abstract regulations. However, it is clear that Best Value legislation will force authorities to challenge current practice and prove that service delivery methods in use are still appropriate and offer good value for money. Already, engagement in Best Value is stimulating a more negotiated approach to tendering and a partnering approach to service in order to generate continuous improvement. (See the Sodexho Defence Services and Sodexho Healthcare case histories in Part 5).

Public sector outsourcing markets

Initially, as a consequence of the IT revolution, public sector outsourcing within Whitehall and the major departments and agencies of the

Civil Service was heavily focused on contracts involving major IT investment. By 1999 the central government sector of the IT market was valued at £378 million per annum in outsourced services, compared to £98 million in local government. The leading suppliers in this market include EDS, Siemens, Sema and ICL. In local government, the majority of IT contracts awarded to the private sector have been finance related, with activities outsourced ranging from the revenue collection of local taxes and benefits administration to payroll, accounting and pensions administration.

In contrast, the outsourcing of physical support services by the public sector is highly diverse, involving an extended range of professional, technical and logistics skills as well as management expertise across a variety of human activities. An example of the wide variety of support tasks in which private contractors may be engaged in a single contract is provided by the definition of activities in Chapter 19 of the partnering arrangements between the Sodexho consortium and Aldershot Garrison.

In central Government, the biggest outsourcing departments for on site services are the Ministry of Defence, the Department of Health and the Department of Education. In defence, there are separate procurement authorities for Army, Navy and Air Force establishments. In the case of the Army, there are five divisions in Army procurement which operate independently. Public health establishments are administered by local National Health Service Trusts. Schools and institutions of higher education, other than universities, fall under Local Education Authorities and are administered through individual boards of governors.

The principal areas of activity for private outsourcing, common to all public service establishments in defence, health and education include, where appropriate:

- catering;

- accommodation;

- cleaning;

- building maintenance and repairs;

- grounds maintenance;

- security;

- car parking;
- transport;
- office support and postroom management;
- fitness;
- healthcare;
- non-clinical support services in healthcare;
- environmental health and safety.

Some of these services fall within the definition of FM, but the list is not exhaustive. Leading edge service providers are dedicated to sound partnerships and the reduction of clients' risk. Within their broader 'good partner' responsibility, they expect to apply their expertise to contribute to headcount savings and manpower efficiencies and as their clients' proactive problem-solvers.

There are several major international multi-service providers who serve both local markets and multinational organisations globally, of which Sodexho and Granada Compass are market leaders. In hospital and healthcare service provision, Sodexho is paramount.

The tendering process in the UK

Public sector procurement authorities operate through publicly issued tenders, according to EU regulations, which are advertised in the bulletins of government departments and the EU Journal. Tenders are open to qualified bidders and these can be, in principle, from any EU member state.

For procurement authorities that are outsourcing for the first time the issue of invitations to tender is preceded by a 'market testing' exercise that involves defining the tasks which are to be contracted and comparing both the tasks and the present costs of delivery with market availability and price. This process commonly takes up to a year but can, in some cases, take as long as eighteen months, depending on the complexity of the tasks and how they are being carried out at the time, either in-house, by civil service providers or by outsourcing to a variety of small contractors.

The outcome of market testing is the preparation of a 'statement of requirement' (SOR) or specification in the case of healthcare. This becomes the basis for tendering and for the contract which is awarded, together with the legal terms and conditions of contract. SORs may be constructed to elicit 'input-based' or 'output-based' tenders. The former are effectively detailed descriptions of how each task is to be performed and what resources are to be deployed in staffing, labour, materials and services. The latter are based on objectives: as precise a description as possible of the services to be provided. Input-based tenders are not popular with service-providers in that they allow no scope for innovation or economies through improved delivery methods. The process has been likened to 'putting a car in for service and telling the proprietor how many mechanics he must use and how much he must pay them if he is to meet the service requirement satisfactorily'.

In deciding whether or not to tender and at what price, service providers are normally given sufficient access to the facilities to evaluate the project thoroughly. In defence, the SOR must be accepted without deviation, as must the contractual terms and conditions. However, in healthcare, there is often an opportunity to present, in addition to a compliant bid, a non-compliant or variant bid which will offer an alternative solution. There is no provision for the tenderer to adjust his price after the contract is awarded, unless the SOR or specification is found to be inaccurate, incomplete or misleading. The interval from invitation to tender to award of contracts may take, typically, up to nine months. Tenders are usually submitted without negotiation on a 'sealed envelope' basis.

Faced with an 'output-based' SOR, a service provider may develop an innovative and more cost-effective approach to delivery which may result in improved service. The only way in which this can be considered is to submit, in confidence, an alternative innovative proposal together with a formal compliant tender against the original, set SOR. The procurement authority may choose to disregard the alternative proposal or, following a contract strategy review, approve the innovative approach. In this case, the proposer is designated preferred bidder and the original SOR is revised accordingly and can, occasionally, be circulated to other selected bidders. The contract is eventually awarded after a period of negotiated competition. The first Sodexho Case History for the Aldershot Garrison Contract is an example of how a rigid FM contract was transformed into a partnering alternative.

Living with public sector contracts can be an uncomfortable experience for all those involved. Some of the discomfort is inherent in the tendering process, because the public authority decision-makers, certainly in defence establishment contracts, are often not the recipients of the service. Difficulties may be compounded where the team responsible for bidding, particularly where there is a consortium of service providers, is different from the management team responsible for performing the contract. Thus, there is potential for conflict between those delivering and receiving the services, and, internally between the operations and business development teams. However, such difficulties are easier to avoid or resolve in a partnering environment where joint management and review teams work side by side and adjustments to the original SOR may be agreed within the currency of the contract.

There is a clear perception that in almost all outsourcing contracts price remains the single determining factor, given that there are no particular risks associated with the employment of one private service provider against another. Ahead of legislation, the Best Value approach is not expected to make any significant impact on pricing, simply because decision-makers are under the constant pressure of tight expenditure budgets and judged by their success in meeting them.

In rare cases, there may be some leeway for wily service providers to allocate costs to their advantage within the fixed price elements of an output-based contract, e.g. if there is an envelope price for the provision of environmental health and safety across diverse facilities. In other cases, where the public authority decision-maker's formula-based evaluation criteria are known, it may be possible to exploit ambiguities in how the price/cost data is presented. For example, relief cover in hospital management contracts may or may not be included in cost per hour calculations.

There are usually provisions for the extension of contracts, where the current service-provider has satisfied the service receiver and is willing to continue. When contracts come up for renewal, the same tendering process applies, although the establishment of an updated SOR is greatly facilitated by the experience of the current term. The incumbent service provider has an advantage, if it wishes to re-tender. There is a cost to the public authority unit in replacing suppliers, generally estimated to be up to five per cent of contract value, and replacement bidders under the pre-Best Value regime expect to have to demonstrate a clear price advantage over the incumbent in order to gain a new contract.

Transfer of Undertakings (Protection of Employment) – TUPE

Without legal protection, local authority members and ministers would be unable to take decisions that would project employees into an uncertain future without incurring massive, unsustainable redundancy costs. Indeed TUPE legislation was a necessary condition for the acceptability of outsourcing to the public sector.

The legal effects of TUPE are discussed in Chapter 13, but the substance of the provisions is the employee's terms and conditions, their salaries, holiday entitlements and length of service transfer with them to the service provider under an outsourcing contract. Although TUPE provides assured protection to employees in the changeover to outsourcing (or from one contractor to another via the original employer organisation on the expiry of a contract) it does not relieve staff from the unease caused in what is often seen as the sale of their jobs without consultation.

Although the outcome for employees may be favourable, and ultimately recognised as an improvement, the motivation of the workforce during transfer is the key to success, and suppliers are well-advised to maintain a co-operative partnership with the trade unions, sometimes in the form of formal agreements committing both management and staff sides to a non-confrontational, problem-solving approach to local and national issues.

For the service-provider, now the new employer, the indiscriminate takeover of staff is not without hazard. The only way of avoiding the burden of unwanted staff is through the abolition of positions and the recharging of redundancy payments to the client under the terms of the outsourcing contract. Even where job descriptions and staffing complements are unchanged, it is probable that working practices and standards will change, and employees accustomed to a public sector work environment may have difficulties in adapting.

However, in the absence of TUPE, many FM contracts would be unmanageable, particularly in high employment areas where the recruitment of staff poses severe problems. The retraining of staff employed through TUPE and management development are critical issues. Sodexho's approach to recruitment and HR management described in Chapter 5 are illustrations of industry best practice.

The advent of the Private Finance Initiative (PFI)

Consistent with the Best Value concept in public sector service provision, but not necessarily a logical consequence, is the trend towards Private Finance Initiatives (PFI). In most cases, the driver for PFI is the high investment requirement which is looming in all major public service sectors including health, education and defence. The replacement of inadequate, outdated and run-down facilities is an imperative for the next decade and the financial burden of bringing Britain up to 21st century standards is beyond the public purse. The Government has recognised this reality and embarked on the encouragement of PFI in all sectors. The alternative of complete privatisation of public services has already happened in some prisons and education authorities and PFI may be a step in the direction of further privatisation. The disastrous Railtrack experience in public transport may be viewed as the consequence of a poor privatisation framework rather than as a result of privatisation *per se*.

Health Minister Alan Milburn has recently announced 29 PFI schemes in healthcare; in this sector, Sodexho Healthcare, currently providing services to more than 130 hospitals within the UK, is already engaged in three major projects. The first of these is the £90 million Wythenshawe Hospital PFI consortium with South Manchester University Hospitals NHS Trust for the development of a 319 bed acute unit, including an accident and emergency department and a 77 bed mental health unit, which brings the hospital's overall capacity up to 800 beds. Incidentally, including 700 staff at Wythenshawe, a total of 7000 people have so far transferred to Sodexho Healthcare under TUPE arrangements.

Sodexho is also a partner with King's College Hospital NHS Trust in the £100 million PFI project to provide a new 147 bed clinical block to house neonatal and specialist women's health departments. Third, Sodexho is an equity partner in Mercia Healthcare, part of the £90 million Hereford Hospitals PFI to develop a new 380 bed acute district general hospital and support services under a 30-year contract.

In education, Sodexho is engaged in PFI projects to design, build, finance and operate three schools in Fife and three secondary schools in Conway, as well as the rationalisation of Fleetwood High School, Lancashire, from three sites into one at a cost of £70 million.

Finally, Sodexho Defence Systems, which already supports the MOD on some 50 sites in the UK, will be the equity partner in the PFI over 35 years to rebuild Colchester Garrison, creating accommodation and support services to some 3500 service personnel.

A common feature of all PFI projects involving bricks and mortar capital investment, whether in defence, education or health, is that the length of contract needs to be in the 25 to 35 year time frame in order to provide for the total recovery of investment and the private investor's return on capital employed and operating profit. This absolute requirement in turn places a special onus on the judgement and policies of government on demographic change and resource allocation a generation ahead. Rebuilding hospital complexes and schools in major conurbations where social demands are relatively assured up to half a century ahead makes sense. Forecasting the requirements of defence establishments or higher education institutions (where distance learning may replace conventional campuses) in even 25 years' time is much more an exercise in crystal-ball gazing.

Acknowledgements

Roger Davie, Business Development Executive, and Cliff Fiander, Contract Director, Sodexho Defence Services and Andrew Isaac, Sales & Marketing Director, Sodexho Healthcare, for their provision of content and contributions to this chapter and related case studies.

7
Tendering Best Practice for Outsourcers

Toby Hirst

There can be little doubt that contractual relations founded on understanding, openness and clarity of mutual objectives create the best environment in which to deliver and manage successful contracts. This is particularly true of 'people' contracts, which result in people delivering services to other people. A common error when starting down the outsourcing route is to assume that the ability to procure commodities implies the ability successfully to procure services. While the underlying principles and processes may have certain similarities, the degree of subjectivity that is involved in a service transaction makes it necessary to treat service contracts somewhat differently. The delivery of a service is all about relationships, and the contractual negotiations are where those relationships can be made or broken.

The following pointers are designed to help you to achieve the best results if you decide to pursue the outsourcing route. This is not an exclusive list but one that reflects experience as both a client and a service provider, where the contractual outcomes have varied from distrust and antagonism to openness and a real spirit of working together. If you can achieve the latter, you will be well served by a service provider who is professional, delivers good quality services and soon becomes part of your team.

Clear objectives

To get the best from outsourcing, its purpose must be completely clear and should be positive in outlook – the aim should be to get added value from the support services and improve core business performance rather than to save money, staff or materials. While the latter may certainly be an outcome, as a declared objective it is likely to send quite the wrong message to employees and is not the most attractive 'come-on' to the better services providers who will be looking for a positive working environment.

Board level commitment

There will be plenty of internal detractors. Much pain and grief can be avoided if the concept of outsourcing has clear endorsement from the board from the outset and if the board's ongoing involvement as an integral part of the procurement process is understood both internally and by the potential suppliers. Both parties will then know that their time and resources are not being wasted. Bidders will be looking for that level of commitment from your senior management when they are deciding whether to bid for your business.

Involve the workforce

While most of your staff will have a degree of loyalty to your organisation, they will be more concerned with 'certainty'. To them, outsourcing smacks of managerial disloyalty to them, and of job uncertainty. Early, informed dialogue with them, and with their representatives, should go a long way to reducing these concerns. It will also help to ensure that the transition period from the initial announcement of intent through to the successful implementation by the new service provider is as smooth and free of impact on the core business as possible. TUPE regulations have, in any case, done much to mitigate the short-term employment uncertainty of any outsourcing process.

Benchmark your requirements

In considering whether to outsource or not, it is useful to benchmark your company against its peers and against successful leaders in other markets, and see how they have approached support service delivery and its outsourcing. Not only will this provide valuable information on the outsourcing market and its general direction but it will also enable you to restrict your expectations to achievable goals and outputs. It will also provide you with guidance on the better service providers and the relevant trade associations.

Be clear of your requirements

Before you go to the market you need to be clear on what you expect service providers to deliver. It may be a specific service such as mailroom or security, or it may be ideas: ie 'come and look at this range of services and tell us how you could help us'. Either way, potential service providers need to have a clear starting point from which to make proposals, and you need to have a defined requirement against which you can compare bids. Asking service providers to submit proposals against differing requirements will make the selection process much more difficult and may damage your credibility as an 'intelligent' client.

Set outputs

If you are intending to outsource some services, it is implicit that you wish to engage a service provider who has the relevant expertise and who is at least conversant with market best practice. Therefore you should set the outputs that you require it to deliver, such as a 24-hour security service or clean offices, rather than lay down how it will do it. However, you may need to engage external assistance to evaluate the bidders' methodologies, since you may not have the in-house expertise necessary to assess best practice in certain disciplines.

Involve the end users

To outsource services without involving the end users of those services will ultimately lead to tensions and misunderstanding between the service provider and its customers, ie your staff. While the process will be driven by the company, its success will depend on a good working relationship between the service provider's staff and the people they serve. You should ensure that what you are inviting a service provider to deliver is what is actually required, not what you, at the centre, think is required. Establishing user groups will help inform you, and at the same time allow you to retain control of the process.

Determine what is affordable

There will be financial limits to what you can pay for the outsourced services. Understanding those limits will ensure that the service outputs you lay down are affordable and not 'gold-plated'. Making the financial parameters clear to potential providers will help to ensure that their proposals are realistically priced. This approach will help you and the service providers avoid being involved in nugatory tendering. An open approach to exposing the financial limits should also encourage innovative bidding from the better service providers. It is unlikely to produce a similarity of bid prices, which is a concern often raised. Even if it did, there will be qualitative differentiators.

Gainshare targets

Initially, your budget and the outputs you place on the supplier will be defined. This should not preclude you from setting gainshare goals that will encourage both you and your service provider to look jointly for ways of delivering improved efficiency once the contract is operational, and then sharing the resulting benefits equitably. The benefits could be financial; or for the public sector client for whom financial benefits might create budgetary problems, the benefits could be in kind, for example as an extra service or an additional piece of equipment. For gainshare to work, you will need an agreed mechanism to be detailed in the contract.

The right team

When setting up your procurement team, look not only for people with the right skills to win the contract but also for those people who will be able to stay on to manage it. Continuity of team members, and particularly of your team leader, will be critical to success. By establishing a good understanding with the bidders and being able to develop it with the successful provider, the eventual working relationship will reduce misunderstandings about the deal and form the basis of a very productive contract. Individual 'ownership' of the contract through the transition period will help to ensure that the service provider can assume responsibility with the minimum of disruption to the core business. You will need to invest in your team to attract and retain the right people, and you will need to train them.

An achievable timescale

It is important that sufficient time is allowed for the procurement process. With too little time you may have an ill-defined requirement and the bidders may produce poorly researched and over-priced proposals. Too much time, and the requirement may be out of date and the bidders may lose interest and look elsewhere. Good quality bidding takes time and therefore costs money, but it is time and money well spent. It is important to remember that the best service providers may be in great demand and also have constraints on their time. A timetable that seeks to accommodate their programmes through early notification may well prove beneficial in the long run.

Don't be too ambitious

It is tempting to try and outsource more than your resources are capable of managing. This is likely to be to your disadvantage, since your potential suppliers (whose core business is bidding, winning and delivering service contracts) come to the table with better and more able resources than you. Outsourcing bite-sized pieces of work and holding out the prospect of more work to come to the successful tenderer, allows you to develop experience and skills and to learn from any mistakes.

A manageable competition

It may appear attractive to have a large number of potential suppliers, but in practice you will only have the time and resources to manage a few. In any case, while many providers may express an initial interest, only relatively few will really be able to offer you what you require – a good quality service – and of these some may already be fully committed elsewhere. Your procurement process should seek to get a wide initial response but be capable of rapidly down-selecting to two or three good suppliers.

Consider the supplier's perspective

When setting up your tendering process consider what you are offering from the supplier's perspective. The good quality supplier will be looking for a professionally managed competition where the risks involved in bidding are reasonably set against the chance of winning. On larger contracts, bidders will initially be evaluating not only the project and your ability to bring it to a successful outcome, but also the type and quality of the competition you are attracting. If they are uncomfortable with what they see, they may choose not to bid. Your organisation would be the loser as a result of such a decision.

An attractive contract term

You should be looking for commitment from the supplier. Innovative suppliers will themselves be looking for a contract term that will enable them to invest in the project, in either human or capital resources, and then to obtain a reasonable return on that investment. There may be a temptation to restrict the term of your initial contract in order to minimise any risk of an incorrect outsourcing decision or of poor supplier selection. This, however, may be interpreted as a lack of commitment and professionalism on your part and result in sub-optimal proposals from bidders. You could therefore seek the bidders' views on the contract term as part of the tendering process.

Sensible evaluation criteria

Given that potential bidders will be assessing the cost of bidding against the likelihood of selection, they will be looking for a fair evaluation process. The more open the evaluation, the better the results will be. At the same time, a well-defined evaluation process will leave you with an audit trail of how decisions were reached and will enable you to debrief the winner and the losers in due course. This process will enhance your reputation as an outsourcing client and ensure you have a good response at the next competition you run. Defining the evaluation criteria will also enable you to check that you have the correct resources to manage it.

Contract monitoring

Contracts need monitoring, but not excessively. Service providers should be tasked with demonstrating self-monitoring regimes that enable you to have confidence that your required outputs are being delivered while at the same time keeping your resources low. Your staff, the users of the outsourced services, also need to be briefed on what the contract is designed to deliver. This will ensure that any customer surveys are properly informed and that 'complaints' are correctly founded. You should try to adopt a positive approach to contract monitoring, which seeks to reward better-than-required outputs (through gainshare) rather than concentrating on penalties.

'Soft' and 'sustainable development' issues

The cultural 'fit' of a potential service provider with your organisation is a key issue, as is its ability to relate to your sustainable development strategy. Your tendering process should seek to obtain evidence that the supplier's corporate strategies are sympathetic with those of your company, and that its approach to sustainable development will enhance your stance on corporate responsibility. Put simply, will you like working with them and will they be happy working in your environment?

Summary

If a common theme runs through all these points, it is the need for open dialogue, defined as an exchange of ideas or opinions. Without dialogue, both internally and externally, the chances of reaching a mutually satisfactory contractual conclusion will be slim. Neither you nor your supplier will be content, and your respective staff, who have to receive and deliver the product of the negotiations, will feel they have been left out of the process.

The delivery of services, whether in-house or through outsourcing, is a 'people' business, with the underlying contract being negotiated by people. As a result, there is significant scope for misunderstanding, misinterpretation and mistrust in the procurement process. The points highlighted above are intended to minimise those potential shortcomings and to help you achieve a successful, long-term relationship with a good quality service provider whose support will enable you to concentrate on improving the performance of your core business.

8

The Changing Workplace – Analysing Property Needs

Dr. Alexi Marmot and Joanna Eley,
Alexi Marmot Associates

When you see other offices that are given all the facilities, it makes you feel pretty undervalued ... It would be lovely to have new office furniture and new layout and even things like fresh flowers in the office. The overall feeling could be calm, uncluttered and positive.

> (Questionnaire quote from employee in a retail company buying department. Source: AMA)

No fresh, clean air in the building whatsoever ... leads to stuffiness, drowsiness. If you're working late your desk never gets cleaned. Windows don't stay open when you open them. Coffee station should be equipped with coffee percolator. Carpet should be nice like the ground floor. Ceiling too low. Totally uninspiring artwork in miserly quantities.

> (Questionnaire quote from employee in a multinational high tech company. Source: AMA)

Does the workplace matter?

Creating a good workplace is important for morale, productivity and company growth. People who answer office questionnaires reiterate time and again how much a decent work environment matters. Creating an indifferent, or worse still, a poor work environment, can turn even the most positive employee into a grumbler. The workplace says a great deal about the company to customers and to employees alike. The strength of feeling displayed when people discuss their work environment indicates that productivity issues are closely involved with workspace quality. Despite little formal research evidence, it is hard to avoid the conclusion that a good environment is a productive workplace. Without doubt, it helps to attract and retain high calibre staff. Exit interviews in companies offering poor workplaces bear this out.

Senior managers are often in the dark about their buildings. They are responsible for the mission statement of the business, but often they are not in close contact with the people whose job it is to see that a building, with its equipment and furnishing, properly supports the business to achieve this mission. The best managers understand the strength of a good workplace. They excel if their work environment supports the way they want their firm to function, if it helps people to communicate and if it gives customers the right image. They know that they have a competitive advantage if their workplace performs better than the norm through efficient design and space management. They seek to make the most of their property assets to support their core business. In this age of e-business, they certainly dare to pose the questions: do we need an office building at all?; can we function with a distributed workforce, electronically linked but working at low overheads from their homes and cars?

Basic decisions on the workplace

Changes in the workspace are costly in time and capital outlay. At every stage, the intelligent manager questions basic assumptions to minimise the risk of wrong decisions. There are many options for the first level of strategic decision:

• How many workplaces do we need? One, none or many?

- If we need none, do we provide our staff with a home or remote office kit of technology and furniture to ensure health and safety is met?

- When and where do we meet up – physically or virtually?

- If we need any workplaces, can we commit long-term, or should we seek a short-term license in serviced offices for all or some of the space?

- If we expect to use it long-term, should we lease or purchase?

- Should we seek to outsource all aspects of procurement, ownership and management of workspace in the same way as we might, for example, outsource all aspects of IT?

The reason these questions must be addressed is that buildings are part of the corporate asset base, have a high financial input – typically 10–20 per cent of annual running costs – and are complicated to procure. Managers are rarely familiar with the process as organisations require workplace changes infrequently. Familiarity with a range of options is always a sound grounding for good decisions.

Current workplace options

The range of legitimate workplaces has increased as a result of technological and organisational changes, as well as the alternative work styles that have accompanied them.

Home office

A den or study for one person, the corner of another room, the kitchen table or a space under the stairs can be turned into a home office equipped with the full range of office machinery or occasionally set up with a laptop and a mobile phone. It may be used daily for regular work or occasionally for 'heads down' work when exceptional concentration is needed.

Working from home sounds idyllic if the home is spacious, in a peaceful environment and well-equipped.

If I've got anything difficult to do, I stay at home — there's too many interruptions, it's too noisy in the office.

(Questionnaire response: management consultant. Source: AMA)

However, many people prefer to keep a distance between their home life and their office.

I view my home as somewhere in which the company doesn't intrude. I would not like to work at home, I like to keep home and work separate.

(Questionnaire responses: management consultants. Source: AMA)

Home is less attractive for work if it is too small to provide a permanent place for the computer, filled with the noise of wailing two-year-olds or discontented teenagers out of work and into reggae, or cold because heating during the day is too expensive. There are numerous difficulties to be resolved such as: who pays the telephone bill?; do benefits, such as an agreement with the employer to pay a suitable proportion of the heating bill, have to be taxed?; who pays insurance, and what eventualities will it cover?

Call centres

Reminiscent of an old style factory with machinery that could not be turned off and needed people present at all times, teams of workers now respond to telephone lines in call centres, offering information, selling goods or services and acting as help desks for almost every sphere of business. The extent to which these services are required by customers determines the size of the teams at different times of day. In some cases, supplementary staff are connected to the centres from home-based workplaces at times of exceptional pressure. The service may be provided on a 'round the clock' basis from a single location using early, late or even night shifts. It is also possible to shift the work location, rather than the work time for the staff, and use teams on the other side of the world.

Satellite offices

The local outpost established by a larger business is acquiring an identity of its own. It may be set up for a variety of reasons – to exploit cheap space for activities that do not require central locations; to provide offices that are more accessible to the workforce and enable them to avoid extensive commuting; to set up in new locations, starting with modest premises to test the local opportunities.

Business centres

Simple or lavish, space can be rented by duration for a few hours or for a number of months, and by area, such as a single desk or several rooms for a team. Business centres can be part of large chains with multiple outlets in different cities and countries; or one-off. They can be located in the suburbs or in central areas. They are suitable for companies establishing a base in a new location or for start-up firms. Services that emulate those in a large organisation – reception, conference suites and other client-focused facilities – are provided on a 'take only as much as you need' basis.

Client locations

A variety of pressures have fostered situations where individuals or groups are regularly located in the office premises of their clients. At the same time, as all organisations grow increasingly conscious of the cost of providing and maintaining office space, so the balance between client and provider constantly shifts: no one wishes to be responsible for accommodation that others can be persuaded to pay for. Many, but not all, of these implants are related to activities that need to be located in the office building, regardless of the identity of the employer, such as reception, security, catering, facilities management (FM), IT related troubleshooting and helpdesks. Other typical 'cuckoos' are consultants providing an in-house role on a short-term basis – leading or manning project teams of a defined duration – and contractors absorbed alongside company employees to maintain a reduced permanent 'headcount' at a low level but enable fluctuations in workload to be taken up.

Telecottages and neighbourhood work centres

Not all work, and not all homes, are suited to home-based work. Some organisations are seeking solutions where the commute is reduced but may not be eliminated; work takes place near, but not at, home. From Sweden to Hawaii via the Scottish Highlands, there are experiments with telecottages and neighbourhood work centres. A telecottage is a community centre – equipped with technology such as computers, faxes and photocopiers – where local people can train or work using the resources provided. City-based companies are realising this, and more and more work is being tendered out to telecottages, reversing the centralising effects of the industrial revolution.

There are examples of workforces in unexpected, unconventional, non-office buildings, such as prisoners in an Irish jail handling the claims forms for an insurance company in the USA, or large companies in India handling data processing and code writing for software operations in the First World countries.

Alternate officing

The world's largest accountancy firms and consultancy organisations, among others, are enthusiastically following another parallel avenue – that of 'alternate officing', 'desk sharing' or 'hot desking' – as a way to acknowledge, and thereby exploit, the change in working patterns. With desk sharing, or pooling, someone who has just walked through the front door settles down at any one of the available desks. The term 'hot desking', borrowed from 'hot bunking' on submarines, assumes that the desk has just been vacated by a colleague and is reoccupied before the chair has had time to cool down. Desks are dubbed 'touchdowns' when it is assumed that people settle there only briefly, like butterflies flitting in and out of the office. The people using these desks are variously described as nomads, road warriors, peripatetic or merely mobile.

Why even consider such a horrendous idea? Isn't it a thin disguise for squeezing people into unacceptably tight spaces? Who wants to give up the ownership of his of her desk? What lunatics are willing to give up their own desks? Who can stand sharing? Will any managers be prepared to give up their own offices?

Desk sharing may or may not operate at the same time, or for the same individuals, as telecommuting. When one worker is at home, or working on an aeroplane or a train, another one can be using the desk in the office. The convention whereby everyone is allocated a place of their own has been effectively challenged.

An active sales force results in a sea of empty desks, an expensive luxury. Consultants, whose task is to understand the business of another organisation, spend part, sometimes most, of their time on client premises. Other examples are inspectors checking that firms are following correctly the rules laid down for them by taxation, health and safety or other employment regulations, who often need to see the organisations actually at work; or journalists away collecting material before crafting it into reports; or researchers out gathering data or interviewing people. All these are among the groups whose work takes them 'out of the office' and may keep them out more than in.

Different workplaces for different economic sectors

Workplaces vary for organisations that are public or private; locally-based or global; profitable or unprofitable; creative or routine; tiny or vast; well-managed or chaotic; steeped in tradition or avant garde; growing, stable or declining. The conduct of work varies enormously in different organisations as does the pace of work, the way in which it happens and how people relate to one another.

The academic office environment

In a university or college, workplaces usually conform to the following characteristics:

- Everyone wants a room of their own – space for heads down concentrated work is the main need. Offices shared by two or three are reluctantly accepted, but open plan is strongly resisted.

- The hierarchy is very important and clearly marked out in different space allocation for full tenured professors, assistant or associate professors, senior or junior lecturers, research associates or assistants and administrative staff.

- Control of space is essential. Each department within the wider university or college tries to cling to its space, denying other departments access. Without space, the department cannot grow. Without growth, additional research projects cannot commence. Without new research projects, steps on the academic ladder cannot be reached.

- Computer power and connectivity is usually high.

- Walls of shelves and filing cabinets to store books and papers can never be too numerous.

- 'Clean desk' policies can never be enforced.

- Budgets are always modest; furniture is functional; style is utilitarian; people are allowed to humanise and personalise their space in their own way.

Offices for large retail organisations

Large retailers have small offices for local managers within each retail outlet, plus a central head office where all of the main business decisions are taken. The local offices tend to be found hidden away in the spare piece of space behind the delivery bays and somewhere near a staff room where sales people stop for their breaks. Head offices are more orderly. They are characterised by:

- large reception areas where suppliers gather before meeting buyers;
- generous offices for the top managers;
- small desks in open plan layouts for buying departments;
- interspersed within office space is space for storing and setting out product lines from household items, clothing and small accessories or food products to large bulky items like sofas and garden furniture;
- suites of meeting rooms well-equipped for audio visual presentations;
- some specialised rooms for storing perishable goods under refrigeration.

Offices for cultural establishments

Museums, art galleries, libraries and theatres all operate thanks to the work done by three populations: front-of-house staff who interact with the public; operational staff who look after the contents (conservation, cleaning, set building, framing and transportation of the works); and office-based staff who determine the direction of the establishment and its collection, keep the organisation solvent, write catalogues, prepare performances or exhibitions and inform the public of its contents. This third group may number several hundred in a large national museum or just a few people in a small organisation. Whatever the size of the establishment, office space comes second to the space for the main activity (housing art, exhibitions, plays or books). Offices tend to be found in 'Cinderella' space: basements, annexes and old wings that are relatively inaccessible; new wings inserted to house a few more people or short-term space rented down the road. Offices for cultural establishments are characterised by:

- communication between different departments is often a problem because of the scattered layout;

- expenditure on office furniture and systems is rather modest;

- management of the office space may be rather amateur as the main space management efforts are directed at the front-of-house;

- some of the office staff prefer to work heads down in cells as they come from academic traditions;

- others are more comfortable with team offices or open plan arrangements for tasks such as cataloguing or finance;

- storage of books and papers in vast quantities is common to both.

Offices for new technology and e-business companies

The companies responsible for creating, marketing and exploiting the new technologies in computing and telecommunications that influence everyone else's office work share common features in the way they house themselves:

- As the companies tend to be quite youthful, they also tend to have few outward shows of difference between top management and the most junior levels.

- Using the new technologies is common within them, even if the best and latest is reserved for customers.

- Impressive customer showcases and training areas for customers, dealers and their own staff form part of many of their buildings.

- Work mobility is common to the way sales teams operate: so, the office is an occasional stopping point in a work rhythm that includes customer premises, cars, planes, trains, hotel rooms and home.

- Storage is primarily electronic.

- Image must be functional, up-to-date and well-organised.

- Software development houses are often youthful and include many relaxed places for solo and teamwork, plus some 'play' space.

Offices for banks, insurance companies and other financial players

Financial institutions come in many shapes and forms from retail, commercial or investment banks, stockbrokers and trading houses, insurers and reinsurers, home loan mortgage companies, asset management operations and credit card companies. Many are long-established representative companies that in one guise or another (and several mergers away) were founded more than a hundred years ago. Others are newcomers created to sell financial services directly to consumers through the telephone and Internet, thus avoiding much of the costly infrastructure of the older companies. Some of the characteristics of the offices are:

- a significant presence in the main trading capitals of the world's finance centres – Wall Street, the City of London, Frankfurt, Tokyo and Hong Kong;

- utter dependence on computers, hence a lot of office space for IT departments;

- trading floors for some of their staff, consisting of tightly packed desks, each equipped with multiple computer screens creating an electronic bazaar for buying and selling stock;

- back office clerical factories for processing transactions, housing large numbers of relatively junior people;

- call centres where queries are answered, housed in suburban centres or office parks away from the expensive metropolitan centres;

- headquarter offices redolent of solidity, wealth and history, with enough artworks and elegant meeting rooms to give the key investors the impression that the organisation is long-established, safe and solvent;

- reduced reliance on paper processing as electronic records gradually dominate all transactions;

- growing introduction of remote work and home work for some parts of the organisation, eg insurance claims settled without any paper work by roving inspectors reliant solely upon laptops operated from customer premises, cars or their own homes.

Offices of the large accountancy and consultant firms

The last twenty years have witnessed breathtaking growth in the dependence of public and private organisations on the services of a few vast international accountancy firms with their allied consultancy operations. Mergers now leave a handful of such partnership companies checking and advising others on how best to further their businesses. Their offices are:

- located in the major cities of the globe with a growing presence in Asia, Africa, Latin America and Eastern Europe;

- path breakers in pushing the limits of efficient space use through their desk sharing for young audit trainees and hotelling for consultants;

- defining a balance between the space demands of partners (ideally large corner offices) and space efficiency (pooled offices and desks, as partners are often away);

- set aside suites of meeting rooms of some elegance to impress key clients;

- happy to announce their presence to the outside world with big lettering and neon signs atop their buildings;

- traditionally providing very clear space increments that parallel career advancement from trainee to auditor/consultant, managing consultant, partner, senior partner, though this is breaking down as space efficiency increases.

Offices for major industries – manufacturing, energy and transportation

Offices in these companies are just a small part of the building stock that also comprises factories, research and development laboratories, processing plants, exploration bases, workshops and maintenance zones, stations and terminals. Yet the headquarters and central office functions accommodate vast numbers of people to keep the organisations ticking over. Offices need to house the board and top management; strategic departments that help define the future directions by examining trends and exploring new product concepts; sales and marketing operations; finance; human resource and training sections; information technology and a miscellany of other central functions, including communications and public relations, property and real estate, legal, purchasing and health and safety departments.

These offices cover many different industries' various preoccupations and locational imperatives. Some themes that typically emerge are:

- main headquarters usually in central city area of a major finance centre, however, some have their HQ on, or close to, one of their major operational sites;

- pressure to reduce the number of staff in the central operations and reduce the costs of the HQ, hence a move to more suburban locations or office parks;

- outsourcing of some activities to other organisations helps the pace of downsizing the HQ;

- HQ to look and feel suitably opulent;

- culture of the company often trying to balance the dominant culture of its skill base (eg, chemistry, engineering, geology) with multi-disciplinary need of the business;

- investment in new technology is essential; hence office buildings and their contents are not allowed to fall too far out of date;

- frequent mergers and acquisitions that involve much effort in uniting the image and processes between formerly discrete companies in different buildings;

- corporate history is a source of pride and may demand space for displaying artefacts and an archive.

Offices for creative industries

Offices for creative industries are made up of a combination of routine and mainstream departments (finance, IT), plus departments more directly shaping the business. The overall image in such organisations is usually youthful and casual.

- Much creative work is done in teams so multiple spaces for teams to get together in meeting rooms, project rooms, coffee bars and chill out areas is essential.

- Image is projected clearly from reception areas and through into the building. Depending on the industry, books will be displayed in every office, a TV will broadcast, music will be played or posters displayed.

- Hierarchies tend to be unimportant in spatial terms.

- Apart from newspaper and TV, locations are usually within a few large cities filled with bright young things whose ideas dominate the cultural frontiers. New York, Los Angeles, London and Boston play a significant role.

- Buildings are often outside the most expensive central areas and creative clients dare to take on slightly difficult structures, converting them to a space that expresses the corporate image.

- Materials, colours and finishes are light hearted and explorative. Cheap plastics or recycled manufactured goods may be used to create internal walls, ceilings (eg, painted TV remote controls, crushed recycled aluminium soft drink cans).

Government offices – federal, state and local

Vast bureaucracies are essential to keep modern social and economic systems functional as they: defend our countries; ensure taxes are paid; the young are educated; the poor receive medical treatment, housing and enough money for survival; justice is served; the environment is preserved; and industries are regulated. At a state or local level, smaller bureaucracies are needed to run and maintain sanitary services, schools, libraries, street lighting, fire protection, roads and highways. What are the peculiar characteristics of offices for the public employees helping to deliver our common infrastructure?

- Vast office building clusters, in small areas within the capital cities. The older of these buildings are likely to evoke associations of the classical Empire of Rome – being built to impress. The modern buildings are more varied.

- Town halls and city administrative buildings are similarly built to impress, both internally and externally.

- Growth of public administration will have resulted in the accumulation of many office properties close by serving to house back office personnel or new developments.

- The ceremonial parts of the Government need their own spaces for elected representatives to meet in committees, debating and voting chambers.

- Modest furnishings and fittings are the order of the day – public accountability suggests that overt signs of comfort and elegance should be avoided.

- Space allocation is governed by clear sets of principles laid down by bodies such as the General Services Administration. Status and job type dictate spatial provision.

- Vast amounts of paper filing are essential in most departments though electronic record storage is starting to make small inroads.

Legal offices

Lawyers and solicitors generally work in a partnership with many other lawyers, trainee lawyers and support staff. Partners still often demand – and cannot conceive of working without – an office of their own. The typical spatial formula for large legal practices consists of:

- a location in one of the world's main financial or manufacturing centres or capitals;

- many small offices around the perimeter of the building for lawyers;

- open plan or small group offices for legal secretaries and other support staff;

- a wing with the meeting rooms for clients furnished tastefully with a balance between traditional (you can trust us with your affairs – we are solid and have been around a long time) and modern (yet we know the ways of the world and are up to date with every new twist of business, government and society);

- paper everywhere starting with a legal library, spreading into every office down into file rooms, basements and off-site archival offices;

- space pressure due to growth may require junior lawyers to share offices. They won't like it, but will find that it still works;

- in a few cases, lawyers are experimenting with fully open plan arrangements plus a number of small rooms for concentrated work. This arrangement is more common for the legal department within a large corporation, which in turn may have moved to open plan throughout;

- space pressure and the desire to reduce overheads will result in many more firms changing their space, experimenting with more open space, more space sharing and more mobile office work off-site/at home/with clients, for best concentration.

Acknowledgements

This chapter has been drawn in part from the book by Alexi Marmot and Joanna Eley *Office Space Planning: Designing for Tomorrow's Workplace*, (2000), McGraw-Hill, New York.

9

The Changing Workplace
– Analysing Space Needs[1]

Danny Shiem-Shin Then
*Queensland University of
Technology*

Business dynamics and the changing workplace

Much of the workspace occupied by business today has, at best, been
developed in response to assessments of work needs that have their
origin in a time when the pace and character of changes in work were
less pronounced than they are today. The workplaces of the future
must not only accommodate rapid changes – economic, technological
and social – but must also strive to reflect and promote new ways of
working.

Work environments in terms of their location, size and configuration are, or at least should be, a direct response to the considered
needs of people and the work processes they carry out or plan to carry
out in the future. Consequently, to ensure that the most fitting work
environments are provided to meet the needs of business, corporate
directors tasked with the responsibility of developing workplace

---

[1] This chapter has been drawn mainly from the book by McGregor and Then (1999) *Facilities Management
and The Business of Space*, Arnold. Special acknowledgment is therefore due to my friend and co-author,
Wes McGregor.

strategies and planning workspace must be constantly considering their needs for the years ahead. The proactive alignment of real estate assets and workplace strategies with corporate goals and objectives of business units will continue to be the driver for corporate directors.

Space as a support resource – workspace to production process

In today's business environment, business support infrastructures are no longer static. Directors of enterprises must now consider the provision of appropriate workspace as an integral part of their overall business delivery strategy. In addition, the ongoing task of managing functional space as business support facilities requires a thorough understanding of the drivers of business occupancy costs and how they can be systematically assessed, evaluated, procured and managed to remain strategically and operationally relevant to supporting the current corporate strategy.

There is clear evidence that supports the view that a sharp strategic direction is needed from senior business managers in their consideration of the management of corporate real estate (i.e. the land and buildings used for workspace infrastructure and investment) as an integral part of business resources management. This view was aptly expressed in the Industrial Development and Research Council (IDRF) Corporate Real Estate 2000 report (Joroff et al, 1993, p.7), which called for a rethinking in the way this resource is managed:

> In the past, corporate management often did not consider the corporate real estate function to be as important as the four corporate resources of capital, people, technology and information. Senior managers had not learned to ask how the function could create value for the company and help to meet the overall corporate mission. Today that goal is being pursued aggressively. Senior managers now are beginning to recognise that real estate is a critical strategic asset, one that supports the financial, work environment and operational needs of the total corporation.

The reference to 'financial, work environment and operational needs' as an integrated task of resources management, which provides for the 'total corporation', is significant in that it acknowledges that land, buildings and the work environment are essential parts of every corporation's strategic planning, and must therefore be managed accordingly to ensure that the financial and operational goals of the company are met. It is also noteworthy that the same report also describes corporate real estate assets as 'the fifth resource', after the traditional resources of people, technology, information and capital.

It is crucial for corporate directors to understand the resource implications of corporate real estate assets in terms of:

- the importance of the workplace environment as an enabling facility that shapes corporate culture and behaviour;

- the economics of the provision of real estate assets as operating resources, as well as in terms of their intrinsic value;

- the relationship between the physical environment, individual satisfaction and organisational productivity;

- the provision and ongoing management of facilities support services and their users' interface with the workplace environment.

Operational management (provided by the real estate and facilities management functions), for its part, has to move from being a transactional-reactive role to a strategic-proactive role, where the emphasis is on anticipating the future in the light of the company's core business and its work processes, and consistently providing value-adding solutions. Some examples of such innovative facilities solutions to emerging business challenges include:

- meeting competitive challenges, for both the business and for the FM function;

- reducing costs associated with acquiring, operating and changing workspace and its layout;

- increasing the quality of the work environment, and hence improving the productivity of its users;

- responding to unpredictable market conditions and, in so doing, have close alignment of the workspace provision with the needs of the business;

- organising workplaces to accommodate a more varied and complex workforce;

- exploiting new information technologies to improve the management of workspace and its related facilities services.

It should be noted that the cost and quality, referred to above, are not alternatives. The days of trading one aspect off against the other are gone: what business expects, in fact demands, is low cost *and* high quality.

Understanding space needs by having a strategic accommodation plan

The planning of all workspace should be a response to specific business needs and corporate drivers. The challenge of managing workspace is to achieve the best match of the functional space supplied to the dynamics of changing business demands. The underlying business rationale of effective workplace management is the promotion of business effectiveness through an understanding that the buildings which accommodate the productive resources of employees, facilities infrastructure and enabling technologies must be aligned to the strategic intent of the organisation that they are intended to support. However, it must be acknowledged that the definition of need, the specification of workspaces, the procurement and management of functional space as a supporting resource of business delivery only entered the strategic management arena in comparatively recent times.

The effective management of workspace is based upon two imperatives: first, the acceptance of the economic reality that every square metre of occupied space has to be paid for by the business; and second, that the space occupied by staff should be directly related to the requirements of the work processes and tasks the person has to perform, rather than based on their seniority and status. It is from this starting point that the relationship between business planning and space planning becomes apparent. The process of addressing the workspace needs of the business is the conscious planning and design of the work environment to facilitate the delivery of products and services, driven by desired business practices (culture and organisation) and operational requirements (tasks and functions).

Just as the aim of a business strategy is to provide a framework which guides the organisation in its decision-making towards a chosen goal, so too an accommodation strategy provides the framework for decision-making relating to the management of an organisation's workspace. Unfortunately, the fact that an organisation evolves rapidly, whether it is by organic means or by acquisitions and mergers, is seen, all too often, as justification for not producing a strategic accommodation plan. The results experienced as direct consequences of the failure to plan can typically include:

- insufficient available workspace;

- inappropriate premises;

- inefficient facilities and services;

- outmoded systems for handling information;

- conflict between facilities providers and facilities users;

- poor staff morale resulting in the achievement of poorer than expected productivity levels.

For success, therefore, there is a need to consider workplace-related issues at an early stage and, in so doing, create the framework around which the organisation's workspace can be developed to function effectively. This is where the need for a strategic accommodation plan becomes critical.

The production of an accommodation plan fosters an atmosphere in which decisions relating to the business's workspace can be made, confident in the knowledge of being able to respond to the varying needs of the organisation through time. The accommodation plan has its roots in the organisation's business plan and is itself a component of the organisation's facilities plan. When well-constructed, the plan not only enables responsive actions to be initiated, but will provide the basis for anticipatory actions by the real estate/facilities manager. This can be said to be the challenge for all workspace planning – to move from a reactive to anticipatory process. (Figure 9.1).

Effective strategic facility planning requires constant and continuing communication between corporate planners, who chart the future path for the enterprise, and the real estate/facilities professionals, who are charged with delivering the physical infrastructure to affect the business plans. The use of scenario planning provides a useful mechanism for promoting the much-needed dialogue between strategic planning and tactical planning. It also provides for the two-way exchange between *business* information and building-facilities information. This informed interface between corporate planners and real estate/facilities managers should be driven by a clear understanding of the business demand variables:

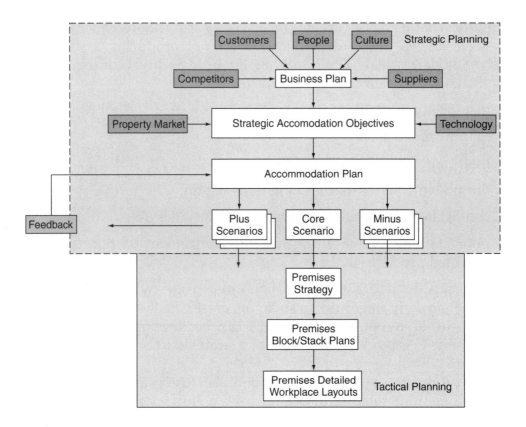

Figure 9.1 Elements of an accommodation planning model (McGregor & Then, 1999)

- The push to control costs and minimise long-term commitments to infrastructure – both of which suggest the consumption of less functional space.

- The increasing need to provide workplaces that enhance productivity, while addressing increasingly complex environmental and technological requirements.

- The provision of satisfaction to the workforce, individually and collectively.

For many organisations, the prospect of preparing a five-year facilities and accommodation plan will be a new departure. For some, it will be considered that this is an unreasonable demand and without any valid foundation. However, when one considers the length of time involved in gathering data, analysing it, preparing a plan and then

Figure 9.2 Creating supporting strategies by promoting dialogue between strategic business management and operational asset management

implementing the plan (particularly if it involves the production of a new building), two to three years may have elapsed before occupation of the building can even begin. It is for this reason that the facilities manager should always be working to a five-year planning horizon, albeit with various scenarios to take account of changes that may arise in the intervening period.

In far too many instances, organisations have found themselves suffering in the medium-term (let alone the long-term) through the failure to plan effectively. Long-term strategic planning does not necessarily involve buying a site or acquiring a building, but rather considering 'what if' each time a decision is being taken to test its validity against the long-term strategic plan. For example, when committing to new premises (whether purchased or leased), consideration should be given to what happens if the organisation contracts within the next five to ten years. Will the premises be let or sold easily? What if the organisation expands: how easy will it be to extend the premises, or acquire the adjoining site or building? Consideration of such matters can save much corporate pain, both physical and financial, in the future. This is where the linkages between the business and accommodation plans are made, and where strategic and tactical plans play a vital role in the successful application of the accommodation forecasts. The scenario models are developed in response to various possible scenarios which the business may encounter.

From the information gathered, a core scenario can be developed, which is the organisation's best view of the future. Best in this context is not 'most optimistic', but is the 'most reliable' forecast based on a full understanding of the business environment in which the organisation operates. From this core scenario, other possible scenarios are developed by applying sensitivity analysis techniques, which have the effect of acting as pluses or minuses in relation to the core scenario. From these 'alternative worlds' of business, several corresponding accommodation scenarios can be developed to meet the needs of different levels of business, different numbers of people in the organisation, different levels of technology usage, different organisation structures and so on.

A major role of FM is the efficient operation of all serviced spaces supporting the delivery of the core business activities. Operational support on an ongoing basis demands a thorough understanding of the work tasks carried out and the criticality of the processes supporting business delivery. Ongoing support tasks can be grouped under two categories of activities:

- Measures to ensure the smooth operation of serviced facilities, in terms of:

  - the range of building-related services – utilities and statutory requirements, building maintenance and repairs;

  - the range of business support services – cleaning, catering, office services, etc.

- Measures to handle short-term fluctuations of demand for workspace – churn management.

Whilst the former functions are essentially transaction-oriented, with the focus on meeting agreed service levels, the latter are more strategically driven by the organisation's culture and vision of 'how we want to work'. The perceived cultural inclination and strategic visioning will influence such key facilities variables as:

- categories of workplaces – enclosure-based, ownership-based, activity-based and time-based;

- design of workspace – variety in work settings (both off- and on-premises), furniture selection and provision for flexibility;

- protocol to support implementation of alternative workplace practices;

- provision and management of essential technical support infra-structure – technology and communication.

Defining space demand and supply

Meeting operational requirements – business demand variables

In defining space demand, it is crucial to understand the relationship between people, workspace and services. All three components are interrelated and must be managed dynamically in order to provide viable facilities solutions to emerging business challenges.

The process of demand assessment in terms of space planning and management is driven by the need to translate business data to work-place (design) solutions (i.e. facilities requirements and workspace specifications). It is discernible that a fundamental rethinking is required about the *definition* and the *use of space*. A key concept in the measurement of the performance of operational real estate assets is the relationship between the cost of provision and the utilisation of workspace. Workspace, measured in terms of square metres or square feet, is a component of the real estate resource. The monitoring of occupancy costs, as a primary component of the costs associated with facilities provision, has focused management attention upon the importance of the *amount, quality* and *utilisation* of workspace as key business measures of a premise's occupancy costs.

Defining workspace as a business resource demands a clear under-standing of the organisation's operational support needs at two levels:

- corporate real estate assets at the *portfolio level* – attributes, location and tenure;

- the characteristics of individual buildings at the *building level* – attributes, floor plate and layouts.

At the portfolio level, matching supply to demand is, or should be, an integral part of the interface between core business planning (i.e. the client) and strategic facilities planning. At the building level, the process is comprised essentially of planning and space management issues, involving the interface between business units (i.e. the cus-tomers) and the real estate/facilities function (i.e. the service provider). The nature of these tripartite interfaces between corporate manage-ment (where executive decision to allocate corporate resources rests), business units (who are the purchasers of facilities and services) and the real estate/facilities function (who are the enablers) suggests that the management of facilities and services provision must be considered as part of a composite whole, and not in isolation. The imperatives of such an interrelated process are:

- in the provision of operational real estate – an increasing realisation that the real estate resource can be managed to promote organisational change; and that productivity of staff, the business's most expensive resource, can be enhanced by the provision of an appropriate enabling working environment;

- in the provision of support services – an increasing awareness of the requirement for a more systematic approach to defining service levels, and in the procurement of facilities support services upon which a business can develop and evolve.

From all of the foregoing it is evident that a need exists for a dialogue between business managers and facilities managers, based upon a common language, shared objectives and a free exchange of ideas, from which overall benefits can be derived through the effective provision and servicing of the corporate work environment. The primary driver of *demand management* of the real estate resource is meeting business objectives through economic space utilisation.

Summary

As a supporting corporate asset, whether owned or leased, buildings attract liabilities if not properly managed. Prudent asset management (buildings are assets) is therefore a prerequisite in order to ensure optimum utilisation of the resource, to sustain its continued functional suitability and to protect or even enhance the asset's intrinsic worth. In this respect, the economics of operational asset management can be viewed from several narrow perspectives: in terms of its exchange (financial) value; its operational (cost) value; and its organisational (utilisation) value.

In practice, the true economic (business) value of a built asset must be seen as a result of composite measures that reflect its contribution to the value of the business, comprising a combination of all three components of value. Buildings must therefore be managed as value-adding facilities, not as consumers of vital resources.

The durability of buildings and their fixed location may conjure a notion of inflexibility. In reality, buildings are creatures of time, and thus of change. As a dynamic business resource, the focus on buildings in use requires ongoing management, which continually adapts in order to provide affordable facilities with appropriate services to their owners and users, whose needs change along with the economic conditions.

References

1. Joroff, M, Louargand, M, Lambert, S, Becker, F (1993) Strategic Management of the Fifth Resource: Corporate Real Estate. Report of Phase One CRE 2000 – Executive Summary. The Industrial Development Research Council (IDRF)
2. McGregor, W, and Then, D (1999) *Facilities Management and the Business of Space* Arnold, UK

10
Outsourcing Health and Safety Management

John Dyson

The Health and Safety (H&S) regime in the UK has crystallised in recent years with enforcement in both the public and private sectors being uniformly administered either by local authorities or the Health & Safety Executive.

Consistency of enforcement by both agencies has substantially improved; however any advantage organisations may take from this is greatly outweighed by the ever-increasing complexity of regulations made under the Health and Safety at Work etc. Act, 1974.

The outsourcing option for H&S management

It is the increasing complexity of regulations that has made both the public and private sector look for expert advisers to act as their 'competent person' in the management of H&S. Even the employment of a qualified Health and Safety Officer may not be enough and such an individual will need external expertise to keep up to date with legislative changes and best practice.

The time when medium sized and smaller businesses could allocate H&S as a small part of the role of a senior manager such as facilities management (FM) or human resources (HR) is now almost over. The responsibility for H&S must always lie with the owner or 'directing mind' of the business and it is not enough to rely on inspections by enforcement officers to pick up defects.

For larger organisations, particularly those with multi site operations, the development of a specialised and fully trained H&S function may still be a cost-effective solution, but increasingly many prefer to outsource this function to organisations such as Safegard, an independent member of the Sodexho Alliance providing services to a wide range of organisations as well as Sodexho itself.

In the public sector, eg NHS trusts, it is possible to set up specialist H&S departments. Equally, within local education authorities or in universities in-house expertise can be used. However it can make sense to outsource H&S as an addition to the outsourcing of FM.

The H&S management role

In outsourcing terms, H&S management may be classified as a knowledge-based 'soft' service, but the failure to adopt best practice can result in substantially increased costs through accidents, incidents which can result in business interruption or fires which can cause property loss and claims both by staff and members of the public.

The penalties for non compliance with H&S legislation can be severe with unlimited fines and jail terms for directors all available to the courts where serious offences occur. Legal liability cannot be avoided by outsourcing services as both client and contractor are liable. Therefore, the appointment of a contractor with fully accredited H&S management expertise makes sense for all concerned.

Where FM services have been outsourced to Sodexho, its H&S provider Safegard will carry out a pre-tender audit of the client's facilities and any defects requiring significant expenditure to rectify can be identified and included as a pre-contract condition. If this is not possible then the contractual terms will provide for rectification at the client's expense, and Safegard will always complete a thorough H&S audit as soon as possible after the contract is signed. In the unlikely event that the client is unwilling to undertake the rectification or renovation work necessary to eliminate identified risk under H&S legislation, Sodexho will, upon advice from Safegard, rescind the contract and walk away.

The H&S management role will vary according to the nature of the client's activities. Food safety advice as well as supply chain management, training and crisis management are well within Safegard's expertise.

In order to improve the management of H&S, client organisations are able to outsource training and guidance on risk assessment activity, key to implementing procedures to reduce accidents, incidents and claims.

In hospitals such as the Hereford hospital complex in the UK where Sodexho has gained ISO 9002 accreditation, the range of services provided can be as complex as the sterilisation of surgical equipment and the cleaning and disinfecting of operating theatres and wards. H&S management is an integral part of these procedures and is necessary to ensure the highest standards of cleaning and disinfection to assist in the prevention of MRSA infections.

In some cases, Safegard H&S management is delivered to clients as part of a wider range of Sodexho services, but an increasing number of clients engage Safegard on stand-alone contracts. A large number of independent schools together with local education authorities are using Safegard's web-enabled management system which covers all of the educational activities including sports, science laboratories, even trips abroad. Indeed, 35 per cent of Safegard's contracts are external to Sodexho and include hotels, leisure, catering establishments and charities, business and industry, as well as educational establishments.

Health and safety management expertise

Safegard is staffed with the appropriate levels of expertise demanded by the more complex role of H&S management. Safegard's team of 27 permanent staff includes 20 graduates who are qualified and have practised as environmental health officers, many with additional qualifications with the Institute of Occupational Safety and Health (IOSH) and the Royal Institute of Public Health (RIPH).

Safegard provides training at various levels from operator level to senior management accredited by IOSH and the Chartered Institute of Environmental Health (CIEH). Therefore, when operators at facility locations are transferred to Sodexho under TUPE provision, they receive formal training from Safegard at Sodexho's Kenley Training Centre.

The involvement of Safegard as a contracted H&S provider has been shown to have a beneficial effect on a client's insurance premium and a joint venture partnership has been set up between Safegard and Aon global insurance brokers and risk managers to take advantage of this.

All organisations recognise that good H&S management incorporating best practice is a key part of their business activity providing assurance to their staff and customers alike. It not only ensures legal compliance but also assists business in a cost-effective approach to the smooth running of the business with reduced risk of claims, incidents, property damage and business interruption.

11

Private Finance Initiatives – a Progress Report

Paul Aitchison and
Jonathan Reuvid

The concept of Private Finance Initiative (PFI) funding and its application to public sector facilities outsourcing was developed under the rule of the last Conservative Government and first articulated in 1994. The Treasury objectives are to relieve the Public Sector Borrowing Requirement (PSBR) and at the same time generate capital assets for the State 'off balance sheet'. The concept was adopted by the incoming Labour government in 1997 and has been refined since. The first wave of PFI schemes is now underway and so far the outlook for successful operation is promising, although it will be some years before a balanced assessment can be made.

Nevertheless, the National Audit Office and the Audit Commission have completed positive reviews of PFI schemes in the NHS and the government has expressed its satisfaction, identifying PFI as the principal vehicle for NHS capital investment in its plans to accelerate health service improvements. In relation to the NHS plan for over 100 new hospital schemes between 2000 and 2010, 64 of the 68 major hospital development projects already committed involve private finance, as do a further 34 of the 36 currently proceeding medium-sized hospital schemes.

Exposing the contradictions

At first sight, there is an irrefutable counter-argument to the claimed benefits of PFI funding. The cost of government borrowing is invariably lower than from any private source including the international market for Triple-A rated bonds. In order to counterbalance this disadvantage and to justify the 'premium' cost of borrowing from private sources, it is necessary to introduce value added benefits. In PFI projects, the benefits are realised by transferring risk from the government to the private investors and service providers and by gaining higher quality facilities and service delivery.

To understand how operational risk may be transferred and best value achieved, it is necessary to compare PFI structure and mechanics with the previous system for commissioning public sector capital expenditure projects and subsequently outsourcing non-core services. Hospital development programmes in the public health sector generally followed the same pattern and provide good examples of the pre-PFI regime.

Each NHS Trust, supported by its Local Health Authority and with input from other stakeholders, including doctors, staff unions and local authority planners, is responsible for generating its own facilities requirement plan and individual hospital plans. These plans are submitted to the Regional Health Authority to which budgeted funds are allocated by central government. Inevitably, the sum total of Trust calls for capital expenditure within a Region exceeds the allocated funds, driving the Regional Health Authority to direct the Trusts to phase their development programmes so that funds can be allocated thinly across the board.

According to the funds made available, each Trust would then return to the drawing board, trim or restructure into phases its hospital development plan and set about preparing the design, materials specification and tendering documents. Sometimes, the hospital would engage its own architects; often there would be pressure to adopt standard public authority designs. In a procurement environment which might best be described as the converse of 'expense is no object', it is not surprising that design and construction quality were not top priority. Poor quality also affected functionality so that the operational efficiency of facilities commissioned under these conditions was often impaired, leading to higher than optimal operating costs. A further factor affecting the planning of phased developments was the lack of certainty that funds would remain available for subsequent phases. Therefore, each phase had to be self-sufficient for longer than the short term and this constraint was not conducive to effective design solutions.

Having completed the tender specification, NHS Trusts would then engage in the formal tendering process described in Chapter 6, culminating in sealed envelope bids from registered contractors. In principle, contracts were fixed price, subject only to inflation, and the process produced keenly competitive tenders. However, as with most construction contracts, there were provisional cost (PC) sum inclusions and the appointed contractor could expect to agree a myriad of variations to the specification after the contract was awarded.

An unwelcome side effect of the system, from the Trusts' point of view, is a general assumption by Regional Funding Authorities that new or refurbished facilities are cheaper to operate – on the basis of lower maintenance costs and expected efficiencies – than those which they replace. This assumption, which tends to result in reduced revenue budgets for subsequent years, is inaccurate in two respects. Firstly, for example, new facilities with a superior specification including more advanced equipment may use more electricity even if the patient capacity is unchanged. Secondly, this assumption takes no account of the cost of servicing the capital investment. In the pre-Thatcher government era, NHS Trusts did not have balance sheets so that there were no charges to revenue for depreciation or interest on capital. Today, they do have capital charges in their revenue budgets, but it is doubtful whether the total budgeted annual operating cost equates to renewed whole life cost spread over the expected life of the facility.

Structuring and financing the PFI

PFI contracts are developed and awarded in a quite different manner to traditional public sector construction or support service contracts. In the first place, the contracting authority, which in hospital healthcare is still the relevant NHS Trust, goes out to tender for a single consortium to design, finance and construct the required facilities, and to equip them and operate them fully for the life of the contract. The Trust undertakes to pay a single annual charge, with adjustments only for retail price index (RPI) changes and agreed variations.

On the supply side, the full commitment cannot normally be undertaken by a single organisation and a special purpose vehicle (SPV) is formed as the contracting party, composed of a consortium of specialists who each hold equity in the SPV, itself a limited company. Typically, the consortium comprises one or more civil construction companies, one or more facilities management and support services providers, and the financial institutions providing 'third party equity' finance for the project. The duration of PFI contracts is normally from a minimum of 25 years up to 35 or more by reason of the time required by the SPV to service and recover the full capital cost while maintaining an operating profit on the performance of the contract and generating dividends to the investors.

Effectively, the SPV is granted a complicated series of leases/licences to take possession of the construction site or facilities in their original condition for the duration of the contract and to develop or refurbish and re-equip them to the contractual specification. The SPV is also responsible for the maintenance and repair of the new buildings throughout the term of the contract. NHS Trust assets are vested in the Secretary for Health and remain the property of the government. Thus, the government retains what may be described as the freehold interest and at the end of the PFI, if the contract is not renewed or replaced by a fresh contract, the SPV's leasehold/licensed rights terminate.

The capital investment in new facilities, amortised over the term of the contract, is on the balance sheet of the SPV and remains 'off the government's books'. Equally, the consortium partners are able to keep the PFI off their several balance sheets provided that none of them has an equity interest in the SPV that would require consolidation: some UK consortium partners have shareholdings as high as 50 per cent. Sodexho currently targets at 25 per cent shareholdings in the SPVs where it is a consortium member).

The lowest cost source of finance available to PFIs, in the present climate of low interest rates, is the commercial bond market for sums exceeding around £50 million. Given the quality of the income stream in the form of unitary payments from government funds (which do not distinguish between capital and support service charges) with RPI protection, SPVs are an attractive investment. As an example, the PFI project for King's College Hospital in south London, in which the SPV consortium members are Costain, Skanska, Noble Finance and Sodexho, attracted a Triple A-rated, index-linked bond with a term of 35 years post-completion of the new building as the primary finance.

The remainder of the finance was provided by consortium members. In general, lending terms over the past few years have also improved as the PFI legal framework has become standardised.

The investment of SPV shareholders, perhaps 10 per cent of total investment, is typically structured as a combination of equity and medium-term subordinated debt. In the event of default on the senior debt, the lender (or bondholders) have step-in rights over equity shareholders' interests. Between themselves, it is common for consortium members to have pre-emption rights over each other's shareholdings in the event of a decision to sell.

The operational obligations of the SPV under the contract are subcontracted according to the functions of the consortium members. For example, at King's College Hospital, all the building and refurbishment works are carried out by the Costain-Skanska joint venture, while Sodexho provides a wide range of support services, including catering, domestics, laundry, portering, environmental services, service centre (help-desk), as well as the operation and maintenance of the new building and technical installations.

Transferring the risks

In hospital PFI projects the transfer of risk from the NHS Trust to the consortium is the key feature which justifies the complicated financial engineering and helps to achieve best value.

Financial risk begins for the consortium members from the moment that they engage in negotiation amongst themselves and the preparation of the project proposal and tender.

Unlike conventional projects, the design of facilities is not undertaken by the Trust or public authorities. The Trust defines its short- and long-term objectives and service requirements and the consortium – in consultation with the Trust, service receivers and local planners – then engages in the design process, employing its own architects and other professionals including lawyers and financial advisers. Under the original procedures, the multi-stage negotiation process was lengthy and time-consuming, involving a long list of six bidders. For example, Sodexho's PFI contract with Hereford Hospitals NHS Trust took three and a half years to develop. Under this regime, the minimum realistic timeframe was probably twelve months to preferred bidder. After the contract was awarded, the consortium may have been able to recover its external costs within the capital investment, but not the management time of its members and other internal costs.

However, these are minor risks compared with the risks which the winning consortium bears. At the outset, the Trust makes no payment until construction is complete, all equipment is installed and the facilities are handed over in fully operational condition.

There is also an implied guarantee that the buildings which the SPV provides are fit for their purpose and will remain so for the duration of the contract. In effect, if the buildings prove unfit for use, the consortium will be responsible for repairing them and for compensating the Trust for the fact that they cannot be used while the repairs are undertaken. Indeed, if areas are taken out of commission at any time, charges to the Trust are reduced pro rata to a pre-agreed proportion.

As a PFI service provider, Sodexho is required in its support service contracts to achieve consistent and exacting performance standards throughout a period of 25 years or even longer. Soft services may be benchmarked or market tested at regular intervals and the penalties for poor service could be severe, resulting in financial deductions and ultimately the loss of the contracts themselves.

On the other hand, there are advantages in being an investor and shareholder in the SPV as well as a service provider. There is an opportunity to influence design and construction quality in the facilities under development so as to improve the cost-effective delivery of support services. Also, through the long-term relationship with consortium colleagues and the client, new approaches and solutions to service provision may be developed. Equity participation in the consortium makes replacement as a service provider unlikely even if an unfavourable market testing or benchmarking comparison is registered, subject to agreement among the SPV shareholders and the client.

Simplifying the process

The NHS has recognised the need to simplify the bidding process, in order to save time and reduce management costs. The lengthy 6–3-2–1 process was replaced by a 4–2-1 process for the 40 schemes announced in February 2002. The Ministry has also agreed, in principle, to amalgamate the Strategic Outline Case and the Outline Business Case, thereby removing one stage from the overall procurement process.

Other innovations intended to streamline the deal-making machinery include the NHS Private Finance Unit working with Trusts to standardise how schemes come to the market, standard tender documents, a standard payment mechanism and standard specifications.

A welcome recent change is that Trusts which consider it necessary to hold further 'clarification rounds' after their stated Best and Final Offer (BAFO) days will have to reimburse bidders' costs. The government has taken the view that if a Trust cannot decide on a preferred bidder on the basis of priced BAFOs it is their documentation and not the bid that is at fault.

A further initiative under consideration is to fund bidders' costs within the contract price, subject to a budget agreed in advance. Bidders would keep any saving they make by concluding a deal quickly and meet any extra costs which result from protracted negotiations.

Sodexho has won all three pilot schemes at Havering, Stoke Mandeville and Queen Mary's Roehampton hospitals.

Employment issues

Government response to trade union pressure insisting that support staff in PFI hospitals, such as catering staff, cleaners, porters, laundry and security staff, retain full employment is less welcome to private contractors. In accepting this submission the government averted an escalation of the strike called by UNISON at Dudley General Hospital but the decision to allow 'soft service staff' to opt out of TUPE arrangements (see Chapter 15) has cast a shadow over PFI bidding for new NHS projects.

One consequence of this proposal which is adverse to employees arises when one contractor takes over from another contractor. Staff are then transferred under TUPE back to the Trust and are offered fresh TUPE employment with the new contractor. If they elect to refuse a transfer they may be seconded to the new contractor but could lose service on their NHS pension entitlements.

The whole issue has been referred for evaluation under the Whitley Council Ground Rules. The minimum requirement by private contractors is that management staff, including supervisors and charge-hands, should remain subject to TUPE provisions. New staff will be recruited on Trust or Whitley terms and conditions rather than the contractor's rates, which may be higher.

Current activity and future trends in PFI contracting

PFI projects have taken root in healthcare, education and defence, and this approach to the development of flexible support services and design, build and funding solutions for asset-based services has applications for the whole range of central and local government, agencies and authorities.

As a prime mover in the field of healthcare support services, Sodexho is involved as an equity partner not only in the £100 million King's College Hospital project referred to above, but also in the two other PFI projects mentioned in Chapter 6: the £90 million Wythenshawe Hospital PFI with South Manchester University Hospitals NHS Trust and in Mercia Healthcare, the SPV for the PFI with Hereford Hospitals NHS Trust.

In education, Sodexho is involved as an investor in two PFI contracts under negotiation at Rotherham and Conwy. Sodexho is also an equity partner in the RMPA Services consortium which is at an advanced stage of negotiation for a 35-year contract to rebuild and provide support services to Colchester Garrison, and it will soon conclude contracts to service Exeter Courts.

Given the up-front costs and management time required to put together a consortium bid and to gain and fund a PFI project, the approach works well for contracts over £50 million in value. For lower value projects the transaction costs are generally too high.

From a contractual and funding perspective it would be possible for a Public Health or Education Authority to bundle together a collection of smaller projects with a combined contract value in excess of £50 million, but it is doubtful whether a single SPV consortium would find such a project operationally manageable. Separate review committees and reporting structures would be required for each individual facility. The members of these joint committees would represent individual NHS Trusts or Boards of Governors and would have differing, if not conflicting, interests and concerns. This is not a partnership environment which many service providers would relish.

However, the NHS is exploring different ways of procuring capital schemes of varying size by grouping them together. Following a similar approach towards PPP by the Department for Education and Skills in relation to school modernisation programmes, smaller scale refurbishment schemes in new and tailor-made PFI packages could be concluded.

Britain is the pioneer worldwide in PFI projects. At present, no other European country nor the US has yet fully adopted the same approach to public sector funding and service provision. However, there is keen interest among French, German and Scandinavian contractors in the PFI process. As indicated above Skanska are already engaged in several SPV consortia and Bouygues and Kvaerner are known to be investors in other PFI projects. These companies are taking the opportunity to gain experience in the UK market now, in the expectation that the PFI concept will in time gain acceptance in their home countries. Indeed, countries from all continents, from South Africa to Hong Kong and from Australia to Canada, which are considering the use of PFI, are turning to the UK for advice and experience.

Part 3

Commercial and Management Considerations

12

Procurement – Best Value Criteria for Selection

Phil Roberts
Hertfordshire County Council

The process of selecting a potential business services support partner is important to the future success of any business enterprise or organisation. The right partner selected for the right reason can provide long-term business benefits to the organisation and improved outcomes for the customer. So, senior managers cannot afford not to be closely involved in the outcomes of the process. However, like many business processes, selecting a support partner is technically complex, and few senior managers will have the time to be involved at every stage. One of the most important ways in which they influence the process is through their involvement and leadership in setting the selection criteria.

The purpose of successful procurement is to make sure that goods or services represent good value for money. The Office for Government Commerce defines 'value for money' as the optimum combination of whole life cost and fitness for purpose that meets the user's requirements. Striking this balance in the purchase of business support services requires a well-structured and robust approach. Support service provision involves a complex range of stakeholders ranging from senior management to business unit managers, end-users and external customers. Each of these groups may have their own needs and objectives. Best value procurement requires that all these stakeholders are fully involved in the process. Senior managers have a key role in helping to balance some of these competing demands in ways that support the longer-term vision for the future of the enterprise. The selection criteria are the way in which this balance of objectives and outcomes are translated into a form that will direct the outcome of the procurement process.

Setting the agenda

Procurement decisions are often taken against tight time schedules. They may be driven by the termination dates of existing contracts, corporate business plan commitments, or where staff may be externalised, the need to end uncertainly. There is a natural tendency to move quickly into the technical stages of procurement. This is generally a mistake. Insufficient understanding of user or stakeholder needs, or the costs and benefits of the service, can compromise value for money from the outset.

The first step is to establish executive authority for providing oversight and decision-making. It is important that the executive sponsor is at the right level of seniority for the scale and scope of the contract to be let. This is for a number of reasons. First, they must be in a position to broker resolution of conflicting or contradictory requirements where there are a complex group of internal stakeholders who are customers of the service. Second, where business objectives are unclear the sponsor may need to work with senior management to clarify planning objectives and agree the scope and objectives of the service contract. Finally, the executive sponsor must be in a position to maintain the integrity of the procurement process. Other senior managers, outside sponsor organisations or bidders themselves, may seek to influence the outcome of the procurement process by developing a range of contacts with the organisation.

The executive sponsor will need to be supported by an individual or group who can provide an external challenge. Their role is to review the process at key points and provide an independent perspective on the process, the selection criteria and the business or service outcomes. External challenge can be provided by other senior managers from inside or outside the organisation, or by specialist consultants not otherwise involved in the selection process.

Reporting to the executive sponsor will be a procurement manager. Wherever possible, the procurement manager should be in a position to take responsibility for the subsequent contract management. The procurement manager will take early advice on the legislative background of the selection decision. A range of UK legislation controls fair competition by placing obligations on both purchasers and providers of services. In some cases, legislation may restrict the selection criteria that can be applied. In others, provision is made for compensation to providers who believe they have been unfairly treated as a result of a procurement procedure.

Approaching the market

At the outset, the procurement team will begin a process of preparation and research. Figure 12.1 shows the flowchart of activities that lead to the defined service scope and selection criteria. At the earliest possible stage the existing service needs to be reviewed. This may include process mapping, surveys of end-user opinion, interviews with key stakeholders and analysis of the service inputs and outputs in terms of cost and fitness for purpose. Specialist consultants can be helpful in analysing and benchmarking existing service levels.

In parallel with these investigations, the procurement team will begin a process of market scanning. This review will show what the market leaders are able to offer, and the current state of best practice. Early and informal discussions with potential suppliers will provide useful insights into the development of the subsequent procurement strategy and selection criteria.

Preparation also involves clarifying the business objectives for the outsourced services. There are likely to be at least five main stakeholders in a major business services outsourcing decision, such as:

- senior management;
- managers of key business units;
- staff and unions;
- end-users who rely on the services provided; and
- other parts of the supply chain that may be affected.

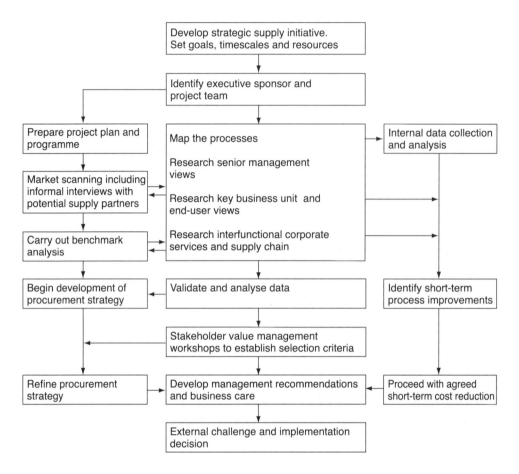

Source: David Burt and Michael Doyle The American Keiretsu
Homewood: Business One Irwin 1993

Figure 12.1 Developing the selection criteria

The executive sponsor will need to set a clear strategy at the outset for communicating with and involving these stakeholder groups. Generally speaking, the best approach is likely to be through workshop seminars to discuss and clarify longer-term business objectives and service requirements.

Developing the selection strategy

Market scanning, stakeholder consultation and research studies will begin to shape the initial procurement strategy and selection criteria.

The preparatory research will have identified a number of characteristics of the service or services to be provided in terms of the size and frequency of the transactions involved. They are summarised in Figure 12.2. Each of these categories drives a different approach to the procurement and selection process.

Low frequency and low value transactions

These are characterised by occasional purchases of small value goods or services, for example, specialised consultancy or inspection services. The best strategy is likely to be to consolidate the number of suppliers where practicable. A conventional tendering procedure is likely to be appropriate, provided that the goods or services can be clearly defined.

Low frequency and high value transactions

These are likely to be one-off purchases of major infrastructure or consultancy services associated with an organisational change, such as relocation or business redesign. The procurement and selection process will be designed around a one-off business case. Specialist expertise and close involvement of potential bidders is likely to be necessary in the procurement process.

Low value and high frequency transactions

Many routine business services fall into this category. Examples include recruitment services or the repair and maintenance of build-

	Low Frequency of Transactions High	
High Value of Transactions	Consolidate Sourcing of Similar Work	Maximise Leverage Long-term Agreements
Low	Package Purchases Consolidate Suppliers	Process Redesign Paperless Systems

Figure 12.2 Developing the procurement strategy

ings. Transaction costs are likely to be a high proportion of the total cost of the operation to the business, and the objective should be to carry out a full process redesign to maximise the benefits of paperless invoicing or the implementation of low cost transaction procedures, such as corporate credit card systems. Potential partners are likely to be selected on their ability to contribute to transaction efficiencies.

High value and high frequency transactions

Into this category fall major infrastructure management programmes, involving joint commitment to mutual investment. The objective here should be to maximise purchasing power through long-term agreements with a consolidated number of suppliers.

As a result of the market research and the preparatory studies, it will become clear whether the procurement option is *market-making* or *market-orientated.* If the approach is within the capacity of the existing market, there will be a wide range of potential suppliers and a well-understood basis for specifying and pricing the service requirement. Selection criteria will tend to focus on quality and cost. Where the approach is at, or in advance of, the capacity of the existing market, the number of suppliers is likely to be limited. Selection criteria will tend to focus on innovation and risk, and emphasise long-term partnering relationships.

Senior management will want to see the outcome of a procurement risk assessment at this stage. The purpose will be to consider the impact of the planned procurement processes on business operations, the risks that are likely to be involved and the means of containing them.

Pre-qualification selection

The conclusions of the first stage of the process will generally take the form of a prospectus for the scope of the contract. In the public sector, the issue of the prospectus will always follow public advertisement. The criteria used for pre-qualification selection are less specific than those used for the final selection. They include:

Organisation

Provides background information on the provider organisation or consortium. It shows information about the principal and relevant activities, a chart of the organisation and the company organisation and holdings.

Capability

Provides details about the number of staff and their qualifications, quality management procedures, the amount of work in hand and the availability of resources. Enquiries may also be made about past or pending litigation relevant to the service to be provided.

Financial assessment

Includes an analysis of the latest available audited and interim accounts, and any other information that may have a bearing on the company's financial position such as credit facilities, debt rating, capital investment and takeover activity.

Reference visits

Reference visits can be made to existing or previous customers of the potential supplier. The purpose is to get customers' views of the supplier and their services. Visits should be carefully planned to include a review of management competence, quality control and training and development.

The purpose of pre-qualification is to make sure that neither the purchaser nor the provider waste time in inviting bids from suppliers who do not have the capacity or financial stability to meet the demands of the contract.

Developing the selection criteria

In parallel with the pre-qualification selection process, the executive sponsor will need to agree the strategy for the development of the detailed evaluation model. The objective will be to build a consensus amongst the key stakeholders and end-users about the choice of criteria and the ranking to be applied to them. There are a number of techniques that can help build this kind of consensus. For example, value management workshops provide a useful basis for decision-making. They allow end users to participate and contribute to the setting of priorities and the methods by which the performance of the service will eventually be assessed. Some organisations will have adopted quality systems, such at the Balanced Scorecard or the EFQM model, which provide an enterprise-wide framework for assessing and ranking selection criteria.

Generally speaking, the selection criteria for business support services can be grouped into five main categories:

- quality management and innovation;

- resource management;

- business management;

- cultural fit; and

- cost.

The first four are often grouped together as generic quality criteria and balanced against cost. However, each individual category has a different emphasis that will be more or less important depending on the selection strategy and the planned business outcomes.

Quality management and innovation

Quality management and innovation are central to effective service delivery, and are normally a key criterion for selection.

Quality management

Delivering effective business support services requires a well-developed quality management regime in which the emphasis is on measurement, user feedback and continuous improvement. Each provider is likely to put forward their own proposals for quality management ranging from externally accredited to provider specific schemes that should contribute to quality management processes within the host organisation.

Innovation

The speed and pace of innovation in support services will need to keep up with innovation in the organisation as a whole. In some cases, innovation in support services can act as a catalyst for wider organisational change. Providers should be able to demonstrate their specialisation and show how it adds value to the host organisation. Generalised outsourcing agencies will not add value unless they can provide specific service delivery expertise, information, quality control or financial management systems that reduce overhead cost or add value to the end-user.

Resource management

Business support service providers manage a range of resources, that may be transferred from the host organisation, and include both people and knowledge. The management of outsourced knowledge is becoming an increasingly significant factor with the increase in the scale and complexity of the externalisation of business support services.

Managing people

Business support services rely on committed, motivated and knowledgeable staff. In many cases, the provider will be taking over responsibility for the management and development of the organisation's own staff, who will be expected to make the transition from in-house to external provider without interruption to service delivery. Amongst the questions that will need to be considered are policies on training and development, equal opportunities, benefit packages and staff involvement in the final decision.

Managing knowledge

The outsourced provider may inherit and expand a range of information related to the key business processes of the client organisation. At an early stage, the client organisation has to decide on what terms information is passed to the outsourced provider, and what information is essential to retain in order to maintain its freedom to act or to innovate at some future date. Amongst the issues that will need to be considered are:

- *Ownership of databases*
  The format, content and ownership of databases are a key issue, both for business continuity and data protection. There is likely to

be a clear distinction between the content and format of the database, which is often best kept with the client side and the application systems, which are likely to be most effectively managed by the provider.

- *Pre-existing records*
  Most contracts for business services involve the transfer of pre-existing records in either paper or electronic form. The record set needs to be covered by a clear inventory, and should be subject to due diligence checks at the time of transfer in order to ensure that there are no issues that would affect the contract or contract price. The client side will also need to clearly define the form in which key record sets have to be returned at the conclusion of the contract period.

- *Knowledge transfer*
  Perhaps the most obvious issue will be the issue of copyright in the information produced for the client organisation over the period of the contract, as well as the rights to innovations or patents arising from the work that the provider carries out in conjunction with the client. However, equally significant is the need to plan for knowledge transfer during the period of the contract to avoid the problem of dependency or 'hollowing out' of the client by the provider organisation.

- *Managing the environment*
  All business support services have environmental impacts of one kind or another. Some organisations will have existing environmental management schemes to which the provider will be expected to contribute. Potential providers will be able to provide information on their own environmental policies and should be expected to show how they contribute to the environmental performance of their host organisation.

Business management

The profile, approach and succession planning of the provider's contract management team are key issues for the successful development of long-term joint relationships. The host and provider organisations may also want to share and agree to a business plan that includes measures of the commercial health of both sides of the relationship.

Cultural fit

Cultural fit is one of the most important, but difficult to define, criteria. Client and provider need to have a close understanding of the context and style of each other's organisations. There is often a tendency for organisations to assume that 'leading edge' or 'world-class' providers will be best for all circumstances. In reality, best practice providers need best practice clients, and host organisations need to be realistic about their own level of maturity. The selection process can provide the opportunity to explore the cultural fit by providing bidders with the opportunity to work with the host organisation through workshop sessions and joint presentations.

Cost

The tender procedure will report on the headline costs for the service delivery. However, traditional contracting has tended to favour cost-added activity, such as price and contract negotiation or competitive bidding. This approach assumes that the whole life price variance is the sum of the purchase price variance. Experience shows that variations in the scope and volume of services over the life of the contract are likely to be more significant than the cost variation at the outset. These whole life costs can include:

- acquisition costs – these include staff, management and consultancy time in bid preparation and evaluation;

- change costs – one of the largest causes of variation from the headline price is change in business or service requirements;

- transaction costs – savings in transaction costs through contract rationalisation can often exceed the benefits achieved through market competition;

- waste – specification terms are often set down without any knowledge of the eventual sourcing of the product or service. Rigidity in specification terms leads to unnecessary or avoidable waste with its associated costs;

- the impact of bonus and penalty payments identified in the contract terms.

- credit/bond charges – guarantees of financial performance are routinely built into contract terms. The cost of the guarantees can be a significant element in the headline price of the service;

- management overhead – this can take the form of both dedicated contract management resources and also the time given by general managers carrying out devolved contract management duties.

Not all of these costs can be identified, nor can savings in them necessarily be translated directly into a cash benefit. Nevertheless, the selection criteria needs to take account of the likely impact of whole life costs on the headline costs.

The importance and relative weighting of each of these five criteria will be determined by the agreed selection strategy and business objectives. It is easy at this stage to lose sight of the main business benefit. Although it is common to adopt a 60: 40 quality: cost weighting when evaluating business support service bids, it is not possible to be prescriptive. Each case needs to be considered on its merits in the light of the business objective. Working with the external challenge, the executive sponsor has a key role in moderating the weighting and evaluation model to make sure that the primary objectives for the outsourcing are met.

There is no point in having well-prepared selection criteria if they are not understood or shared with the bidders or other members of the supply chain. The bid teams can be involved through participation in the development of the bid documents, through presentations to share the business objectives and assumptions behind the evaluation model, and through joint workshops involving all the bid teams to deal with points of clarification and further information. In this way, bidders will have a good understanding of the basis on which they are being assessed and the benefits the purchaser is expecting to achieve.

The ethical background

Procurement and selection procedures for business support services are resource intensive for both the purchaser and the provider. The purpose of best value procurement is not simply to obtain value for money for the purchaser; it is also to promote the competitiveness and commercial health of the supply side, on which all purchasers ultimately rely. The ethics of best practice procurement require that purchasers should not waste the time or resources of the supply side needlessly, nor extend the selection process by asking for excessive or irrelevant detail. The reputation of purchasing organisations in the market place is shaped by their reputation for fair dealing. Purchasers with a poor reputation will not attract bids from leading service supply organisations. Well-prepared criteria make sure that the eventual selection of a supply partner is evidence-based and allows informed feedback to unsuccessful bidders.

Summary

Best Value selection criteria for business support services need to be closely aligned to business outcomes and objectives. The key to identifying the right criteria is good preparation and close involvement of the stakeholders who will be users or purchasers of the services. Senior managers have a key leadership role in advocating and championing the benefits of innovative service delivery. However, more importantly still, they will shape the eventual outcome through their skill in matching the procurement selection process to their long-term vision for the future of the business enterprise.

13

Smart Outsourcing – the Legalities; How to Negotiate the Best Contract

Robin Baron
Fox Williams

The legal process

Function of the contract

The economic function of a contract is to regulate the risk: reward balance between the parties. For each party, a well drawn contract should be part of their risk management policy. It is important not to lose sight of this point, although many experienced business people see the contract as a safety net, to be considered only if something goes wrong, when they ask 'can we sue on it?'

In practice, an outsourcing contract moderates the parties' behaviour in relation to possible disputes arising out of the outsourcing. This is often half recognised by statements from the parties such as 'once it is signed, we will put it away in a drawer and won't look at it again'. Of course, they will look at it, if there is a problem or if they become unhappy with the other party's conduct but they will look at it on the quiet from time to time asking their lawyer 'what's the effect of this if we have to go to Court?' The legal advice received will then affect how they behave in relation to the particular current problem.

Function of the lawyer

Simply put, a commercial lawyer's function is to help his client achieve the client's business objectives.
He does this in three main ways, namely:

- drafting the contract or amending it;
- advising on risks;
- negotiating.

Lawyers live by their wits and an outsourcing negotiation is not primarily a battle of wits. The common objective of both parties in conducting a successful outsourcing should be to aim for a bigger pie which the parties can share. A lawyer, while looking after his client's interests, should be helping the parties to achieve a win:win situation, not as in so many other legal situations, a win:lose situation.

The lawyer is often brought in late to a transaction and so should be given a full briefing, including particularly the business objectives which the client was hoping to achieve from the proposed outsourcing. Ideally, this instruction should be in writing to act as a brief to which the lawyer may refer back. This activity may present an opportunity for you to reassess the current position in relation to the anticipated business objectives, compared with your original intentions. It is all too easy for everyone, not just the lawyer, to lose sight of the objectives.

Tell your lawyer of those objectives when you first instruct him and ask him to report on how the contract in its final form covers those objectives, before you sign it. By understanding the other side's objectives as well as those of his own client, the lawyer can help engender a constructive approach to negotiating the contract and thus a win:win situation.

Defining the services

The specification of services is arguably the most important element of any outsourcing contract. All too often we find that the customer has spent a significant amount of time, effort and money in negotiating a comprehensive services contract which is undermined by having a loose specification of services. The specification needs to be both comprehensive and detailed. As with all areas of contracting, the devil is in the detail.

In defining the services, it is better to define the deliverables, that is the output of a given procedure, rather than the method by which the procedure is to be carried out. The reason for this is that the specification will then better stand the test of time and be susceptible to improvements in efficiency by the supplier adopting new procedures. Only where the method to achieve the deliverable is of critical importance to the customer should it be defined within the specification. It would then still be possible for improvements to be made by changing the procedures, but this would be subject to the change control procedure in the contract. Inevitably, this process will take time and add expense to the change.

Tenders

Two methods of organising tenders are common. The first uses a detailed invitation to tender (ITT) and an outline of the proposed main terms of the contract. Suppliers are then asked to tender against this and a preferred supplier is then selected by the customer, based on a combination of price, quality and compatibility. At this point, the customer is in its position of greatest strength in relation to the contract negotiations and all too often, once the preferred supplier is chosen, the contract negotiations have the effect of gradually eroding the customer's position. The supplier knows that the customer will not want to reopen the tender process if this can be avoided, due to the delays and extra costs likely to be incurred.

Contrast this situation with the position where the tender documentation includes a fully worked up draft contract and where the supplier is asked in its response to tender to indicate variances, not only against the specification of services but also against the contract. A supplier may try to hedge its bets by giving responses to the legal contract such as 'agreed in principle, but subject to detailed negotiation'. If this method has been selected, then the customer should resist such responses and ask the supplier to propose specific amendments to the draft contract. The advantage of this method is that in making a final decision, the customer is aware not only of price, its own perception of quality and compatibility but also of the form of contract that can be signed. However, this method is likely to be significantly more expensive in terms of time and legal fees as the customer's lawyers are likely to have discussions with each of the supplier's lawyers and to keep track of each of the various amendments which each supplier is proposing. For some reason, it is fairly common for a customer, if it accepts an amendment from one supplier, to adopt this in the contract which is to be used for each supplier. I do not fully understand the logic of this, save that it may make the contract management process simpler. It does not make commercial sense to give every supplier an advantage just because one supplier had the sense to negotiate a significant concession.

The involvement of a preferred supplier in preliminary consultancy work, often paid, with a view to scoping the work and, in many cases, preparing the specification of services is fairly common. For the reasons already explained, the specification of services is vital and is not something which should be left to the supplier to write unsupervised. If the customer has the appropriate specialist knowledge to write the specification, all well and good. Otherwise, a suitably qualified consultant should be employed to write the specification or to amend and comment on the specification written by the supplier.

Due diligence

Due diligence is a term which originated in the US in relation to corporate acquisitions. It is the process undertaken by the supplier to ascertain that the resources to be used to provide the services are sufficient, taking into account their size and state, to enable the supplier to provide the contracted services. The resources to be subjected to the due diligence process should include tangible assets, intellectual property and the work force. Clearly the sufficiency or otherwise of the assets affects price because, if there are deficiencies, the supplier will have to apply his own resources to make them up. In many cases, the supplier will insist on warranties from the customer as to the extent and condition of the assets, employees and resources and the due diligence process should assist in defining the extent of the warranties required.

Often, due diligence is a necessary exercise both from the supplier's and the customer's point of view because the customer is not aware of the extent of the inventory or precisely what is used to provide the services. For example, in many companies, the precise extent of IT hardware and software content and the capabilities of the persons by whom it is used and for what purpose, are not accurately recorded.

Computer software presents particular problems in that in many cases the licensing terms will not extend to an outsourcing supplier. Typical phrases in a software licence such as 'by the licensee and its employees at the licensee's premises for its own business purposes' create these difficulties. In many cases, the due diligence investigation will lead to a full software audit by the customer.

Due diligence reduces uncertainty and, therefore, risk. In the case of Government contracts, where no warranty as to assets will be given, full due diligence prior to contract is essential as otherwise the contractor may commit and find shortcomings in the assets, intellectual property and workforce which have not been taken into account in the contract prices.

Typically due diligence will cover:

- licences to proposed customer;

- licence from proposed customer;

- infringements/disputes;

- inventory of assets;

- inventory of employees – and their terms and conditions of employment, particularly pensions;

- premises.

Key issues

The observations which follow are based on English law and English practice. International outsourcing is now becoming increasingly common and, as in the case of any trans-border transaction, the appropriate local legal advice will be necessary in order to advise on the impact of local laws. Nor does this overview deal with public procurement law or the additional factors to be taken into account where the outsourcing is being funded under PFI. Appropriate advice is also needed in both these situations.

Value

Price

There is no standard model for the pricing structure of an outsourcing contract. Typically, there will be a fixed charge for the provision of a core service. This may generate much discussion and legal drafting on what is or is not included within the core service. Some contracts provide for pricing based on input and output, so that charges are related to actual usage. Additional services are likely to be charged on a time and materials basis.

It is common to include a price indexation formula in outsourcing contracts which will apply either automatically on the anniversary date of the contract or may form part of an annual negotiation procedure. Possible indexation formulae include the Retail Price Index published by the Central Statistics Office, the Index of Earnings for the Electrical, Electronic and Instrument Engineering Industry published by the Department of Employment, or the UK Office for National Statistics New Earnings Survey – Part A for Computer Analysts and Programmers Matched Sample. The latter indices, which are related to labour rates rather than product prices, are probably more suitable for an IT outsourcing contract.

Fixed charges are normally paid in advance in instalments, either quarterly or monthly, while usage charges, additional charges and reimbursable expenses are normally invoiced monthly in arrears.

Time for payment of invoices must be clear, which will be within a specified period of delivery of a correct and properly due invoice.

In relation to non-payment of invoices, the supplier will wish to charge interest on outstanding sums in addition to its other rights and remedies for default. Where continuity of service is critical to the customer's business, the supplier should be prevented from suspending the service due to non-payment by the customer pending a cooling-off period, or an appropriate period of notice to be given by the supplier of the proposed suspension.

If the price structure provides for a customer entitlement to credits or reimbursements, the contract needs to specify how these credits will be dealt with and at what frequency.

The question of VAT needs to be addressed at an early stage. The imposition of VAT on outsourced services in the banking and financial sector, where the VAT is normally irrecoverable, may make a proposed outsourcing more expensive or not viable.

Service level agreements and compensation

Service level and compensation provisions can vary widely, and there is considerable scope for creative thinking.

Typically, a 'normal' level of services is defined at which the supplier is paid the contracted price and no more. There may also be a 'bonus' level of service which triggers additional payments to the supplier. There will almost certainly be a 'lesser' level of service which triggers service compensation payment or credit, so that the customer is recompensed to some extent for a lower level of service. Finally, there is a 'termination' level of service which triggers an opportunity for the customer to terminate for bad service.

One method which is quite often used is to have a points system, rather like driving licence endorsement points. The supplier may be allowed a certain tolerance on a low level number of points which can be incurred in any given period. If that is exceeded, then compensation by way of payment adjustments is triggered and, if a higher threshold is exceeded, then the right to terminate arises. The advantage of the points method is that it can be used to accommodate a wide variety of service level performance factors. For example, where a service might involve a combination of live running and overnight batch processing, down time on the live network below, say, 99 per cent availability, may attract 10 points for each percentage below that threshold, while the failure to make an overnight batch process on any particular night might attract 25 points. In this way, the breakdown of the components in a complex service can be dealt with through a single compensation mechanism.

Quality

The customer can seek to achieve quality in the contract in a number of ways. The first and most important, as already stated, is the provision of a comprehensive and detailed specification of services, coupled with well-defined service levels and an effective mechanism for compensating for the supplier's failure to reach such levels.

Failure to put these ingredients in place may well lead to opportunistic behaviour by the supplier.

Most suppliers also have quality control procedures which they should be asked to declare. The supplier's compliance with its own quality control procedures can be made a term of the contract.

Customers should resist arguments from suppliers such as 'Of course we'll do that, it's part of our ISO9001 registration'. Compliance should be a term of the contract.

Often one of the objectives of the outsourcing is to use technology which is and continues to be leading edge. This may not be confined to IT agreements but could apply to any service which has technological features. In these cases, provision should be included in the outsourcing contract that the supplier will keep the customer informed of technological changes relating to the service which both parties will review, and if they agree, will incorporate them into the contract. Implementation would be subject to change control procedures. In practice, this clause may not be of great benefit because we know that new technology tends to reduce the cost of the provision of most services, so that most suppliers will want to keep up with technological developments.

Change control

The change control procedure is one of the most important parts of the contract. Typically, it will provide that 'any requirement for a change to the services shall be subject to the Change Control Procedure'.

Most outsourcing contracts have lives of three to five years. Some are longer. The manner in which services are delivered is changing all the time and a well-drawn outsourcing contract needs to cater for such changes otherwise the benefits to both parties from technological change will be wasted.

The primary purpose of the change control provisions is to provide a framework whereby the definitions of services and service levels and price may be amended to take account of change of circumstances. Normally, this amendment has to be by agreement.

Customers will be concerned to see that they retain control over the definition of the services. Suppliers will be concerned that they may find themselves subject to too rigid a requirement for the customer's consent to changes in service provision. These potentially conflicting interests underpin the suggestion that the services should be defined in terms of output rather than method.

The change control procedure may vary, depending on whether the procedure is initiated as the result of a recommendation made by the supplier or a request made by the customer. In each case the supplier must provide a change control note, setting out the following:

- details of the change proposed;

- the originator and date of the request, or recommendation for the change;

- the reason for the change;

- the price, if any, of the change;

- a timetable for implementation;

- a schedule of payments if appropriate;

- details of the likely impact, if any, of the change on other aspects of the services;

- the date of expiry of validity of the change control notice (which shall not be less than three months); and

- provision for signature by the customer and the supplier.

Typical points in the negotiations arise out of how each party must respond to a change control notice where provisions such as 'neither the customer nor the supplier shall unreasonably withhold its agreement to any change' may be appropriate and also the question of who pays for the supplier's work in evaluating a change.

On the question of payment one possible compromise is that, where the supplier makes a recommendation, he pays the cost of preparing the change control notice. Conversely, where the customer makes a request, the supplier is entitled to charge for the work involved in evaluating the change and producing the information required for the change control notice.

Risk

Guarantees

One or other party, usually the supplier, is often asked to procure a guarantee from its parent company, of its obligations under the agreement. This is best done either by the parent company becoming a party to the agreement to stand as surety or by the guarantee being given in a separate document. An assessment of each party's balance sheet should be carried out by the other party in deciding whether such a guarantee is appropriate.

Limitation of liability

The negotiations on the provisions relating to the limitation of liability will often be prolonged and sometimes heated. The issue is the classic trade-off between cost and risk.

Some customers start from the position that the supplier should have unlimited liability. This is an unrealistic demand; where a supplier is readily willing to accept unlimited liability a customer would be well advised to look very carefully at the financial strength of the supplier. A supplier who is willing to 'bet the farm' on every contract, is likely to come unstuck at some stage to the detriment of his customers as a whole.

A prudent supplier will link his limitation of liability to his existing insurance cover. Customers should realise that seeking to increase the limitation of liability is likely to result in an increase in the charges for the services. Both parties should make a realistic assessment of the potential likelihood of loss and the potential scale of loss before settling on a limit of liability.

Limitations can be in terms of a 'per event' cap, a 'per contract year' cap or an 'aggregate lifetime' cap. Contractors are likely to prefer the 'aggregate lifetime' cap because it puts a predefined limit on the potential exposure. However, customers should probably resist this because, if there are multiple significant claims, then it is highly likely that the customer would at some point have terminated the contract so that the right to make multiple claims in respect of multiple events of loss becomes irrelevant.

Commercially, the starting point for the supplier may be the contract value or in other words, the aggregate amount of payments which the customer is due to make. The customer may well feel that this is an insufficient deterrent to the supplier from providing bad service. In the case of IBM, it has led a trend in the software industry to move from price paid limitations towards 'price paid plus' limitations, in IBM's case 125 per cent of price paid, in order that a supplier who is seriously at fault will have to return what it was paid plus a certain amount more as a deterrent.

Legally, both parties should consider whether the limitation figure they are minded to agree will satisfy the requirements of the Unfair Contract Terms Act 1977 ('UCTA'). Briefly, the Act renders void and of no effect, contract terms which seek to exclude or limit liability or negligence resulting in death or personal injury. Furthermore, where one party contracts on the other's written standard terms of business (and in outsourcing this may possibly happen where the supplier's standard terms are adopted) then any limitation of liability must satisfy the requirement of reasonableness. This is of concern to the supplier as, of course, the customer is likely to be pleased if the supplier's toughly negotiated limitation on liability is found by a Court to be invalid because it fails the reasonableness test. UCTA contains five guidelines for determining whether a contract term satisfies the requirement of reasonableness. Case law has indicated that one of the factors likely to be taken into account is the level of the supplier's insurance cover.

Intellectual property

The ownership and licensing of intellectual property needs to be considered carefully. The due diligence process suggested above should have given both parties an understanding of the particular issues which will arise in each case in relation to the existing intellectual property. If the outsourcing involves a system build or system enhancements, then negotiation will centre around who should own the intellectual property in the new system and, if this is to be the supplier, the customer will be seeking wide licensing rights and a source code escrow agreement so that it can take over maintenance of the system itself, or through another supplier, in the event that the first supplier is terminated.

The customer should have a full indemnity from the supplier in relation to breaches of intellectual property and this is one of the provisions that may well be taken outside any limitation on liability clause. The customer will also want a tightly drawn confidentiality clause in respect of not only its data but also its business affairs, as well as a provision providing that, in the event of the supplier losing the customer's data by reason of default, the cost of reconstituting the data will be borne by the supplier. Again this is a provision that may well be taken outside the limitation on liability clause.

Finally, regard must be had to the data protection legislation. Each party will have obligations under the Data Protection Act and responsibility must be allocated appropriately under the terms of the outsourcing contract.

People – TUPE and pensions

Pensions

It is appropriate to deal with pensions first because they are one of the issues which is usually the last to be resolved. The sooner that the process of understanding the nature of both parties' existing pension arrangements is started and an actuary involved in considering the best way to deal with the pensions transition, the earlier this process is likely to finish. It is still likely to come late to the negotiation table.

As a general rule, there is no legal requirement on the supplier as a transferee under TUPE to continue to provide an equivalent level of pension benefit under an occupational scheme (although it must be borne in mind that an employer's contractual obligation to make contributions to a personal pension scheme will transfer across to the transferee). However, the pensions issue, such as it is, is an industrial relations one. There is a risk that employees in a transferring workforce may leave or be disaffected if they are not given equivalent pension benefits.

Regulation 7 of TUPE and recent legal decisions support the view that the transferee is not, in most cases, obliged to provide pension rights on the same basis as the transferor but nevertheless the usual practice is for the transferor to require the transferee to provide equivalent benefits to those provided prior to the transfer. The position is more formalised in the public sector as a result of the advice provided by the Treasury Solicitor's Department. In the case of the first outsourcing at least of a public sector contract, transferees are required to provide equivalent pension benefits. Changes to the TUPE Regulations resulting from the revised EU Directive must be implemented by July 2001. The Government has indicated that it will, as one of those changes, require transferees to provide equivalent pension rights for transferring employees. Progress is slow and the outcome will only become clear once consultation on the changes starts.

I do not propose to deal with pensions in any great detail, save to say that this is an area where detailed due diligence is necessary and that the outsourcing contract should contain appropriate warranties and appropriate pensions transfer provision. These will require detailed drafting, which will vary in each particular case.

TUPE

Most outsourcings involve detailed considerations of how the Transfer of Undertakings (Protection of Employment) Regulations 1981, otherwise known as TUPE, apply to the proposed outsourcing and detailed negotiation over the relevant drafting provisions.

There is not time in this chapter to deal with TUPE in any detail. The purpose of the original legislation, namely the EU acquired rights directive, was to protect the workers in circumstances where the internal market within Europe would lead to important changes in employment patterns. Paradoxically, the effect in this country of the implementation of the acquired rights directive by TUPE is in many cases to cause resentment amongst employees who find that the identity of their employer is changed without their consent. The resentment arises out of the fact that they feel that they are being treated like slaves, to be sold on from one employer to another.

The relevant questions in relation to TUPE are as follows.

Has a relevant transfer taken place?

In answering this, we have to look to see whether there has been a change in the natural or legal person operating the undertaking and in answering this, to look at the criteria set out by the Court of Justice in *Spijkers v Gebroeders Benedik Abattoir* (Case 24/85 [1986] ECR 1119) which were as follows:

- the type of undertaking or business in question;

- the transfer or otherwise of tangible assets such as buildings and stock;

- the value of intangible assets at the date of transfer;

- whether the majority of staff are taken over by the new employer;

- the transfer or otherwise of customers;

- the degree of similarity between activities before and after the transfer; and

- the duration of any interruption in those activities.

The Court of Justice in *Spijkers* said that each of these factors was only part of the assessment. One had to consider the overall picture, to examine what had existed before the transfer and then examine the entity after the change, in order to decide whether the operation was continued.

Another relevant case is *Süzen v Zehnacker Gebaudereinigung GmbH Krankenhausservice* (Case 13/95). The *Süzen* decision concerned a second generation competitive tender for a school cleaning contract. The Court of Justice considered whether a transfer of an undertaking had taken place and whether one could distinguish between an entity and an activity. The transfer of an activity only may not be a relevant transfer. The Court came to the conclusion that the directive did not apply to the situation where a person had entrusted the cleaning of premises to a first undertaking, then terminated his contract and, for the performance of similar work, entered into a new contract with the second undertaking, unless there was a concomitant transfer from one undertaking to the other of significant tangible or intangible assets or taking over by the new employer of a major part of the workforce in terms of their numbers and skills, assigned by his predecessor to the performance of the contract. This last point on the workforce is, of course, something of a circular argument. Süzen has been followed in some, but distinguished in other, UK cases. Initially, the courts and tribunals were inclined to follow Süzen slavishly. More recently, robust decisions have consigned the apparent requirement in Süzen (that a major part of the workforce must be taken over for there to be a TUPE transfer) to its rightful place as one item on the list of relevant factors (rather than being the determining factor). Uncertainty continues, but one thing is clear; a transferee cannot now deliberately refuse to take on employees so as to avoid the impact of the TUPE Regulations.

If only a part of the business is transferred, one needs to examine whether there has been a transfer of an identifiable entity that has retained its identity and, secondly, which employees work for that entity. The transfer will then include all the employees devoting 100 per cent of their time to the activity transferred and it may include others who spend the majority of their time servicing the activity, even though not based within it. A transfer may take place in two or more stages.

The second question is:

Who is protected by the TUPE regulations?
The acquired rights directive's effect is to extend existing national provisions for the protection of employees to include protection against dismissal by reason of a relevant transfer. TUPE extends to all those

persons who are treated as employees and who have a contract of service, as opposed to a contract for services with the transferor or the transferee. This will include shareholders and directors who are also treated as employees. Protection is extended to those employed at the time of the transfer. This includes persons employed when the transfer takes place and those persons who might have been so employed, had they not been dismissed by reason of the transfer.

Who is not protected in TUPE transfers?

In the first category are employees who choose not to transfer. They are free to object to the transfer and to cease working, but will not be treated as having been dismissed for any purpose by the transferor or the transferee. Exempted employees include sea-going crews in certain circumstances, and those employed exclusively outside the United Kingdom.

Regulation 10 in TUPE provides that the parties must inform and, in some cases, consult employee representatives. All elected employee representatives must be informed (the Regulations specify what must be provided) and consultation with those employee representatives may be required. In those workforces who do not have appropriate elected representatives, then affected employees should be invited to elect representatives so that effective information and consultation can take place. Notification and consultation should begin long enough before a relevant transfer, to enable consultation to take place.

Failure to consult can lead to the payment of compensation to employees who should have been consulted and this can be up to a maximum of 13 weeks' actual pay. Based on current case law, that liability can pass to the transferee – suitable protection should be considered.

Outsourcing usually produces a wish on the part of both customer and supplier to reorganise their workforces. This can give rise to a difficult situation in that only dismissals that take place for economic, technical or organisational reasons, entailing changes in the workforce, are legitimate. This applies both to pre-transfer organisation and post-transfer reorganisations and, in each case, to the customer and the supplier. It should be borne in mind that harmonising or changing terms of employment in connection with a TUPE transfer will not be effective, even with employee agreement. In one case, changes made two years after a transfer were reversed.

In looking at the provisions in the outsourcing contract relating to the workforce, an understanding of TUPE is absolutely essential. Typically, the provisions in the outsourcing contract will contain cross-indemnities providing that the supplier will indemnify the customer in respect of actions taking place after the point of transfer, while the customer indemnifies the supplier in respect of actions taken prior to the point of transfer. If there is a large potential redundancy cost inherent in the workforce, then the supplier may seek to have a notional fund set aside provided by the customer, which the supplier can draw on in the event that it becomes necessary to make part of the workforce redundant. In order to make this work realistically, it is usually advisable for the supplier to bear part of the redundancy cost himself, with only a proportion of the cost to be provided out of the redundancy fund.

Exit

Remedies

I have already talked about pricing penalty mechanisms. If these fail to produce a remedy then termination has to be considered.

In preparing the contract, termination and the effects of termination require care and attention. By the time these provisions come into effect, the parties are likely to be taking a strict view of their respective obligations. Any ambiguity is likely to be exploited.

Careful consideration should be given to different termination consequences, depending upon which party is in breach.

Standard events of termination are as follows:

- if the other party ceases to carry on business;

- if the other party goes into some form of insolvency;

- material breach of a term of the contract which, if capable of remedy, is not remedied within 30 days of written notice specifying the breach and requiring its remedy;

- material breach which is not capable of remedy.

The customer should be careful to have specific provisions dealing with failure to pay on the due date as otherwise this is likely to be a material breach which is not capable of remedy.

Other possible events which may give rise to a right to terminate include:

- change of control of one party;

- the aggregation of a certain level of penalty points as mentioned above.

The change of control provision is there to protect one party who is concerned about either providing services to a customer who may pass into the control of one of its competitors or, more likely, the customer who does not wish to have a very close relationship, involving in practice a considerable amount of mutual trust, with one of its principal competitors.

In some contracts the customer may be in a strong bargaining position and able to negotiate that the supplier cannot terminate, unless the supplier has first had the matter in dispute adjudicated by the Courts, by arbitration, by expert determination or by alternative dispute resolution as provided for in the contract. In other words, no right to termination arises until the matters in dispute have been adjudicated by a competent authority.

Standard drafting provisions should provide that termination is without prejudice to the rights of the parties accrued prior to termination and that various provisions of the contract (particularly confidentiality requirements and the effects of termination) which survive termination should be included.

Transition

We have already seen that termination is a remedy not to be exercised lightly. If the outsourcing contract does not provide adequately for proper transition of the services, either back to the customer or to a new supplier, then termination is likely to be an empty remedy which the customer is unwilling to exercise.

The precise drafting of the transition arrangements depends totally on the type of services to be provided. In IT outsourcings, for example, any software running on the supplier's operating system and network will have to be ported to that of the customer or new supplier. Any such transitional services will normally be charged for by the supplier on a time and materials basis, although different charging provisions may well apply if the termination is due to the supplier's default. The transition provisions may vary, depending upon which party is in breach of contract. A software licence from a supplier could reasonably be expected to be the subject of a continuing licence to the customer after termination if the termination were for the supplier's breach, but not otherwise.

Typical provisions include transition assistance, a right to purchase the supplier's assets used in providing the service at net book value, porting of the software, assignment or licensing of intellectual property rights, continuation of services for an interim period until alternative arrangements have been put in place, return of confidential information, a provision to provide reasonable assistance in transition and so on.

Conclusion

This chapter started by explaining the effect of the outsourcing contract, both in its economic function and in its function affecting the behaviour of the parties. The centrality of the contract should be re-emphasised. In practice, weak contracting, based on poor practice and a poor document, leads to unanticipated higher costs and can create major problems for customers.

In many cases, suppliers talk in terms of 'partnering', but this expression should be viewed with some cynicism. It is a notion often relied on to offset any difficulties arising from loose contracting and in many cases the customer believes in the rhetoric of 'partnering' much more than the supplier. Faced with a supplier who continually harks on about the benefits of partnering, it would be tempting to suggest to their lawyer that the contract, so far as the supplier is concerned, is made *uberrimae fidae*, that is of the utmost good faith, so that the supplier has to disclose every relevant piece of information to the customer, behave with the utmost good faith in all its dealings with the customer and account to the customer for any profits made in excess of those provided for in the contract. No well-advised supplier would ever agree to this, but it might have the effect of removing any mention of partnering from the discussion.

14

Outsourcing: Defining the Need; Managing the Decision

Francoise Szigeti and Gerald Davis

Performance-based selection: jacking up the procurement process

In the last eight to ten years, the focus in the corporate world has been on doing more with less, and for less. Wall Street is asking for higher profits for shareholders. Corporations have to identify their core businesses and steer clear of doing anything in-house that is not part of their core competencies and that others can do better – or cheaper.

In this environment, outsourcing is here to stay, whether it is understood as out-tasking a specific activity or forming a strategic alliance or partnership with an organisation that brings special expertise to the table. But that doesn't mean outsourcing always works. In a recent IFMA survey, 20 per cent of the organisations surveyed reported that they were doing tasks in-house that they had formerly contracted out. The reasons for this included improved service and quality, better control and in some cases decreased overall costs.

The key is the process used to decide whether to outsource or out-task, what to outsource and which service provider to use and, most importantly, how to select the suppliers and providers.

What separates success from failure?

In the evaluation of whether to outsource, the first step is fully to identify the goals. This sounds obvious, yet in practice it is not an easy task.
Is the real goal to reduce absolute overall costs? To decrease headcount
and get staff off the in-house payroll? To improve or decrease levels of
service? To benefit from best practices used elsewhere? To gain access
to locked-in capital? Some of these questions touch on very sensitive
matters, and it is not uncommon to find that the real answer is masked
by other objectives.

At this stage, talk of outsourcing can be demoralising to current
staff, but there are ways to limit the damage – even to find a silver
lining. One key is to decide early on which staff you will want to keep,
whether or not the decision is made to outsource. Select the best
people and re-assign them to the positions you will want them to hold
in the future. Then involve these people in the decision-making
process to help them evolve into a strategic management team.

In the analysis of whether to outsource, one question is: what functions could potentially be outsourced? A place to start might be to establish what should definitely *not* be outsourced – for example, strategic
planning and relations with the core business units. Changes in levels of
facility/real estate services can have a significant impact on the core
competencies of the core business units. It is therefore important to
involve the business units in the decision-making process: after all, they
know what support they require. But be careful: without careful planning, good communication, careful implementation and effective management of the entire process, involving the business units can backfire.
Do *not* involve the business units if you and senior management are not
serious about taking their advice and recommendations into account, or
if the purpose of the outsourcing exercise is to reduce the level of service to the business units, regardless of the impact on their mission.

As part of the outsourcing analysis, take a close look at the needs of
the occupants of the space, not just the business needs of the various
departments. These occupants are the real customers of facility and
real estate services. If those services and the products that they provide don't meet occupant needs, the overall department will suffer.

A crucial question to ask in the outsourcing analysis is whether a
function can easily be defined and provided by the marketplace. The
best candidates are functions for which it is relatively easy to describe
output and performance in quantitative terms, the levels of service can

easily be measured and audited, and there are many well-qualified service providers.

Defining needs and evaluating potential providers: focus on quality

Preparing the RFP is a key step. The services and products to be provided must be clearly identified, yet without giving too much detail. The trick is to adequately define the requirements of the organisation in functional and performance terms.

More importantly, the level of service and the performance indicators need to be spelled out so that the service providers and suppliers know in advance how their response to the RFP, and their services and products, will be assessed. New standard tools can help to do just that.

A few years ago, we predicted a fundamental shift in the way providers and suppliers are selected and workplace facilities and services are provided. Great strides have already been made since the ISO 9000 series of standards were promulgated in the early 1990s. In the next few years, quality will become one of the key criteria to determine how corporate resources support the core business, and how service and products providers are evaluated.

As core business managers increasingly focus on quality, they and their purchasing agents will demand consistent, coherent, and appropriate levels of quality from their service providers and suppliers. They want value for money. Core business units of owned and leased space – ie workplace occupants – perceive the corporate facilities provider, as an *internal* purveyor of products (the physical setting of their work) and services (the workplace operations and support services), and as an intermediary to the external providers. When dealing directly with a landlord as tenants, or with a design team as buyers, they have the same focus.

These customers want to measure and compare their workplaces and associated services against their functional requirements. More importantly, they are now looking outside the organisation to see what potential external suppliers might offer. Competition for their business among landlords and suppliers of everything from office supplies and facilities to security services is constantly increasing.

Providers of workplace services and constructed assets need to join the quality movement. We call for teaming with occupants and other stakeholders. Cost effective management and approaches are no longer sufficient – only cost effective delivery of *appropriate* services and constructed assets will ensure customer satisfaction.

Decision makers at all levels, from project managers to top executives, need a standard way of comparing the functionality of the options they are considering. This applies equally to buy, sell, keep, vacate or rent decisions, as well as to the procurement of products and services. Lacking any systematic way of measuring functionality, most top executives and core business managers have just tried to ratchet down occupancy costs for workplaces, rather than leveraging workplace costs by paying attention to the effectiveness of the occupants. In the absence of comparative information, this was reasonable, although often counterproductive. So, when deciding to outsource, and when evaluating outsource suppliers and providers, the same is true. Paying undue attention to cost and not enough to quality is counterproductive.

Now, however, there is a standard way to target quality. Now you can compare facilities required to facilities delivered, and performance defined to service provided.

Customers expect constructed assets, products and services to meet new, rigorous standards and *measurable* demands for quality. They will want providers of workplace facilities and services to show how corporate real estate assets link to the overall business strategy.

Many corporations and organisations already use the ISO 9000 series of standards in some parts of their core business activities. Most facility providers have seen this as an interesting and positive part of quality improvement programmes but have tended to watch from the sidelines. No longer.

Organisations are installing processes that measure quantifiable quality, value for users and improved customer satisfaction. You can, you should, and you soon will be expected to apply the same approach to your own facilities and support services. The cornerstone is to determine customer requirements in a systematic, coherent and consistent manner. This is now feasible with respect to facilities because of new FM tools. Standard practices and scales from ASTM E06.25 were approved in 1995 and recognised as American National Standards in 1996. These standards provide a way to measure and benchmark fitness for purpose.

To convince your customers – including top corporate executives – that you understand, you need to know more about the sets of standard documents that have been developed to deal with quality and functionality in the past few years. These documents are:

- The quality management system (ISO 9000 series – revised edition 2000);

- The process for determining functional requirements and for rating the serviceability of facilities (Compendium of ASTM standards on Whole Building Functionality and Serviceability – revised edition 2000);

- The functionality and serviceability scales (Compendium of ASTM standards on Whole Building Functionality and Serviceability – revised edition 2000);

- Constructed Assets – Methodology for defining demand and assessing supply (Performance standards in building – Levels of functional requirements and levels of serviceability – Part 1: Principles – ISO CD–291933–1, document number 59/3 N474).

Checking the financial stability of potential providers

Before a corporation selects one or more service providers, it is important to understand a good deal about each of the firms being considered. Financial stability is a good starting point. In the 1970s and 1980s, a significant number of companies that entered the outsource business were on a wobbly financial footing and were later taken over, merged or failed outright, leaving a wake of disruptions and service quality problems. Today, the largest service providers generally seem to be financially stable. Nevertheless, it may be worth evaluating the chances of merger or acquisition for each provider being considered; a merger could produce changes in culture that would affect a provider's suitability for some customers.

Careful financial analysis extends to all parts of the outsourcing process. That means examining current costs (explicit and hidden) and total budget (including transfers from internal charge-backs and contracts) as well as the costs estimated in the proposals to ensure that the comparisons are 'apples to apples'. For example, review the current overhead allocation to ensure that the in-house facilities group is not carrying overhead costs that the service provider would not carry.

Bids should receive the same close scrutiny. For example, watch for charge-backs, pass-through costs and internal transfers for which the bidders may demand extra cash payments, claiming that they did not provide for these costs in their proposal because they did not have adequate information. And when comparing in-house costs to the estimates in the proposals, be sure to take into account the cost of the management team that would remain in-house.

Of course, it is not just the numbers that matter. The facility executive will have to spend enough time with the finalists to understand whether they would work comfortably with the corporation's culture and would take similar approaches to the inevitable problems.

Avoiding traps and pitfalls

- Do not assign 'spare' staff to the outsourcing or transition team. Many enterprises foolishly choose 'direction committee' staff – who can be made available with least disruption to current work and projects – for their outsourcing project. One multinational did this, and quickly lost its key leadership staff in real estate and facilities. These people wisely refused job offers from the newly appointed service provider, with predictable negative consequences.

- Don't ask the service provider to clean out the organisation's dead wood. This strategy inevitably backfires; companies that have tried it differ only in the degree to which it damaged their core business.

- Maintain effective, high-level management of the facility/real estate function. The corporation must retain sufficient in-house intelligence to understand what questions to ask, stay aware of developments, and judge the potential impact of these developments. Corporations must retain the institutional memory and the information systems built in-house – unless the service provider has systems that work better, in which case the information from the in-house system must be poured into the new system.

- Watch out for pass-through costs, project or transaction management fees and mark-ups. The extent of these unbudgeted costs will depend on how the contract has been negotiated, what incentives have been included, and what fees are fixed for basic services.

- Contract for and measure outputs, not inputs. Use measures and provide incentives that encourage the staff of the service provider to do a good job and to be proud of being on the site. If the contract is too tight, or treats the provider staff with mistrust, the relationship will get off to a bad start, the work will suffer and the operations of the core business units will be affected.

- Don't sign up for too long – or too short – a contracting period. Three to five years, with an option to renew, seems to be an optimum contracting period.

- Don't reinvent the wheel. Learn as much as you can from the experience of other companies. Obviously that means talking to other companies that have outsourced facility/real estate services to find out what they did and whether they are happy with the results. But it is also worth talking to potential suppliers about their other contracts and how they were hired.

Making the decision

Once the bids have been received and the service providers have been interviewed, it is important to ask again the question of whether or not to outsource. Asking that question again at this point in the process is very important. In a number of cases where we have first-hand experience, analysis of in-house costs versus bids from service providers showed that the in-house real estate and facility management group was actually very competitive in terms of costs, even when compared to the low end of the bids. What is more, the analysis showed that the in-house staff was doing a good job of delivering service. The process was valuable because it focused the attention of senior management and proved the value of the in-house support function. It also forced the in-house group to sharpen its accounting and processes.

Assuming that a decision is made to outsource a major function, and that the facility executive is comfortable with a service provider, it is time to examine that firm's plans for staffing. Typically, a large provider will install its own senior person on site within days of taking over responsibility for that function. The new on-site manager is often one of the best in the firm, who in some cases, is moved on to the provider's next big new contract. The corporation should insist that the incoming manager be permanently assigned to the site, not to be moved elsewhere without permission of the enterprise, unless that manager does not perform.

Another aspect of staffing is taking over existing employees and contracts. This is difficult but very important; how it is handled will colour the whole relationship between the corporation and the service provider. Investigate how the service provider has handled the transition for other clients and whether the results have been appropriate.

There is also the issue of corporate restructuring. There may be a need for restructuring and re-engineering some of the facility and real estate management functions that are being considered for outsourcing. If so, the corporation should usually proceed with the re-engineering exercise before making decisions about outsourcing.

It is probably healthier for the corporation to deal with its current staff and resolve all labour issues and contractual issues by itself, ahead of time. Deal with the severance process quickly and fairly, and involve the relevant unions where necessary to avoid ending up with serious labour problems.

There is another good reason to treat current staff fairly: they may well still be the people who will be doing the work once the service provider takes over. It is common for the successful firm to hire at least some of the current staff from the client organisation, who are more knowledgeable than anyone else about the buildings and the organisation. For them, the transition to outsourcing is likely to be very stressful but there may be a long-term benefit: a career path that includes senior management positions, all the way to the CEO slot of the service provider.

What about the core facility and real estate staff who will now be responsible for managing the service providers? Of course, simply giving the remaining in-house staff new titles and new responsibilities isn't enough. They will require tools, training and support to handle their new responsibilities. In most cases, the facility and real estate organisation must be redesigned to focus on its new mission.

Too good to be true?

If the decision is made to outsource, examine the bids carefully. If the proposals are significantly less than the current budget, find out about the qualification of the staff that will be assigned to work for the corporation. Be sure to get the hourly costs, numbers of people assigned to the work, levels of service etc. Be confident each service provider has access to a pool of staff with adequate qualifications at salary levels compatible with their proposal. Look at all the costs that you will incur and what they are for. Check that provisions have been made to cover those costs.

Managing the provider

Performance reviews are crucial to the long-term success of an outsourcing arrangement, and it is important to agree with the provider up-front on a system of measurement. In large organisations, performance reviews should include surveys of customer satisfaction as well as more objective measures of performance. Use rewards as drivers rather than penalties in a system of incentives.

Facility executives should also examine carefully the way in which the service provider will subcontract work. Make sure that those subcontracts or alliances are in place before the start of an outsource contract.

There are also important contractual issues concerning subcontracting:

- The service firm should not be able to change subcontractors without advance approval from the corporation.

- The corporation should have the same authority to enforce specific performance requirements on the allies or subcontractors as on the prime.

- Incentives between prime and allies or subs should be compatible with the interests of the corporation.

While you're at it

In conjunction with the outsourcing analysis, top management may want to address the question of ownership of the properties. Perhaps some owned properties should be sold and leased back. It may also be worth exploring different kinds of leases offering different benefits, such as those that can provide access to capital while retaining control (eg synthetic lease arrangements).

While it is of course vital to pay attention to the needs of the corporation, it is also important that the contract be balanced and fair. If the service provider is squeezed excessively, the corporation will pay for that later, one way or another.

An outsourcing relationship is a long-term commitment. Although the facility executive will legally want the flexibility to change service providers relatively easily, the relationship should be constructed and started on a basis of mutual trust and support.

One-stop shopping?

It is certainly rational for large corporations to set up national accounts instead of hundreds of small local contracts. But using only one 'strategic' service provider or partner requires careful analysis, since the corporation will be very dependent on the performance of that one external entity. One national company subdivided its regions into large outsource contract units, and awarded about two thirds of the business to one service provider, and the balance to another. Each provider had different strengths and shortfalls. Each turned out to excel at some parts of the work, but initially was only marginally acceptable on other parts. By having the two firms compete for performance incentives, the enterprise was able to avoid having to suffer from the weaknesses of either, and was able to upgrade the performance of both.

Whatever the decision about outsourcing, do it because it makes sense for the long-term health of the whole corporation, not because of the lure of alleged immediate cost savings or reduction in headcount. Done correctly, outsourcing can be an effective tool for supporting the core business, improving services and ultimately reducing overall costs. But when outsourcing doesn't work, it will become evident that the operations of the core business have paid an unexpectedly high price in all, and more, of the following penalties:

• reduced effectiveness of the facilities/real estate operations;

• negative impact on the ability of the core business units to deliver its mission;

• rising facilities costs.

Finally, your new job

Even after a significant portion of the facility and real estate function has been contracted out, the corporation still needs to have an effective leader for the facility function. That person must be able to:

• advise the corporation on sensitive matters related to facilities;

• provide knowledgeable, interested executive oversight, and supervise audits of the work provided by the outside firms;

• manage the preparation of budgets, the procurement and management of the contract, and presentations to senior management;

- manage strategic planning with a small but high-powered cadre of highly competent people who know the corporation;
- recognise issues and spot trends related to that service function which might affect core businesses;
- be heard by senior executive management;
- manage the relationship with service providers.

Acknowledgements

This chapter is based on a prior article published by Building Operating Management (BOM) in 2000. We would like to take this opportunity to thank Ed Sullivan, at BOM, for his careful, knowledgeable and sensitive edit of our material.

The following individuals were interviewed in preparation of this article:

Su Halas, WorkingSpaces Consulting Ltd.; Joe Incognito, Creative Management Solutions; Walt Flannery, Chevron; Rob Lowry, formerly with Ontario Realty Corporation; Martha O'Mara, consultant and author of *Strategy and Place*; Ed Pagliassotti, United Technologies, Sikorsky Aircraft; Bill Sims, Cornell University.

make your school smile

By offering a range of services from catering and housekeeping to grounds maintenance, Sodexho is improving the daily quality of life in schools. This can cut staff turnover, enhance academic performance and enhance your school's reputation – which means not only more contented staff and pupils but a happier, healthier look to your finances. **Call 0800 169 49 59.**

sodexho.co.uk

Sodexho
Catering and Support Services

turning a cost into a value

15

Living with TUPE

Martin Gash, Chris Piper and
Jonathan Reuvid

The complications for service providers entering into contracts with public service employers in respect of the transfer of employees under Transfer of Undertakings (Protection of Employment) TUPE are highlighted in Chapter 6. This chapter focuses on the practical HR issues arising from the administration of transfers and the impact on service providers' planning.

Aspects of human relations

Pre-contract

The pre-contract negotiating and tendering stages of both public service and private sector projects are driven, from the service provider's side, by the sales function. A preliminary assessment of staff skills is made from the information the client makes available: broadly, the backgrounds from which they come and their employment records, in addition to the terms and conditions of their current employment.

In cases where the tenderer is bidding to take over from an existing contractor, levels of skill can be assessed further: sometimes from supplementary information provided by the incumbent service provider, more generally from prior knowledge of the competitor and the skills levels which it normally applies to a range of jobs. Environmental standards and the quality of management at the client's facility may also be evaluated by inspection prior to tender which will, to some degree, reflect levels of staff skills.

Post-contract

Following the award of contracts, responsibility within the service provider for the delivery of services, and communication with the client and staff, passes from the sales to the operations functions. Contracts are seldom for less than three years and the first six months is normally treated as an implementation and review period in which thorough consideration is given to any changes in staffing and terms of employment.

At Sodexho the immediate emphasis – beginning with an induction process for all managers and staff transferred – is on staff motivation. Induction training is focused on best practice in relevant disciplines, and on the delivery of Sodexho's contracted service offer. Sometimes, as in education service provision contracts, only managers are transferred.

Training for managers often extends beyond the skills related to their specific disciplines to education in financial systems and professional management skills and there are many cases of managers transferred under contracts who have found unparalleled paths to career development within the organisation. All staff transferred under TUPE to operational roles in Sodexho are trained in customer relations and in health and safety to best practice standards .

Throughout the implementation and review period, transparency in staff relations is treated as crucial. The review includes the use of Sodexho's own in-house O & M resource to evaluate and improve all processes in the delivery of the services which Sodexho has contracted to provide.

Legal aspects of employee relations

As a part of the commitment to transparency, consultation is undertaken with employee representatives on all issues of staffing and terms of employment. Recognition of public service unions is universal at all public service facilities and at an average of 50 per cent of the facilities in business and industry served by Sodexho.

During the initial six month period the changeover team addresses any issues regarding employment terms concerning areas such as holiday entitlement, sickness pay and other benefits/procedures in consultation with employee representatives. If for ETO (economical, technical or organisational) reasons redundancies are considered necessary, they may also be confirmed after this period of review.

One 'grey area' in employment conditions has been pensions, which may be subject to new regulations from July 2002. There are three possible outcomes to the recent government review: an obligation to provide an individual pension scheme for each group of employees transferred to an economic entity; an obligation to provide admission to the contractor's own pension scheme; or no change to the status quo where pensions are at present not transferable due to the complexities involved. Among these complexities is the difficulty of providing for the eventuality of further transfer.

The impact of TUPE on planning strategy

The competitive pressures in tendering for private sector business have intensified and business is moving increasingly towards fixed-price outsourcing contracts. Therefore, it is of paramount importance to evaluate staffing requirements and the quality of staff to be transferred under TUPE before bidding. Incumbent contractors are not bound to give TUPE detail to their competitors in the pre-tender phase. They are usually cooperative in the catering areas although this is not always the case. There is a growing need to determine the rationale for planned cost savings when finalising the bid price. Some clients provide no pre-tender TUPE information which makes cost analysis and the planning process even more difficult.

The bidding process

Current terms and conditions of employment are discovered during the pre-tender survey, although private sector clients may not reveal the details of staff employed until the final bidding stage when the client demands that bidders declare their plans for managing TUPE if they are awarded the contract. In formulating the sales proposition there is a delicate balance between bidding competitively and costing for best industry practice. Clients may be anxious to avoid becoming vulnerable themselves to trade union criticism, so bidders are well advised to take the approach of maintaining rates of pay.

Post-award of contract

Sodexho makes a point of meeting with staff affected by the transition process, with the client present, as soon as possible after the contract is awarded. There is then normally a four to six week interval before the contract is taken on and staff are transferred to Sodexho under TUPE. Inevitably, there is unease among the staff about the consequences of their transfer of employment and about their new employer, so initial contacts and continuing close communication are essential during the transition period and the following months. Feedback is maintained through regular staff meetings and quarterly reviews.

One measure of success is a high staff retention rate, particularly when a contract is taken over and the previous service provider may be interested in transferring the higher quality staff which they have trained to another site or establishment managed by themselves.

In many respects, movement under TUPE from one contractor to another is generally easier for employees than the experience of moving from the company which employed them. Retraining for management roles is often carried out by providing staff with a 'buddy' to work alongside : this is a quick way to instil the Sodexho standards and ethos and assures quality delivery to the client from the outset of a contract.

The obvious benefit of longer contracts is that start-up costs, as well as the cost in management time initially to secure the contract, are amortised over a longer revenue stream. A less quantifiable benefit, which Sodexho can offer to new employees and which few of its competitors can match, is that of career progression to outstanding managers and staff through other contracts or divisions within the organisation – an effective defence against re-recruitment by former employers.

16

Multiple-site Management Issues in Delivering Business Support Services to a Range of Customers

Peter Cordy

Introduction

An essential ingredient for business success must be the recognition by the board and top managers of an organisation of the importance of property and the benefits of sound asset management in supporting the delivery of business results.

The effective use of resources and the delivery of business support services to a range of customers are at the centre of any successful enterprise and so senior managers and directors need to regard property as a core activity – not, as is sometimes suggested, non-core.

There should be a personal commitment at the very top of the organisation to ensure that property and business support services are recognised as a significant influence when making strategic decisions about business direction.

The author uses his experience of working with the 'top team' at Hertfordshire Constabulary to develop an estate strategy to illustrate how the effective management of assets underpins service delivery.

This chapter will highlight some of the issues involved in providing a strategic direction to the management of property assets in complex organisations, and in arranging and managing the integration of business support services across multiple sites to different customer profiles and by a range of providers and suppliers.

Determining the preferred model of service delivery – some issues and questions

Before taking decisions regarding the model of asset management to be applied and the preferred procurement option to be adopted, it is important to give detailed consideration to a number of fundamental issues relating to the organisational culture of the business. The answers will influence the delivery and integration of asset management with the provision of business support services.

These issues include:

- The role of the local premises manager and the extent of local decision making/empowerment to be allowed. This must include consideration of the relative merits and importance of maintaining an on-site or remote presence;

- The role of the account manager or property/facilities professional as an interface between the client/end user and/or the contractor/supplier;

- The role of the service provider – eg headteacher, operations director etc – in determining service standards and levels of provision;

- Establishing the procurement matrix for services and providers and defining the interfaces, cross-overs and boundaries;

- Developing a shared understanding of the preferred relationship model, eg partnership, alliance, client/contractor;

- Defining reporting lines – delegation of authority to end users/customers and suppliers; authority limits and controls; effective management of reactive maintenance; need for responsiveness; accountability and monitoring;

- Access to information – availability of timely and relevant management information on utilisation and cost of assets to inform investment decisions;

- Securing customer/stakeholder engagement and feedback – achieving involvement and satisfaction; monitoring and performance measurement/management;

- Contract monitoring – compliance and conflict resolution;

- Incentivisation – including profit sharing between users and suppliers resulting from innovation and improvement;

- Communication – two way flow of information;

- Establishing clear lines of responsibility;

- Service standards – range and quality of services;

- Security, resilience and business continuity – corporate and local responsibilities;

- Balancing on-site management and delivery with affordability – access to services; frequency of use and demand; required skill levels; market availability; specialism; cost of services; business impact resulting from failure.

A strategic context for the provision of assets – using available 'best practice'

Once the fundamental issues outlined above have been considered, it is possible to begin developing a strategic approach to asset management.

A useful start to providing a strategic context and direction for the use and deployment of assets should be an audit of current practice measured against best practice advice relating to property management. Two possible starting points are provided by the Audit Commission Reports *Local Authority Property – A Management Handbook*, 1988 (Table 16.1) and the useful audit and planning tool in its report *Hot Property*, May 2000 (Table 16.2).

Establishing the purpose and vision

Before embarking on the development of an asset management/estate strategy it is imperative that each business establishes its purpose and

Table 16.1 Best practice in property management *(Audit Commission, 1988)*

Management Arrangements

- Define responsibility for property at member (director/board) level: set up a property committee or equivalent body to determine strategy for managing the resource;
- Set up an executive unit at officer level to review property holdings and property running costs;
- Use incentives to persuade users to improve utilisation and control of property running costs;
- Set out property management responsibilities:
  – of the property committee and other central support committees, and relevant chief officers;
  – of service committees and service chief officers;
  – of building occupiers.

Property Ownership

- Identify all property owned (or otherwise controlled), together with location, size and use;
- Define criteria and measure the use of direct service property;
- Survey the condition of the stock;
- Prepare a five-year maintenance plan taking account of the age profile of the stock;
- Identify the full extent of vacant property;
- Ensure that premises managers do not re-use surplus property for some other purpose without reference to the property committee.

Property Running Costs

- Define 'cost-centres' for each (major) property;
- Produce regular and timely cost data that can be linked to non-financial data (man/hour usage; floor area etc) to facilitate performance measures;
- Ensure that the different cost elements (cleaning, maintenance, energy etc.) are separately reported and that the information is available to building users;
- Produce league tables of unit costs for properties;
- Identify programmes to improve efficiency in respect of energy, cleaning, maintenance etc;
- Review the rateable value of properties.

Property Review

- Institute a programme of reviews, either on a service or area basis, or both;
- Bring information on utilisation and property running costs into the review process;
- Ensure that such reviews are undertaken by staff of sufficient seniority to speak and bargain for their department;
- Ensure that these reviews are short and focused;
- Ensure that users are aware of the opportunity value of their sites where these are significantly higher than present use value.

---

vision for the use of assets/property. This will provide the context in which these will be used to support business objectives and will inform decisions on the procurement and delivery of business support services to support the organisation.

As an example, Hertfordshire Constabulary's purpose and vision for its built estate is reproduced below:

Hertfordshire Constabulary Estate Strategy – Policy objectives

Table 16.2 *Hot Property:* Checklist for Action (Audit Commission Report, May 2000)

What needs to be done?	Possible first steps	Position Assessment	Action Proposed
Enhance awareness of property as a strategic resource that needs to be actively managed at both corporate and service levels. Provide appropriate and timely information to elected members to aid decision-making.	• Policy statement in corporate plan; • Training for officers and members.		
Clearly identify responsibility for strategic asset management.	• Establish corporate policy covering officer and member roles.		
Develop a council-wide property strategy/asset management plan (AMP) setting out the sufficiency, suitability and cost of existing assets, needs for the future and how these will be achieved.	• Circulate DETR guidelines; • Agree corporate priorities; • Identify roles and timescales for further work.		
Put in place information gathering and monitoring processes to support the AMP.	• Inventory what information is currently held, and by whom.		
Review assets and challenge whether they need to be retained. Dispose of assets that do not support core service objectives or fail to make an adequate return on investment.	• Pilot a series of property 'questions' in an upcoming best value service review; • Target 'easy hits' – eg vacant land.		
The use of property resources should be considered in every (relevant) best value service review.	• Include basic property review questions in internal best value process manuals		
Investigate innovative methods of service delivery, maximising the use of information and communications technology to improve accessibility and drive down property costs.	• Brainstorm possibilities at team meetings; • Look at relevant private sector examples.		
Pursue opportunities to share property with other local agencies, balancing cost, quality and user demands.	• Obtain member commitment in principle; • Plot location of various public agency buildings in a sample area.		
Set measurable targets for non-operational property, on the basis of internal and external comparisons.	• Consult individual property managers to identify possible measures.		

Table 16.2 *cont'd* *Hot Property:* Checklist for Action (Audit Commission Report, May 2000)

Review office accommodation across the council and set departmental targets for reduction, to be achieved through the adoption of hot desking or other innovative practices.	● Identify all office buildings, then ask the person responsible for each to record occupancy levels on a sample day.		
Establish sensible incentives to ensure that departments use property in the wider corporate interest.	● Identify source and nature of recent disposals.		
Within devolved financial management structures, align budgets for property with managerial responsibilities wherever possible.	● Trace 'audit trails' for common premises-related transactions.		
Subject property services to best value review, challenging the current structure and testing competitiveness against other suppliers. Consider locating all services under a single director.	● Join one of the local authority property benchmarking clubs; ● Consult clients on satisfaction with current structures and processes.		
Adopt a stronger customer focus for property services, matching provision to frontline service delivery needs.	● Run an open forum to discuss service needs.		

Purpose of the estate

Hertfordshire Constabulary holds property for the purposes of:

- *providing a Local Public Interface;*
- *accommodating the operating base for the delivery of local police services;*
- *providing accommodation for Corporate Support for delivery of a local service;*
- *residential Accommodation for police officers;*
- *recreational facilities;*
- *police Authority Accommodation.*

Our vision of excellence

We shall pursue the objective of an 'excellent' estate which:

- *is safe and secure;*
- *is user friendly and welcoming (for both public and staff);*
- *is in good repair and well maintained;*
- *is readily identifiable and visible;*
- *is in the 'right' places;*
- *is the 'right' size;*
- *is energy-efficient – 'green';*

- *enhances the local environment;*
- *offers optimum use of space;*
- *reinforces the Constabulary's corporate identity;*
- *complements our long term strategy.*

Developing agreed policy objectives and action points

Having established the purpose and vision, a number of policy objectives/statements can usefully be developed to provide an operational direction within which the deployment, use and management of assets is conducted. These statements must be approved and owned at the highest level within the organisation, ie board, individual directors and chief executive. An example of such a statement, drawn from Hertfordshire Constabulary's Estate Strategy, follows. It illustrates some of the agreed objectives and action points adopted by the senior management team, which could be adapted to suit individual needs.

Strategic overview and general findings

Statutory planning context and major development proposals

We will make representations to ensure that the policies and proposals for new development contained in the County Structure Plan and district-wide Local Plans take account of the likely impact of additional development on policing and include provision for securing developer contributions.
Action points:
Estates Manager to coordinate planning response to Structure Plan and liaise with District Councils.

We will research the likely impact of development proposals on policing in the locality.
Action points:
Estates Manager to liaise with Divisional Commanders regarding research on the impact of development on policing

We will actively seek developer contributions towards provision of additional local facilities or extension of existing facilities where the need for additional resources can be directly attributed to a particular development.
Action points:
Estates Manager to lead on seeking developer contributions.

We will hold early discussions with developers and local planning authorities with a view to securing support for measures to enable policing of developments to occur.

Action points:
Estates Manager to liaise with Architectural Liaison Officer to establish arrangements for monitoring development.

Building condition; maintenance need and the R&M budget

We will continue to monitor the condition and suitability of property to allow early identification of work required to maintain buildings in a suitable condition for operational use.
Action points:
Full condition surveys of operational property will be carried out on the basis of a five-yearly 'quinquennial' in-depth survey.
Surveys will be updated annually (between July and September), and the priorities and costs of work required will be reassessed to inform the budget setting process commencing in October each year.

We will set the Programmed Repair and Maintenance budget to allow for the work identified by the condition surveys to be carried out on the basis of agreed priorities.
Action points:
Agree with Property Partnership arrangements for monitoring condition of buildings and costing maintenance need.
Annual monitoring of programmed work carried out will be assessed on the basis of its relative priority and cost as established in the condition survey.

We will make budget provision for maintenance work of a responsive (unplanned) nature, to meet unforeseen needs that arise during the financial year on the basis of past experience.
Action points:
Identify appropriate level of resources to meet responsive (unplanned) maintenance.
Annual monitoring of responsive (unplanned) work and cost to assess the proportion of the programmed maintenance budget.

We will review alternative property solutions before significant expenditure is committed.
Action points:
Initiate strategic reviews of alternative property solutions as appropriate jointly with users.

We will study property running costs to establish value for money measurements for each property and will benchmark the findings against norms for similar properties.
Action points:
Liaise with Finance Department to identify premises related costs and appropriate benchmarks.

Space utilisation

We will regularly assess the use of space within the context of the Constabulary's agreed Accommodation Standards and Statutory Guidance to ensure that appropriate conditions for the public and staff prevail and that best use of available space is being made.

Action points:
The local senior management team will be responsible for ensuring appropriate utilisation of available space.
The local premises manager (Senior Administrative Officer or departmental equivalent) will be responsible for advising the management team on measures to optimise use of space. Estates Manager will monitor the use of space against agreed standards and statutory guidance and support management teams in developing proposals for improving use of space.

All proposals involving additional staff and/or new areas of service provision will be subject to preparation of a business case, which will include an assessment of the likely impact on the need for additional accommodation and associated premises running costs, before approval is granted.
Action points:
Estates Manager to liaise with Personnel Manager to prepare a report for FPG on requirements for considering accommodation needs in all new proposals for additional staff.

We will retain a proportion of total available space as a strategic reserve to provide flexibility to meet urgent short term needs. This space will not be permanently allocated for a specific purpose and will be allocated and managed on the basis of a specified (renewable) 'let' by the Estates and Administration Department.
Action points:
Identify suitable accommodation and write a practice note for the allocation and management of space held as a strategic reserve.

Statutory compliance – Health & Safety; disabled access; asbestos; legal requirements

We will comply with all Health & Safety legislation in respect of property matters and will implement plans to assess and restrict the Constabulary's exposure to risk. Where compliance with any provision is unavoidably delayed through lack of available resources, we will agree and document a programme identifying interim measures to limit risk, and target dates for achieving full compliance.
Action points:
Estates Manager to liaise with Health & Safety Officer to arrange for an audit of Health & Safety in buildings and prepare plans for securing compliance

We will comply with statutory requirements for disabled access to our buildings and will implement a programme of work to provide suitable facilities for the disabled in all our public reception areas. Where compliance with any provision is unavoidably delayed through lack of available resources, we will agree and document a programme identifying interim measures to limit risk, and target dates for achieving full compliance.
Action points:
Commission the Property Partnership to audit disabled access in public reception areas of buildings and prepare plans for securing provision.

We will review and update our information on the presence of materials containing asbestos in buildings. The record of the presence of asbestos will be maintained and a copy will be made available for inspection at each of our premises.

Action points:
Commission the Property Partnership to survey asbestos and provide a record of materials together with a Code of Practice to be kept on site.
Introduce arrangements for updating the survey.

Before work is undertaken which could involve disturbing asbestos, the appointed premises manager will ensure that the presence of asbestos is communicated to a representative of the contractor, and that all appropriate safeguards for the handling of the material are in place before work commences.
Action points:
Premises managers (SAOs) to ensure contractors are aware of the presence of asbestos and have made suitable arrangements before work commences.

Management

We will adopt the report *Property Management* as the basis for managing property within Hertfordshire Constabulary.
Action points:
Update Property Management *document to take account of comments.*

We will move towards devolution of the responsibility and budgets for internal (non-structural) maintenance to Divisions commencing in the 1997/98 financial year.
Action points:
Discuss with SAOs practical aspects of devolving internal maintenance and recommend suitable procedure.

We will move towards a Facilities Management approach to the management of the Stanborough Road site.
Develop the Facilities Management approach and recommend appropriate working arrangements.

Force-wide issues

Security

We will review our risk / threat assessment and carry out a security audit at operational property across the Force area which will assess the level of risk and identify the need for remedial action.
Action points:
Estates Manager to liaise with Emergency Planning Officer to update the threat assessment and security audit and commission the Property Partnership to produce costed proposals.

Environmental issues

We will develop an Environmental Statement for the Estate and adopt it for implementation.
Action points:
Develop an Environmental Statement and Strategy to encompass Estate issues for incorporation within the Estate Strategy Report.

Topics to be covered will include:

- *Enviromental policy;*
- *Environmental legislation;*
- *Recycling, use of recycled and sustainable materials and waste reduction*
- *Waste materials and reducing waste;*
- *Energy;*
- *Emissions;*
- *Purchasing;*
- *Visual amenity and heritage;*
- *Training;*
- *Local Agenda 21 – Green issues*

Adopt policies for implementation.

Delivering Business Support Services – Premises Management Activities

An audit of how premises management activities are undertaken provides a possible context for deciding the most appropriate delivery and procurement model for any business. The premises management activities identified in Figure 16.1 (adapted from the Touche Ross report *Getting your college ready* prepared for the Further Education Funding Council) provide a suggested basis for determining the roles and focus for attention by those with responsibility for asset management at various levels of responsibility within an organisation.

Defining responsibilities for managing the delivery of Business Support Services adapted from Hertfordshire Constabulary report – 'Property Management'

Premises management activities: summary of responsibilities

General estate management and property records (information and monitoring)

Board/Directors

- Agree overall strategic direction for efficient and effective management of the estate;
- Approve property management policies and standards;
- Approve the estate strategy;

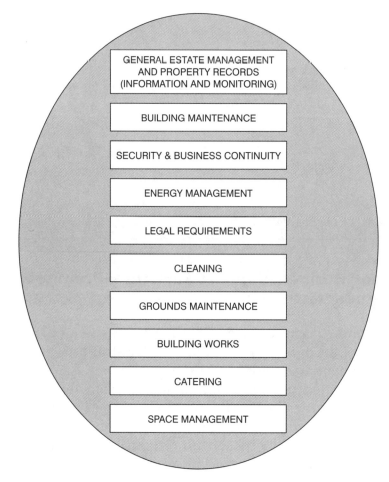

Figure 16.1 Premises management activities
Source: Touche Ross report *Getting your college ready*

- Approve terms of property transactions outside of chief executive's delegated authority.

Chief Executive/Property Director/Finance Director

- Translate board's strategic direction for property into estate management priorities;
- Recommend standards and policies to board;
- Recommend the estate strategy to board;
- Approve terms of property transactions within delegated authority;
- Approve appointment of estate management/valuation consultants.

Estates Manager

- Develop and maintain the estate strategy as part of the business plan;
- Secure arrangements for maintenance of property terrier and asset register (including floor plans);
- Ensure safe keeping of title deeds (through Legal Services);
- Prepare documentation for procurement of construction related services;
- Commission and manage estate management/valuation consultancy services;
- Monitor performance of consultants to ensure quality and report to board.

Property/Facilities Management

- Devolve budget for payment of minor outgoings;
- Monitor and process payment of major outgoings eg rent, rates etc;
- Manage the investment estate (if any).

Local Premises Managers

- Monitor and process payment of minor (delegated) outgoings;
- Hold copies of floor plans and management profiles;
- Notify estates manager of building alterations.

Property Consultants

- Understand the business's strategic needs;
- Undertake estate management and valuation commissions to achieve value for money;
- Recommend transaction terms to property director/estates manager for approval.

Building maintenance

Board/Directors

- Approve maintenance strategy and budget for maintenance.

Chief Executive/Property Director/Finance Director

- Approve policies and standards for maintenance;
- Recommend budget for structural and internal maintenance to board;
- Approve programme for structural and internal maintenance.

Estates Manager

- Develop and maintain a maintenance plan as part of the estate strategy;
- Secure arrangements for maintenance of property;
- Prepare documentation for procurement of maintenance services;
- Commission and manage maintenance consultancy services;
- Monitor performance of consultants and contractors to ensure quality and report to chief executive/board.

Property/Facilities Management

- Devolve budget to local premises managers for internal (non-structural) maintenance;
- Monitor and process payment of major structural maintenance;
- Manage the maintenance programme.

Local Premises Managers

- Notify consultant of needs for remedial (unplanned) maintenance as they occur;
- Agree with consultant timetable for surveys and maintenance works;
- Administer and process payment of devolved maintenance works.

Property Consultants

- Undertake annual and quinquennial surveys;
- Recommend and agree programme with property director; estates manager; property/facilities management and local premises managers;
- Coordinate contractors to undertake work in liaison with property/facilities management and local premises managers.

Security and business continuity

Board/Directors

- Approve strategy and funding for security and business continuity.

Chief Executive/Property Director/Finance Director

- Approve security policies and standards;
- Advise board on cost implications of implementing security and business continuity policy;
- Approve appointment of specialist security/business continuity advisers.

Estates Manager

- Develop and maintain a security/business continuity plan as part of the estate strategy;
- Secure arrangements for maintenance of security of property;
- Commission and manage security and business continuity consultancy services;
- Monitor performance of consultants to ensure quality and report to chief executive/board.

Property/Facilities Management

- Devolve local security budget to local premises managers for minor works;
- Monitor and process payment of major security improvements;
- Manage the programme.

Local Premises Managers

- Day to day implementation of security and business continuity policy;
- Rehearse plans;
- Maintain and update business continuity plans.

Property Consultants

- Note security issues as part of annual and quinquennial surveys;
- Advise on feasibility and costs of proposed security improvements;
- Coordinate contractors to undertake work in liaison with local premises managers.

Energy management

Board/Directors

- Approve strategy and funding for energy saving initiatives.

Chief Executive/Property Director/Finance Director

- Approve strategy and energy management policies and standards;
- Advise board on cost implications of implementing energy policy;
- Approve appointment of energy management consultants.

Estates Manager

- Develop and maintain an energy management plan as part of the estate strategy;
- Secure arrangements for improving the energy efficiency of property;
- Commission and manage energy management consultancy services;
- Monitor performance of consultants to ensure quality and report to chief executive/board;
- Establish an energy management advice service to local premises managers.

Property/Facilities Management

- Devolve local energy budgets to local premises managers;
- Monitor and process payment of energy improvement initiatives;
- Manage the energy improvements programme.

Local Premises Managers

- Day to day implementation of energy policy.

Property Consultants

- Undertake energy efficiency studies as part of annual and quinquennial surveys;
- Advise on feasibility and costs of energy efficiency improvements;
- Coordinate contractors to undertake work in liaison with local premises managers.

Legal property requirements

Board/Directors

- Agree Risk Management strategy;
- To be aware of legal obligations and responsibilities;
- Approve funding for health and safety, insurance, security, etc.

Chief Executive/Property Director/Finance Director

- Approve policies and standards;
- Advise board on cost implications of health and safety, insurance, security obligations;
- Approve appointment of legal consultants.

Estates Manager (acting with the Company Solicitor and Health & Safety Coordinator).

- Advise on statutory requirements (e.g. asbestos; legionella; dangerous structures; planning; building regulations; capital finance regulations; property agreements etc) as part of the estate strategy;
- Advise on the need for specialist surveys eg asbestos; legionella etc;
- Advise on need for health and safety and risk assessment studies;
- Secure arrangements for ensuring safety and security of property;
- Commission and manage consultancy services;
- Monitor performance of consultants to ensure quality and report to chief executive/board.

Property/Facilities Management

- Devolve local health and safety budget to local premises managers for minor works;
- Monitor and process payment of major health and safety improvements;
- Manage the health and safety programme.

Local Premises Managers

- Identify day to day health and safety issues;
- Instruct consultants to take immediate action;
- Day to day implementation of health and safety policy.

Property Consultants

- Be aware of the legal obligations of the business;
- Address health and safety issues as a priority;
- Coordinate contractors to undertake work in liaison with local premises managers.

Cleaning

Board/Directors

- Approve procurement strategy;
- Approve funding for cleaning.

Chief Executive/Property Director/Finance Director

- Approve policy and standards;
- Advise board on cost implications;
- Appoint cleaning contractor(s) in accordance with procurement requirements.

Estates Manager

- Prepare documentation for specification of cleaning services;
- Agree arrangements for cleaning of property with local premises managers;
- Commission cleaning contractor services;
- Monitor performance of contractors to ensure quality and report to chief executive/board.

Property/Facilities Management

- Advise and support local premises managers.

Local Premises Managers

- Monitor and process payment of cleaning contract;
- Day-to-day monitoring of standards;
- Liaison with contractor to ensure access to buildings etc.

Contractors

- Ensure maintenance of contract standards and compliance with specifications;
- Coordinate work in liaison with local premises managers.

Grounds maintenance

Board/Directors

- Approve procurement strategy;
- Approve funding for grounds maintenance.

Chief Executive/Property Director/Finance Director

- Appoint grounds maintenance contractor(s) in accordance with procurement requirements;
- Approve policies and standards;
- Advise board on cost implications.

Estates Manager

- Prepare documentation for procurement of grounds maintenance services;
- Agree arrangements for grounds maintenance with Local Premises Managers;

- Commission grounds maintenance contractor services;
- Monitor performance of contractors to ensure quality and report to chief executive/board.

Property/Facilities Management

- Advise and support local premises managers.

Local Premises Managers

- Monitor and process payment;
- Day to day monitoring of standards;
- Liaise with contractor to ensure access to property etc.

Contractors

- Ensure maintenance of contract standards and compliance with specifications;
- Coordinate work in liaison with local premises managers.

Building works

Board/Directors

- Approve capital investment programme requirements and priorities and funding.

Chief Executive/Property Director/Finance Director

- Recommend schemes for inclusion in building programme to board;
- Advise board on cost implications of building programme;
- Approve appointment of design consultants.

Estates Manager

- Interpret operational needs for new buildings as part of the estate strategy;
- Prepare client briefs for design projects;
- Secure inclusion of capital building projects in business plan;
- Advise on selection process for design consultants ;
- Commission and manage design consultancy services;
- Monitor performance of consultants to ensure quality and report to chief executive/board.

Property/Facilities Management

- Manage the minor works and capital programme.

Local Premises Managers

- Involvement in project briefing process to translate operational needs into accommodation requirements;
- Liaise on implementation aspects of building projects.

Design Consultants

- Understand clients' strategic needs and develop design brief with client;
- Produce design solutions to meet client needs;
- Advise on feasibility and costs of projects;
- Supervise the tendering process;
- Manage individual contracts on behalf of the client;
- Coordinate contractors to undertake work in liaison with local premises managers;
- Monitor works and approve payments to contractors.

Catering

Board/Directors

- Approve procurement strategy;
- Approve funding for catering.

Chief Executive/Property Director/Finance Director

- Approve policies and standards;
- Advise board on budget needs.

Estates Manager (through Procurement Manager).

- Prepare documentation for procurement of catering services;
- Agree arrangements for catering with local premises managers;
- Commission catering services;
- Monitor performance of contractors to ensure quality and report to chief executive and board.

Property/Facilities Management

- Ensure kitchens comply with Health & Safety requirements.

Local Premises Managers

- Day to day monitoring of standards;
- Liaise with contractor.

Contractors

- Ensure maintenance of contract standards and compliance with specifications;
- Coordinate delivery of service in liaison with local premises managers.

Space management

Board/Directors

- Approve strategy and funding.

Chief Executive/Property Director/Finance Director

- Approve policies and standards;
- Advise board on cost implications of space utilisation policy.

Estates Manager

- Develop and maintain space standards as part of the estate strategy;
- Secure arrangements for ensuring efficient use of property;
- Highlight opportunities for optimising space utilisation;
- Commission and manage accommodation reviews;
- Monitor performance of consultants to ensure quality and report to chief executive/board;
- Advise local premises managers on space utilisation.

Property/Facilities Management

- Coordinate implementation of building alterations/adaptation;

Local Premises Managers

- Day-to-day implementation of space management policy;
- Liaise with staff to agree efficient use of space;
- Refer requests for accommodation to estates manager.

Property Consultants

- Coordinate contractors to undertake building alterations in liaison with local premises managers.

Part 4

Building on Experience

17

Measuring the Value of Facilities and Facilities Management

Professor John Hinks
CABER

This is a difficult issue for business. Ultimately, the challenge of measuring the value of facilities and the facilities management (FM) function lies in looking beyond facilities as simply a cost item, and in seeing them and their management as potential value-adding components for the business. This appears to be alien to the business mindset generally, and so represents a largely untapped, potentially competitive edge for those directors willing to grasp it.

The challenge is two-fold

First, the strategic potential of achieving the right facilities and FM service for the business is not always apparent if the FM function is outsourced. This is especially so if the rationale for outsourcing was to minimise cost and/or risk, and/or to remove FM from the director's task list. This often results in an 'out of sight, out of mind' mentality. The matter of divergent goals and the potential disclosure of strategically sensitive information can also tend to restrict the depth of communications in outsourced arrangements, thereby compounding the lack of clarity. Second, assessing the value of facilities and the FM function is complex and highly particular to the business context.

This chapter will raise some of the general issues which should be considered when thinking about how to get the best support services for your business needs. Creating a business-specific solution is something that directors need to work out individually with their facilities managers.

Conventional approaches to evaluating facilities performance

There are several levels at which the issue can be addressed. It is common practice to deal with what is being measured first. Historically, the FM profession tends to measure performance from an operational efficiency perspective – referring to data which are facilities-oriented, and focusing on the efficiency of the facilities spent in terms of factors such as running costs, energy consumption, maintenance costs and rental costs per square foot, etc. This works well for prioritising the operational management of the facilities and for checking how the outlays relate to the norms for the industry, budgetary targets or legal requirements. The approach is convenient for facilities managers, yet it does not tend to relate directly to business drivers. The data also has a propensity to reduce the assessment process to checking for deviation from the lowest common denominators of running facilities efficiently. What it does not do is to illuminate the potential differentiating competitive edge of tuning the facility to the business process; or to support any analysis of the correspondence with the strategic value of the FM service as a lever to help facilitate the strategic priorities facing the director. So, whilst these conventional measurements allow the director to assess outlay against budget, and even to compare this with the industry norm alone, they do not make it clear whether the organisation is spending the right amount for its needs or if it is getting maximum support advantage or potential flexibility.

Some of the aspects regarding the impact of facilities on the business may need to be measured using more than one indicator. The same data may have different meanings in different contexts, and the actual and relative importance of facilities services will vary over time according to the current business climate driving the organisation.

Consider workspace, for example, an operational asset that is increasingly becoming recognised as having profoundly strategic dimensions, especially with the rise of the virtual organisations, 'hotelling' and 'hot desking'. Popular measures use area and cost to assess the efficiencies of space allocation. It would also be appropriate to look beyond efficiency to the effectiveness of the facilities for the business needs. For example, how much more business performance would you get from allocating more space per person, per task, or by spending more on various aspects of the comfort and flexibility of that space? Logic suggests that eventually you would get no marginal benefit. On the other hand then, at what point does reduced space, or reduced comfort, start to detract from the operation of the staff, and hence the performance of the business?

More precisely, when does 'efficiency' eat into effectiveness? More strategically still, at what points do more or less spending on comfort, or on the quality of the internal environment, make little or no marginal difference to business performance? To the point, do you know where your space provisions lie on this spectrum? Bearing in mind that some companies are much more facilities-based than others, a more complex picture emerges of the important issues needing to be measured. What about the organisation that is changing its work processes, say by moving towards virtual or hot desking approaches for some of its operations? With which space solutions will it work well? Which less well? Which not at all? Who is currently involved in making this decision, and how?

As Robert McNamara reflected, the real issue is measuring the important aspects, not the importance of measurement. In the absence of a set of performance indicators, which correspond to the current and foreseeable strategic business priorities and directors' understanding of the business climate, facilities managers do the best they can and monitor that the facilities are not managed in a financially inferior way compared with industry norms. Competitive opportunities abound for those directors who can engage with the facilities director and, even better, correlate the provision of support with their needs. However, since most existing facilities indicators tend to be designed by, and for consumption by, the FM profession, any initiative to correlate the facilities and FM service provision with the business priorities is going to need some supplementary input from the core business director. This is the blocker that I mentioned earlier.

Another major disincentive to measuring this strategically important aspect of business support services is its complexity. Yet, it is not so much an issue of collecting different data as of knowing where to look. Many FM performance issues are the result of a complex interplay of factors, only some of which are directly related to the facilities or fall within the remit of the FM brief. For example, many factors in the impact of facilities on business effectiveness are probably related to the psychophysical responses of staff to space and the internal environment. Lots of facilities issues are known to be complex and interdependent, but how do we disentangle the role of facilities from the business process, and the business climate from the morale of the staff? Supporting business needs is a cross-display issue and assessments of need and performance have to recognise this. It may be best to approach the issue jointly with HRM and IS managers, too, but this needs the patronage of a director.

This is not an insignificant issue for the director, even if it seems functionally non-core. Facilities can be in the order of 10–20 per cent of total costs. Getting the best by spending strategically could add much more value than simply minimising spending. Certainly, there are companies that are already experimenting with increased or radical expenditure on facilities and the impact that this has on business effectiveness. Nevertheless, many more are exploring the risks of decrement to business performance from arbitrarily reducing the level of facilities provision on a cost basis alone. A sort of unacknowledged experiment. Of course, not addressing it doesn't mean that it doesn't matter.

Looking at the appropriateness of facilities

A more targeted approach to measuring the value of facilities would be to consider the appropriateness of their contribution to business performance. This is important because it deals with the relative worth of the facilities and FM to the particular business, and because it measures whether the quality of fit is right, getting better or is getting worse. Such an approach will need to consider the balance between several indicators, each of which are dependent on the particular business and its circumstances.

The nub of thinking in terms of the 'right' facilities is that the actual value of the facilities to the business is completely particular to the actual circumstances. That is, that the nature of the services required by a particular business; the prioritisation that gets attached to them; and the contribution that their adequate performance (or failure) make to the business all depend on the exact profile of the business needs. Quality of fit is what matters.

Cost-based benchmarking, using standardised sets of FM indicators, can only go so far in helping to assess this. This is because wrapped up in the interpretation of these measures are other important aspects – such as the sensitivity of the particular business to superior performance or failure in one or more aspects of its facilities. A more sophisticated and strategic form of benchmarking is needed, and directors will need to help with this since they will be able to contextualise the assessment in terms of the corporate drivers and the business environment.

The first step in designing a set of measures which tell the business director how appropriate their business support services are, is to identify the critical elements of that support for differing scenarios. For example, facilities requirements vary as organisations upsize, downsize, diversify, restructure physically, introduce a new technology or simply stabilise after a recent change. Just as the business priorities will differ for these circumstances, so too will the value of certain FM aspects. A balance needs to be struck.

Facilities and the stable business

Take the case of the ongoing, relatively stable business support need of an organisation which is operating a relatively stable business process (probably a rarity nowadays). A business which is operating in a broadly unchanging state may be able to make most use of an operationally efficient and cost-minimised form of FM. Facility usage and demands on other aspects of the business support services may be stable. The FM function may provide best value for the business by being stable. For this type of organisational situation, the commonly used FM benchmarking indicators such as running costs, energy consumption, maintenance costs and rental costs per square foot may be appropriate. This is modelled as Scenario 1 in Figure 17.1, which represents FM in an environment of business stability and driven by conventional FM output criteria.

Facilities and the dynamic business

However, it is in the field of the dynamic business where changes in the business demand need to be facilitated by creative business support solutions. Change drives business, and it is this reality that current approaches to measuring FM performance tend not to acknowledge.

Consider the business that needs an agile support service to allow it to adapt with market pressures, perhaps to restructure its processes or service delivery, to move to flexible working, downsize or adjust to a geographically changing market. Here, the value of FM to the business is more likely to be associated with innovation than minimal cost and stability. Indeed, high cost will matter less than speed of delivery or the capacity for bespoke attunement of the service to the organisation's individual competitive needs. This is especially likely to be the case for industries where distinctiveness of process (or speed of business adaptation) is a key element of their competitiveness. One of the most obvious singular indicators of this comes from looking at the rental premiums that organisations are increasingly ready to pay to retain flexibility of their operational property. This sometimes involves 20 per cent premiums. Is this an unfortunate cost increase or a wise investment in business agility?

Staying with the same type of situation, where innovation and flexibility in business support are keystones of competitiveness, consider what aspects of business support are really critical to the successful operation and flexibility of this business. Whilst spending on some aspects can be safely minimised, other functions may justify increased investment to ensure business process agility. Better criteria for measuring the value of facilities, and the FM function, in this case may be: continuous improvement, reliability, consistency, lowest cost and timeliness. Rather than helping to refine the FM role to suit the business needs, directors' continued acquiescence of conventional benchmarking indicators could leave attention focused away from the most efficacious FM service for their business. Returning to Figure 17.1, now compare Scenario 2, which models the role of FM in achieving business flexibility for competitiveness in a dynamic market, with that of Scenario 1.

A more strategically potent opportunity to use FM appropriately arises where the same business enters the options-analysis stage of planning a change in its core process or production. Here, the director has the opportunity to get the facilities right – the adaptability of the processes and their support may be more critical to the future competitiveness of the business than some aspects of the cost of supporting that provision and its transition. Of course, the business directors interpret what value means – should cost efficiency take second place to effectiveness? Does FM offer best value to the organisation by taking a cost focus or a business support focus? Proactive FM foresight and a strategic understanding of the interrelationship between the business and the FM may actually be very valuable to the business, whereas any stagnation or unresponsiveness caused directly by the nature of FM provision and outlook could severely limit its usefulness to the business. Such unresponsiveness may limit the change options, speed and/or ultimate effectiveness of change.

Finally, consider as a further example the potential adaptability of FM. This may be crucially important for an organisation that is trying to protect the stability of its core process or production via changes in the nature of the facilities it uses for this. Downsizing (or rightsizing) is one example. Here cost efficiency is also likely to defer to operational effectiveness, to robustness of the transitionary or new service provision, and to the quality of alignment between the support service and the re-stabilising needs of the core business. Spare capacity may be a key measure here, and the convention of sweating the asset to its maximum capacity may actually impede short timescale business flexibility. The right solution depends on your circumstances.

Plainly it is important to understand the overall picture, and this is where some proaction on the part of the director is needed to move things forward. Compare Scenarios 3 and 4, Figure 17.2, which contrast the innovative, agility-oriented FM strategy for survival in a dynamic market with a more conventional cost-minimised approach to FM. The question is, do you and your facilities manager know what shape of profile you are assuming for your strategic planning purposes?

Clearly then, the key performance indicators of facilities and FM performance could differ for the same business and same FM organisation operating in different scenarios (or at different phases of its life cycle). Directors who do not accommodate the subtle variance in priorities of the FM service and rely on general indicators, or fail to involve their FMs in the strategic scenarios facing their organisation at planning, are likely to frustrate the potential of their own business support service to provide them with optimal support. How can you value an options analysis without thinking about the scope and limitations of your facilities?

The challenge of achieving best performance from facilities and the FM function lies in the measurement of the whole rather than the mere summation of the parts. The key performance indicators for FM are not independent of the drivers affecting the business. Directors who work with their facilities managers to design strategic agendas and performance targets, which correlate with the core priorities of the business, are most likely to experience the competitive edge of synergy between core and non-core processes.

Figure 17.1, Scenario 1 – stable FM and stable ongoing business needs

For an organisation operating in a stable business environment, the success criteria for FM may relate to reliability of service quality and a dependable speed of response set against continuous improvements in cost efficiency. Note that these measures represent FM outputs, however, and not business outcomes.

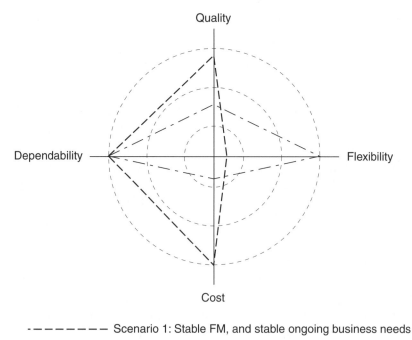

Figure 17.1 An output-oriented approach to FM for various business scenarios

Figure 17.1, Scenario 2 – FM for dynamically changing business needs

This is a more realistic scenario for most businesses. The value of FM arises from a combination of its support for the ongoing needs of the business and its support for changing business needs. Key observers of business competitiveness are remarking that speed and appropriateness of change are becoming increasingly relevant elements of competitiveness in a global business market. In such circumstances, it is reasonable to assume that the future competitiveness of a significant proportion of the business world will become increasingly dependent upon dynamic competitiveness – that is agility and competitive change in business processes (and products). In these situations, relative business advantage in a dynamically competitive sector is likely to be derived from the strategic application of FM in a customised manner. The indicators for assessing this aspect of FM performance will have to be more high-level, more transparent to business and will tend to represent the integrated output of a range of interrelated FM services, probably the result of a complex interactivity within and with the core business.

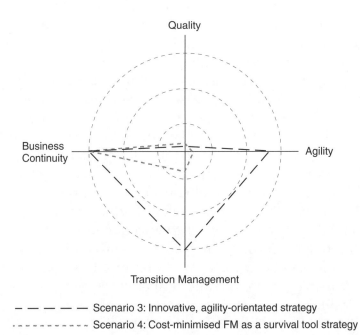

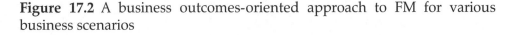

Figure 17.2 A business outcomes-oriented approach to FM for various business scenarios

Note the relatively low emphasis placed on cost efficiency. Repeatability and consistency may be less important dimensions within the assessment of FM quality than the degree of fit of the service to a varying business need. This places the emphasis on FM fundamentally in the arena of business innovation, where the predominant features of good FM may rely on adaptability, novelty, support for new processes, and/or timeliness. This situation differs considerably from the first scenario. Note how the FM output indicators used for Scenario 1 now need some further qualification in their interpretation before the assessment of FM performance can be compared.

Figure 17.2, Scenario 3 – FM for survival in a dynamic market

To extend this further, imagine the market for FM within the dynamically changing business sector in Scenario 2. The performance of this type of FM will probably be more intricate and therefore more difficult to assess – yet more relevant to the future of global business competitiveness and global FM. In this scenario, the survival of the organisation depends on agility rather than cost-efficiency. In these circumstances, the target business value of FM may reside in its efficacy or usefulness when applied strategically for competitive business advantage based on change. Here, the key performance indicators for FM may have to be more oriented towards business outcomes, and could converge with core business performance indicators such as agility rather than flexibility; business continuity rather than FM dependability; fitness for purpose as a qualifier of quality; or the ability of the service to contribute to changing the business. Note how the poles in this figure relate to business outcomes, not FM outputs. In such circumstances, the FM output measure of cost (compare with Figure 17.1) could be of minimal concern within the bigger strategic picture of the overall business outcomes. In this scenario the emphasis moves from efficiency and output to effectiveness and outcome, and the possible needs are measured using a different set of indicators than the stable needs. Once again, attempts to make performance assessments using generalised and reductive FM indicators will not be especially valuable.

Figure 17.2, Scenario 4 – alternate survival strategy in a dynamic market

An alternate survival strategy in the same circumstances as Scenario 3 may hinge around the reduction of all costs to an absolute minimum at the opportunity cost of flexibility and dependability, and with no intention to manage transition, merely to streamline the existing operations. Here, cost becomes the predominant measure of FM outputs and is likely to be the performance driver affecting the business-level outcomes. Achieving FM performance may involve shedding facilities that were highly efficient when measured against generalised criteria. In contrast to Scenario 3, the emphasis moves from effectiveness and efficiency to cost minimisation. Note the equally high priority placed on the business outcome of business continuity in both scenarios, but the implicit need to consider the nature of the FM outputs differently in each scenario. So, given any of the above scenarios, the FM relevance to the business will differ significantly, as should the assessment criteria for evaluating performance.

make your university smile

By offering a range of services from catering and cleaning to retail, Sodexho is improving the daily quality of life in further education. This can cut staff turnover, enhance academic performance and enhance the reputation of your college or university – which means not only more contented staff and students but a happier, healthier look to your finances. Call 0800 169 49 59.

sodexho.co.uk

Sodex*ho
Catering and Support Services

turning a cost into a value

18

Risk Management and Value Assessment

Professor John Kelly
Glasgow Caledonian University

The current growth in demand for value and risk management services results from the recent shift in public and corporate focus from the lowest cost option to the one giving maximum value. This widening of focus seeks to maximise the benefits of a project to the project stakeholders, where the definition of the project is 'the investment of resource for return' and the project's stakeholders are 'those who contribute to or will be directly affected by the project'. In this context, investment is measured in terms of capital or other resource input and a return in units of social, economic or commercial gain.

A value and risk management service is one that maximises the certainty of the functional value of a project by managing its development from concept to use through the audit of all decisions against a value system determined by the client. This chapter will review the development of value and risk management and outline its application to a project through a description and illustration of key tools and techniques.

The development of value management

Value management has its foundation in the manufacturing sector of North America. The concept began in the late 1940s when shortages of strategic materials forced manufacturers to consider alternatives that performed the same function. It was soon discovered that many of the alternatives provided equal or better quality at reduced cost. This led to what was then defined as value analysis:

> *Value analysis is an organised approach to providing the necessary functions at the lowest cost.*

Value analysis was always seen to be a cost validation exercise that did not affect the quality of the product. However, it was recognised that many products had unnecessary cost incorporated by design and it was this that led to the second definition of value analysis:

> *Value analysis is an organised approach to the identification and elimination of unnecessary cost where unnecessary cost is defined as a cost that provides neither use, life, quality, appearance nor customer features.*

In 1954, the US Department of Defence Bureau of Ships became the first US government organisation to implement a formal programme of value analysis. It was at this time that the name changed from value analysis to value engineering for the administrative reason that engineers were considered the most appropriate personnel to undertake the task. The term value engineering was formalised in the title of the Society of American Value Engineers, which recently changed its name to SAVE International. Value engineering in the UK began in the 1960s manufacturing sector, and led to the establishment in 1966 of the Value Engineering Association. This organisation changed its name in 1972 to the Institute of Value Management. Value management is commonly used to define a value activity from the strategic to the technical/operational stages in the development of projects. Value engineering is a subset of value management, which relates to the technical and operational aspects of projects only. Value management is the term in common use throughout Europe, except France where the term 'value analysis' is used.

An overview of risk management

Risk is commonly defined as being a hazard, the chance of a bad consequence or loss, or the exposure to miss chance. However it is defined, it is normally considered to be those issues that prejudice the outcome of an event. Risk management is a planned and systematic process of identifying, analysing and controlling the outcome of a particular event to achieve the planned objective, thereby maximising value. Risk management therefore incorporates three distinct stages:

• risk identification;

• risk analysis;

• risk response.

The characteristic development of projects

All projects, defined as 'the investment of resource for return', pass through four characteristic stages of development. These are:

• strategic planning and business definition;

• project planning and the establishment of systems;

• service definition of the component parts of the project; and

• operations and use.

Maximum value is achieved when value and risk management services are applied pro-actively at each stage as the project develops. As demonstrated in Figure 18.1 (the lever of value), maximum value is attained when effort is applied to the lever at each stage in turn. Also illustrated is that a given amount of effort at the strategic planning stage will give a higher value return than the equivalent amount of effort at the operations stage. It is an unfortunate fact that value and risk management studies undertaken re-actively at the later stages of a project (usually as a result of an overspend) often require a painful and wasteful, in respect of abortive work, climb back up the lever of value to endeavour to understand what lay behind the strategic planning of the project.

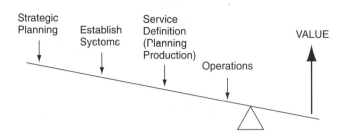

Figure 18.1 The lever of value

The value and risk management workshop

The most common form of a value and risk management service is as a facilitated workshop. This implies the appointment of a facilitator, skilled in value and risk management techniques, to lead an appropriate team. The membership of the team will comprise all of those stakeholders with an input relevant to a particular stage. The ACID test, as shown in Table 18.1, is used to determine who should be a member of the team. Generally, team membership tends to be greater in number at the strategic stage of projects when a large number of issues are being considered, and smaller when the technical details of the project are being investigated.

Table 18.1 The ACID test for team membership

A *Authorise* – include those who have the authority to take decisions appropriate to the stage of the development of the project.
C *Consult* – include those who have to be consulted regarding particular aspects of the project during its evolution at the workshop.
I *Inform* – do not include those who have only to be informed of decisions reached during the workshop.
D *Do* – include those who are to carry out the tasks specified at the workshop.

The structure of a value and risk management service

Irrespective of the stage of the project at which a value and risk management exercise is carried out, it will follow a set number of identifiable steps. These are:

- *Information* – all issues, information and strategies pertaining to the project are obtained through structured interviews, detailed document analysis and the contribution of information by key stakeholders at the workshop.

- *The client's value system* – once all the information has been obtained, the client's position with regard to the project is analysed by reference to a number of key criteria; namely capital cost, operating cost, environment, exchange or resale value, aesthetics, esteem and fitness for purpose.

- *Functional analysis* – all of the information is processed by reference to the client's value system into a number of key functions. At the commencement of the project these functions tend to be of a strategic nature and structured as a function logic diagram in the form of a felled tree, where the trunk is the mission of the project and the branches are the functional requirements of the project separated into needs and wants. At the later stages, functions are listed under each technical and operational need.

- *Innovation* – ideas are generated, usually through a brainstorming session, to satisfy all of the functional requirements identified in the previous stage.

- *Evaluation* – the large number of ideas generated at the brainstorming session is reduced to a manageable number and a risk analysis is developed. The result of the risk analysis may require a return to the innovation stage.

- *Conclusion* – the end of the workshop stage is characterised by the completion of the risk register and a value action plan.

A description of the tools and techniques illustrated by example

This part of the chapter describes some of the tools and techniques of value and risk management and their application by reference to an example case study.

Case study

A small but growing company offering investment advice to the general public has recently taken a lease on the first, second and third floors of a 1960s office building. The company anticipates conducting most of its business by telephone and via the Internet. Nevertheless, the company wishes to present a professional face to the public through its entrance, waiting area and interview rooms. The company's investment in the building will include rewiring, some form of environmental cooling and redecoration as well as computers, fittings and furnishings.

It is to be noted that the case study illustrates a departure from the recommended procedure in that the company has already taken a strategic decision to lease office space without a value and risk analysis. In practice, it is difficult to attract clients to the value and risk service before such a move has been taken and therefore the illustration is a typical example.

Information

The facilitator may either undertake a document analysis through a study of the project correspondence files, drawings, etc, and/or interview the key client stakeholder to become familiar with the background to the project. Following this the facilitator will interview a representative sample of those people regarded as being project stakeholders with the following objectives:

- To identify those whose membership of the workshop team would be an advantage, an exercise undertaken by reference to the ACID test described above.

- To refine the understanding of the background to the project including any covert or hidden agenda.

- To predetermine the tools and techniques required for the workshop and thereafter to compile the agenda of the workshop.

At the workshop, the information stage is a structured gathering of facts and opinions surrounding the project. This may be undertaken by brainstorming issues, by presentations from knowledgeable stake-holders or by interrogation by the facilitator. Whichever method is used it is important that information on at least the following is obtained:

- The context and definition of the project – a short description of the project and how it is to achieve a strategic fit with the overall objectives of the organisation.

- The location of the project – a short description of the geographical location of the project including any restrictions with respect to noise, vibration, working hours, offloading restrictions, storage of materials, etc.

- Near-neighbours and local community – an overview of the nature and likely attitude to the project of near-neighbours and the community as a whole.

- Political policies – a view on whether central and local government are for, against, or neutral towards the project.

- Financial planning – any restrictions with regard to cash flow and/or expenditure profiles.

- Timing of the project— any issues with regard to the project commencement and completion date.

- The form and type of project procurement – is there a preferred contractual arrangement?

- Environment— does the project impact global or local environments and/or does the client have an environmental policy with which the project must comply?

- Specific client policies— with regards to internal organisation and executive control of the project, communication routes and policies relating to technological solutions which may have an impact on safety and security.

Case – study development of description

The project entails refitting three floors of an existing 1960s office building to accommodate a financial investment company. The office is located on the perimeter of the central business district of the town, is well served by public transport and is close to a public car park. The office will become the sole location of the business, which currently operates from two leased suburban shops. Refurbishment work to the office is only permitted outside of the nine to five working day. Loading restrictions apply between 8am and 6pm. A block of up-market residential apartments faces the building across the street. The project is too small to attract any political comment. There are no restrictions with regard to cash flow or expenditure profiles; however, the lease includes a six months' rent-free period and it would be advantageous to complete within this period. The lease on the two existing shops terminates at the end of the six-month period. The client has no preference for any particular type of contract for the refurbishment work. The client does have its own environmental protection policy to which it wishes to adhere. Executive control for the project rests with the managing director.

The client's value system

The client's value system is at the heart of the mission of any project and remains central to any audit process. Exploring the following seven elements and ranking them, using pairs' comparison, exposes the client's value system:

- Time: the time from the present until the completion of the project.

- Capital costs (CAPEX): all costs associated with the procurement of the project.

- Operating costs (OPEX): all costs associated with the FM of the project.

- Environment: the extent to which the project is to be sympathetic to the environment measured by its local and global impact, its embodied energy, the energy consumed through use and other 'green' issues.

- Exchange or resale: the monetary value of the project determined by its sale value post-project less the sale value pre-project. This concept requires the client to think about the future of the project and its economic redundancy.

- Aesthetics/esteem: the extent to which the client wishes to commit resources to an aesthetic statement or to the portrayal of the esteem of the organisation. Many office towers are built for esteem.

- Fitness for purpose: the level to which the project supports the operation of the business in purely utilitarian terms. A very high rating under this heading would imply that a minor part of the budget would be used for art or an architectural statement.

Case study – client's value system

Through discussion, an overview of the client's value criteria is obtained and a pairs' comparison diagram completed.

- Time: there is a requirement to be up and running as soon as possible. Although the business plan takes no account of the six months' rent-free period from signing the lease, to be operational during this time would be a bonus. Not to be operational within six months would be a disaster.

- CAPEX: under no circumstances can the budgeted cost be exceeded.

- OPEX: the operating cost, although important, is a soft area as it is to be paid out of the revenue.

- Environment: the major shareholders of the company have insisted that this be a hallmark project of the company; therefore, no risks are to be taken in this area.

- Exchange: the business plan anticipates terminating the lease at the end of its five-year term. Dilapidations are to be avoided.

- Aesthetic/esteem: only in the public area.

- Fitness for purpose: every square metre must earn money.

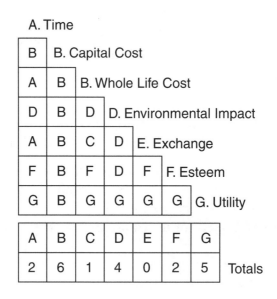

Figure 18.2 Pairs comparison used to rank elements of client's value system.

Functional analysis

Functional analysis is undertaken at two levels: the strategic level, which requires a function logic diagram; and the technical/operational level, which requires a function list.

The method usually employed to construct a function logic diagram is for the facilitator to conduct a brainstorming of functions recording the team's required functions as a simple verb–noun description on sticky notelets for later sorting. The verb–noun description is a useful discipline as it forces a concise and exact description. The notelets are ordered to present a function logic diagram.

To construct a function list it is first necessary to focus on an element or component of the project and then ask 'what does that element do?'. Often the element will perform more than one function.

Case study – functional analysis

The strategic functions generated by the team and recorded on sticky notelets are as follows:

- be accessible;
- promote website;
- enhance image (of company);
- control environment;
- furnish comfortably;
- enhance efficiency;
- locate in CBD;
- attract customers;
- advertise locally ;
- advertise nationally;
- comfortable working environment.

These functions are re-ordered from high order needs and low order wants as follows:

- enhance image (of company);
- enhance efficiency;
- attract customers;
- locate in CBD;
- comfortable working environment;
- promote website;
- be accessible ;
- advertise locally ;
- advertise nationally;
- control environment;
- furnish comfortably.

The functions are structured as a function logic diagram with functions 1 and 2 becoming the mission of the project and the remainder ordered from high order needs to low order wants, i.e. the project needs to attract customers otherwise it will fail. However, without a comfortable working environment the company may have disgruntled staff but may not fail.

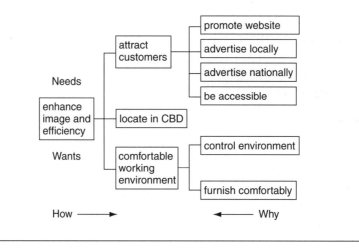

Case study – element function analysis

An illustration of the function list of an element or component is, as follows, with reference to the element 'control environment'. It should be noted that functions are only sought. Technical solutions such as 'open window' would not be permitted but 'infiltrate external air' would as it is a function with more than one solution.

Control Environment

- cool air;

- reduce external noise;

- reduce heat emitting equipment;

- cool structure;

- infiltrate external air;
- heat air;
- heat structure;
- reduce solar gain.

Innovation

The facilitator normally conducts an innovation exercise as a brainstorming session focusing on each of the functions in turn. This will, for example, look for ideas at the highest strategic level such as 'how do we enhance our image and efficiency?' (The answer to this may not be the leasing of office space in the CBD). Brainstorming can also be directed to seeking innovative solutions at the technical level such as 'how do we reduce heat emitting equipment?' At whatever level brainstorming is carried out the same rules apply, including: record every idea no matter how stupid, no judgement or discussion during the brainstorming session, no criticism of contributors, no negative comments.

Case study – brainstorming on control environment

- install double glazed solar reflecting windows;
- install solar film and secondary double glazing;
- install blinds;
- use low voltage lighting;
- install air conditioning;
- open fires;
- install mechanical ventilation;
- retain existing radiators;
- remove wall lining from masonry.

Evaluation

The brainstorming session will end with many suggestions for each function, often amounting to over a hundred ideas in total. At the evaluation stage these are reduced and grouped to form a suitable number for risk analysis and subsequent development. The first exercise is to quickly reduce the list of ideas to a manageable number of good ideas. This can be achieved through voting, asking the team for a show of hands in support of the idea. Alternatively, and more efficiently, the facilitator will read out the ideas and wait for no more than 2 seconds for a champion amongst the team to shout out 'keep it'. This may result in over a hundred ideas being reduced to, say, 70.

The next step is to determine whether the ideas that remain are:

- functionally suitable (**FS**): that is, they exactly meet the functional requirement that gave rise to their suggestion;

- economically viable (**EV**): based upon a first impression, the idea appears to be one that can be afforded;

- technically feasible (**TF**): again based upon the knowledge of the group the idea can be achieved technically, without resorting to innovation in manufacturing or installation. Obviously, some projects by their nature call for this but the majority of projects do not;

- client acceptable (**CA**): the idea is conducive with the client's value system.

Ideas that meet all of the above criteria are carried forward to the next stage; those that do not are re-considered to ensure that there was a good reason for their rejection. The next stage involves grouping and combining ideas to generate an entire solution that can be subject to risk management. There are three steps to a risk management exercise: risk identification, risk analysis and risk response.

Risk identification

During the risk identification process, the facilitator will undertake a brainstorming of risks associated with a particular solution resulting from the evaluation stage. Generally, these risks will fall under four headings:

- Changes in project focus – this will result in a change to the project mission and could result from, for example, a reorientation of the client's core business.

- Client changes – these are brought about by unforeseen changes in the client organisation. However, it is common for client changes to result from poor communication structures leading to an incorrect briefing of the project in the first place. The client change is not so much a change as a correction to the project's course.

- Design changes – these result from an incorrect analysis of data or the exposure of some unforeseen circumstance; for example, forming a doorway in a wall which was assumed to be plasterboard on a timber stud frame but when the plasterboard is removed it turns out to be plasterboard dry lining to a reinforced concrete structural wall.

- Changes in the project environment – these changes are brought about by bad weather, non-delivery of materials, unavailability of labour, new legislation, planning restrictions, etc.

Upon completion of risk brainstorming, some form of ranking exercise is undertaken to highlight those risks which have a high probability and a serious consequence, based upon the opinion of the team. The consequence can be determined at three levels: irritating background noise, turbulence in the project's progress (the project can continue but is severely disrupted) or a blocking force which is capable of halting the project until contained. A suitable method is to rank each risk on a scale of A to F as illustrated below:

Rank	Probability	Consequence
A	High	blocking force
B	Low	blocking force
C	High	turbulence
D	Low	turbulence
E	High	noise
F	Low	noise

Those risks ranked D, E and F are examined to make an immediate assessment of whether further action is necessary, in which case they proceed to the next stage, or whether the risks can be taken on board during the development of the project. Risks ranked A, B and C are taken forward to the next stage, risk analysis.

Risk analysis

The first stage in a risk analysis is normally qualitative in which the following are analysed:

- a brief description of the risk and the stage of the project when it could occur;
- the factors that could cause it and the likelihood of those occurring;
- the extent to which the project will be affected.

Even where the qualitative risk analysis is considered sufficient, the action of undertaking it will sensitise the team towards the recognition of the risk and prompt an appropriate risk response in the event that it occurs. The team, however, may decide that a qualitative risk assessment is insufficient and require a quantitative risk assessment. This is an activity normally not carried out within the workshop; it may therefore be necessary to adjourn the workshop at this point.

Quantitative risk analysis seeks to mathematically model the probability of the risk occurring in two ways: objective risk analysis and subjective risk analysis. An objective risk is when the probability is known exactly, for example, the loss of £10 relies on the flip of a coin landing tails up. The probability of this is 50 per cent. A subjective risk is when the probability is not known exactly but can be estimated, for example, a loss of £10 relies on more than one hour of continuous rain next Thursday. While reference to weather data records will allow an assessment of the probability of continuous rain next Thursday this could not be relied on exactly. Quantitative risk analysis becomes mathematically complex when a number of risks are combined. Computer software is available to calculate probability curves for this situation, usually based on a simulation. It should be emphasised that the results presented by the computer software are merely an aid to decision taking.

Risk response

At the end of the risk analysis exercise, the team will undertake a risk response categorised as one of four actions being:

- to avoid the risk by undertaking that part of the project in a different manner;
- to reduce the risk by taking action to lower the probability of the risk occurring;

- to transfer the risk to a third party, commonly an insurance company;

- to accept the risk and manage its consequences. This is a valid course of action. If the risk event were to arise, the team is sensitised to its recognition and mentally prepared for some form of action.

This stage is characterised by continual reference back to the functional analysis and, particularly, the client's value system. All decisions must accord with the functional requirements and fulfil the requirements of the client. This is a vital part of in-workshop recap and audit.

Case study – evaluation

In the case study, a number of ideas were generated for the control of the internal environment where the primary concern is over heating of the workspace. These ideas are subject to a two-stage evaluation, selection by a champion and the four stage evaluation, FS, EV, TF, CA. These are demonstrated in the table below where the first stage results in one idea being crossed through. In completing the table the team were not confident about low voltage lighting and this was deleted.

The ideas are then grouped for risk analysis – for example, consider the window options and the ventilation/air conditioning options.

Idea	FS	EV	TF	CA
Install double glazed solar reflecting windows	✔	✖	✔	✔
Install blinds	✔	✔	✔	✔
Use low voltage lighting	✔	✖	?	?
Install air conditioning	✔	?	✔	✔
Install mechanical ventilation	✔	✔	✔	✔
Retain existing radiators	✔	✔	✔	✔
Remove wall lining from masonry	✔	✔	✔	✔
Install solar film and secondary double glazing	✔	✔	✔	✔

Case study – risk identification and qualitative risk analysis

Install new double glazed window units	A	B	C	D	E	F
Need planning permission – may take time	✔					
Need landlord's permission			✔			
Must be first activity undertaken	✔					

Secondary glazing & solar film	A	B	C	D	E	F
Need landlord's permission		✔				
Restricts natural ventilation					✔	

Install mechanical ventilation/air conditioning supply at ceiling, return air through floor plenum	A	B	C	D	E	F
Need landlord's permission		✔				
Position of new plant room			✔			
Must be an early activity				✔		
Duct layout may be compromised by beam positions	✔					
Heavy plant must be craned in					✔	
Need sufficient under floor depth		✔				
Raised floor detail at lifts/staircase	✔					

Case study – Risk response

- *New double-glazed windows considered too expensive and too risky; therefore, adopt application of solar film to existing windows and install secondary double glazing with vertical blinds within the gap.*
- *Natural ventilation by opening windows not an option.*
- *Early discussion with landlord essential.*
- *Position of plant room to be established with landlord.*
- *Ask existing tenant for permission to inspect existing suspended ceiling void to determine structural beam layout.*
- *Begin thinking about a design for a perimeter ventilation duct in the event that ducting cannot be accommodated behind ceilings.*

> - *Accommodate plant room at point on perimeter of building where plant can be craned in if necessary. Investigate with landlord now.*
> - *Assess size requirement of under floor return air plenum now.*
> - *Design raised floor to such that no changes are required to existing lifts and stairs positions.*

Conclusion – risk register and action planning

The output of a value and risk management workshop is a risk register that summarises the deliberations of the team and records:

- a description of the risk;

- the impact of the risk and the probability of its occurrence;

- the nature of the solution agreed by the team;

- the person responsible for action to the next stage; and

- the time or cost contingency which is to be built into the project at this stage.

Action planning requires the team to select the best value for money solution from the evaluation stage and decide:

- who is responsible for taking action; and

- by when is the action to be taken.

At the end of the workshop all stakeholders should have a task commensurate with their ACID test responsibilities, i.e.:

- those responsible for authorisation should either have authorised action at the workshop (the preferred option), or will authorise in accordance with the agreed action plan;

- those who were attending the workshop to be consulted have been consulted and will have no active part in the action plan, unless another team member's action activity requires further consultation;

- those who were to 'do' will take away most of the actions on the action plan.

Conclusion

This chapter has briefly outlined an approach to value and risk management based upon a workshop facilitated by a person skilled in the tools and techniques required. The chapter gives an overview sufficient for the reader to be able to identify with the process should they become involved in such a workshop. The training schemes operated by SAVE International in USA, or the Institute of Value Management in the UK, lead to qualifications for facilitators seeking to offer a value and risk management service.

In considering when to use a value and risk management service always remember the lever of value. The service is most effective and efficient when it is used pro-actively and incrementally at each stage of the process.

19

The Role of Facilities Management in Business Continuity Planning and Management

Dr. Marie-Cécile Puybaraud and
Professor John Hinks

It has been assessed that around half of all businesses that experience a disaster and have no effective plans for recovery fail within the following 12 months. To stay in business after disaster strikes requires careful pre-planning. To believe that you will easily be able to sort things out on the day will mean that your business, you and your employees will unnecessarily suffer.

(Home Office, 1996)

This chapter discusses the issues that you should consider when planning for business continuity, and will introduce the scope and importance of involving your facilities manager in business continuity planning and management. It will help you to formulate an in-depth understanding of the principles of business continuity planning, and to consider how to apply business continuity planning processes which depend on your business support services and infrastructure.

The relevance of facilities management and other support services in business continuity planning

While facilities management will be a central element in business continuity planning, perhaps taking the lead responsibility in the coordination of preparation or post-event expediencies, and continuity or recovery of the key business support functions, business continuity planning should be viewed as being broader in scope than facilities management. It is also a highly integrative function. Successful business continuity planning will require the coordination of many, if not all, of your non-core business support services. Consider it a key management task: it requires a good degree of forethought about the interrelationship and interdependency between core and non-core functions – not least in terms of functionality in the business process, but also in the critical areas of communications and responsibility lines.

The key message here is that if business continuity is dependent on the continued or recovered inter-operation of core and non-core issues, you need to think in these terms during the consultation and pre-planning stages. Holistic solutions require holistic planning.

Business continuity planning is systematic forethought about responses during and immediately after an event, and is usually based on pre-planned and optimised solutions. Its function is to minimise the consequences of disasters for the core business.

Business continuity planning is usually concerned with singular events, rather than the day-to-day issues with which business support services management is concerned. Hence business continuity planning is an extension of the business support services management's remit. It involves securing continuity of communication, IT support and real estate and facilities. This is usually seen as the limit; however, business continuity planning may also relate to relatively intangible issues affecting business capital and human resources management (HRM).

Events triggering business continuity tasks

Many events can affect your business: not only the core business of your company but also the supply chain or your outsourced providers of key support services. The first thing to recognise is that the more interdependent your business and business process are on other organisations, the more chances there are of being affected by the spin-offs from another organisation's business disaster. So the decision to outsource business support operations may lead to the outsourcing and the transfer of control over vulnerability as well as risk.

Start by thinking broadly about the profile of risk and disaster consequence that your business is potentially subject to. Your core business needs to be protected against a direct and collateral loss of business facilities – which can be series of events such as the direct or collateral loss of:

- *production facilities* (from fire, explosion, bomb, flood, earthquake, insurrection);

- *access* (from bomb warning for instance);

- *staff* (temporarily through strikes, or permanently following illness, death, or headhunting of key personnel);

- *knowledge and information* (including records and IT-based material, but also through the loss of key personnel).

There are also major potential implications for the core from financial turbulence, and other political, social, or technological changes affecting your organisation, your suppliers and/or your customer base.

The Business Continuity Institute (BCI) distinguishes between business continuity management (BCM) and business continuity planning (BCP):

Business continuity management: those management disciplines, processes and techniques which seek to provide the means for continuous operation of the essential business functions under all circumstances.

Business continuity planning: the advance planning and preparations which are necessary to identify the impact of potential losses; to formulate and implement viable recovery strategies; to develop recovery plan(s) which ensure continuity of organisational services in the event of an emergency or disaster; and to administer a comprehensive training, testing and maintenance programme. Note the distinction between BCP and disaster recovery planning. BCP relates to ensuring that an organisation can survive an event that causes interruption to normal business processes – disaster recovery planning is the process

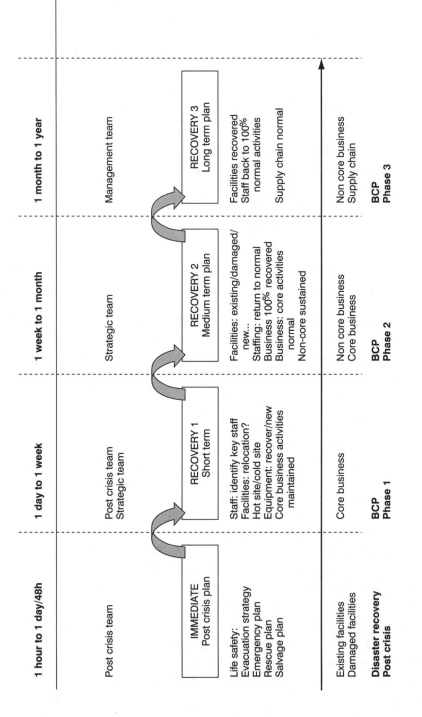

Figure 19.1 Business Continuity Planning: strategic framework

that takes place during and after an organisational crisis to minimise business interruption and return the organisation as quickly as possible to a pre-crisis state.

So, is your business protected?

Protecting your physical and informational assets should be a major issue for anyone running a business. Some companies have learned the hard way the importance of safeguarding their information. It is estimated that more than 40 per cent of banks have no recovery plan, yet for a call-centre based business the IT system and the facilities which support its availability and use by core staff at all times is its main working tool. Not only is such a business critically dependent for its core processes on these facilities and their associated support services, there is also the secondary issue of customer confidence. Romano (1995) estimated that *'within ten days of an extended computer outage, a company loses an estimated two to three per cent of its gross sales and most companies will never fully recover from ten days without computers'*. Innocent events could greatly damage a business as much as vandalism, theft, sabotage, personal assault and other criminal acts. The challenge is to think broadly enough about your vulnerabilities, and then put in place the provisions and authorities essential for the necessary contingencies.

Fail to plan; plan to fail

There are five initial steps in the business continuity planning process:

- Initiation of the business continuity planning process and risk assessment;
- Conduct of a business impact analysis;
- Analysis of critical processes related to the identified key business impacts;
- Creation of an initial business continuity plan;
- Testing and revision of the business continuity plan and management system.

There is one further vital stage: the updating of the business continuity plan and management arrangements, which will usually also require all the other phases in the business continuity planning cycle to be systematically revisited.

Step 1: initiation of the business continuity planning process and risk assessment

A thorough understanding and analysis of your business process is a prerequisite for a successful business continuity planning process. Your facilities manager or business support services managers should be in the best position to inform you on the support implications for business-critical areas of the core company, and should also be able to relate these to business-critical aspects of your business support functions – ie those that could easily disable the core functionality if they were to fail or be collaterally affected by a disaster.

However, the quality of their foresight is entirely dependent on the level of understanding they have of the core business operations and relationship with support services and facilities. It is therefore important for the business director to reflect on whether their non-core services managers have access to sufficient knowledge about the day-to-day operational requirements of the core business process. This may be a challenging integration issue for those non-core services that are not strategically partnered, but if left unaddressed this vulnerability will remain and planning may be seriously jeopardised. This dimension of ensuring business continuity will also arise later in the operational phase, when the issues of authority and communication chains across interdependent operations are considered, and these both have to be clear and unbroken.

Consider also the associated needs of core and support service employees, including the implications of normal security arrangements on their post-event flexibility, balancing the particular needs of the moment against possibly enhanced vulnerabilities of your business to other security issues following an event. Clearly there are many possible combinations of event and follow-up implications which need to be considered, and a second dimension which this should be flagging up to you is the need to know where to draw the line on pre-planning and to defer to the thoughtful delegation of authority.

A number of key issues will need to be explored during business continuity planning, for example:

• The nature of your business and business process;

• Main activities within the business process;

• Types of work;

- Types of risk exposure (including any that those dealing with an initial problem may face and which could exacerbate an otherwise controllable problem);

- The multi-faceted needs, consequences and relationships between the various elements of the process and its sub-activities with respect to different aspects of your core business. This may flag up a critical path for the re-starting of business processes, some of which could perhaps be left for longer than others to make organisational and communications 'space' for the critical operations;

- The financial, HRM and facilities implications of discontinuities in provisions (individually and as part of the system).

A brainstorming and scenario planning session may help with this. Think of the consequences as well as the risks, and try to identify the central or repetitive nodes which reappear in analyses of the causal chains in process vulnerability. The business continuity managers should give these special attention.

Step 2: conduct of a business impact analysis

The business support services managers and facilities managers will be central to this. Facilities management, the practice of coordinating the physical workplace with the organisation's people and work, requires integrating the principles of business administration, architecture and the behavioural and engineering sciences (Gregory, 1994). The role of the facilities manager and/or business support services manager in preparing the business impact analysis is critical – they should be alert to the key issues required to evaluate and implement plans that meet the numerous demands and objectives of their core business. In order to analyse the impact of a possible 'disaster', accident or other interruption to the business, they should look at:

- Who and what (internally and externally, core and support services) is likely to be directly affected?

- Who and what is likely *not* to be directly affected?

- Who and what will be indirectly affected?

- What is the time scale of disruption and consequences? (consider supply chain interruption implications here, too)

- Analysing the business process and identifying the critical components, what are the constraints and resource implications? Which of these vulnerabilities do the critical components depend upon?

- How do these issues differ for immediate impact analysis, which should be considered in a post crisis plan; which are the subject of longer term effects and will require consideration as part of a recovery plan?

- What scope is there for back-up functions, facilities, and systems:
  - hot and cold sites
  - duplications in IT facilities and information records (how out of date would your records have to be before your business could not operate on an interim basis?)
  - duplication in staff expertise
  - facilities generally, in suppliers and in your products/services supply, for instance through the strategic design of work in progress, stockpiling, and the retention of expertise.

Step 3: analysis of critical processes related to the identified key business impacts

Before you start to draft your business continuity plan, it is vital to define the functions that are critical or in some way irreplaceable to the continuity of your business. This is where your deep vulnerability lies.

In conjunction with thinking about this issue, you should consider whether the existing balance of in-house and outsourced provision and management/coordination of the business-critical support processes is an appropriate balance between dispersal of vulnerability versus level of control and coordination. There is no universally right combination (there are plenty of wrong combinations!) – it depends on your business needs. Bear in mind that the robustness and resilience of any business support services to any disaster of their own as well as to your core business must be considered very seriously where these services are themselves critical to your core business. Think about the potential for a domino effect.

To help with this, consider some of the conventional facilities management or business support services issues which may be related to process vulnerability, for example:

- What facilities are core and cannot be temporarily contracted out? Which are non-core and non-critical and could be substituted?

- What facilities can operate temporarily with minimal attention, thereby allowing diversion of normal efforts to assist the critical post-event efforts? (This might stimulate a review of the prioritisation of business support services efforts, and also of the outsourcing philosophy.)

- Space management and allocation is also an important issue and usually held under the facilities manager's control. Consider in conjunction with your facilities manager what is core space and how it is used. Could alternatives be created temporarily or perhaps sourced elsewhere? A mutual arrangement for emergency sharing may be feasible with another local organisation operating a similar set of facilities. So, where is your core business space-critical? Could an IT/IS back-up allow remote working of a significant portion of the process and allow re-shuffling of the remainder to support the site-locked critical operations? This might also lead to a more general review of the facilities strategy.

- Communication is another aspect which may be under the control of the business support services manager. Here you should assess issues such as the critical and core communication routes. How are the remainder of communications achieved? Could alternatives be created temporarily or sourced elsewhere? What would be the value or implications of permanently or temporarily outsourcing some of your IT systems?

- How critical is the visible product/image of the company?

- Look also at the facilities management and business support services management arrangements themselves – are these the possible victims of an event? The consequences for the business of problems in the 'non-core' business support services could still be disastrous.

- What aspect of the process (and people) is the *memory* of the business support services department?

- Who and what are the highly critical facility/communications and HRM issues?

Consider also business support services other .than the facilities-related aspects, for example critical HRM issues – there have been cases where a disaster such as the death of a person or the failure of a single facility has led to the collapse of a company. However, most companies require more than a single entity to run. It is important to identify what would be needed to maintain a business at a minimum and allow for the recovery plan to come into place.

Business directors should ask themselves a number of important questions, which should also be asked of their business support services managers. For example:

- Who is critical to the process and cannot be substituted or temporarily contracted out? Who can safely be temporarily ignored (location or process-wise)?

- What supplies or suppliers cannot be substituted? Bear in mind that the loss of a monopolistic key supplier could be very damaging…and the same applies to your customer!

- What sub-processes are on the critical business process path? Which are safe and which unsafe? Do you have a list of contingency suppliers?

- Who in the company, eg the CEO or the key designer, is irreplaceable?

Lessons from events

Our experience and knowledge of business continuity planning is mainly based on lessons learned from major events. Daily newspapers are full of anecdotes and feedback from mini-disasters occurring frequently: an increase in interest rates destabilising a company, the change in unit prices for construction companies, mergers and take-overs operations between companies, bad weather conditions, fires, vandalism, personnel head-hunting, terrorist attacks, etc. From these a number of lessons have emerged:

- **The safety needs of staff:** evacuation and shelter are paramount, especially in a progressive event;

- **Robust and transparent alert mechanisms:** to have established contact points and communication routes within the company and to and from the outside world;

- **Communication and control:** coordination meetings are essential to implement and operate the business continuity plan;

- **Cordons and access:** planning for operation within the cordon is a priority. Access to your building to assess the damage and losses and recover core data and information may be restricted, meaning that your business will be affected indirectly even if it has escaped the main event;

- **Transition:** establishing a transition management team is an option considered by many companies;

- **Parallel business continuity planning and disaster recovery plans:** immediate measures following a disaster should be compatible between the various sub-plans and authorities to avoid duplicate work and responsibility, gaps in responsibility and other problems;

- **Emergency services roles:** liaison is critical to allow them to help you;

- **Business continuity planning contracts:** if you make prior arrangements with, say, a specialist salvage firm to operate a business continuity plan, will they be over-extended, and how do you get priority?

Step 4: creation of an initial business continuity plan

The characteristics of a business continuity plan will of course be specific to your organisation and business activity. Assuming that the aim of business continuity planning is to recover your business, then the emphasis is probably going to be on rapidly reoccupying your premises in order to ensure the continuity of your business activity with as much being left to the longer recovery period as is acceptable. Striking this balance correctly is not easy, but there are some general issues that can be identified.

Consider the business continuity plan a 'live' document. It needs to be adapted as the business changes, or as the circumstances in which the business operates change. In order to create a business continuity plan you will probably need to consider at least the following issues:

- An accessible and authorised budget for immediate use, with arrangements for increasing this as required if the circumstances exceed those anticipated. Think carefully about who is given authorisation and their accessibility by the key business continuity managers;

- A clearly identified business continuity management team, comprising the key business continuity planning members (probably as a standing committee). Membership is likely to include the CEO or MD, financial director, marketing, key engineers and technicians, and representatives or managers for the business support services that affect all the key operations of the core business as well as any other people representing and having knowledge of any part of the core business. Identify the line of authority and delegation, and the responsibilities for up-chain and down-chain communications clearly. You will also need an individual or individuals charged with external communications and HRM-related communications with the rest of the business;

- Any other specialist knowledge, and for the planning team a business strategy planner, a business process manager, and a risk analyst. Plan also for the handover of responsibility with job moves (especially if your organisation's HRM policy requires people to leave immediately rather than work their notice);

For the creation of your business continuity plan:

- Think who, what, where, when, why, how…

- …and how much. Rationalise your provision across the risks and knowing where the domain of core and business support services finish, especially the delineation between in-house and outsourced functions, and between functions which conventionally fall under separate coordination or communication channels;

- Be careful to avoid over-providing for the controllable at the expense of the highly critical or unstable. Focus on instability.

- Plan your real time communication chains (with back-up);

- Set your business continuity targets, for example time to recovery. What level of partial recovery can you actually cope with in the first instance?

- Create a detailed, chronological, hypothetical scenario or scenarios to help you design and brainstorm the business continuity plan. Focus on realistic scenarios in sufficient detail to make the planning worthwhile.

The next stage after the creation of your initial business continuity plan is to plan its operation and management. There is no point in writing a plan if you are not going to be able to operate it on the day of the event. Consider the following:

- Who decides to activate the business continuity plan? How, and with what back-up, from whom? Is a single person to decide, and if so what is the immediate communication chain? Who decides, and how, which version of a staged or flexible plan is used?

- How, and by whom, is the plan to be interpreted in an event which differs materially from the scenarios which were used to design the plan? Do they know?

- What can be left until after the event and what is better planned live? This depends on the level of confidence that you have in your team and their understanding of key business issues. Within the business continuity plan, reserve the resources and try to create the scope for mental 'space' to allow this to be done properly under stress.

- Assess the likely consequences of an event and the plan on staff, work in progress, access to equipment, materials, records, documents and stock.

Step 5: testing and revision of the business continuity plan and management system

As stated above, your business continuity plan should be a 'live' document, and so must be tested and updated regularly since the needs and resources of any organisation or business will change. Continuously testing and updating the plan is an excellent way to assess its strengths and weaknesses, and to gain an appreciation of the safety factor of your operations. There are likely to be spin-off benefits in terms of the formalisation of better internal communications (especially between the core and non-core) and the scope to test your own company and resources. If it is done properly, it will not be cheap, however, especially if the plan is refined as changes in circumstance arise, especially those which involve delayering or fragmentation of the core and non-core processes. However, not having a plan could ultimately be fatal for the company, and not maintaining and updating a plan could also seriously limit its value.

Concentrate on the key characteristics of your business continuity plan – flexibility, realism in terms of timescales, effort and resources compared with the seriousness of the event; a process designed to suit the chain of consequences and adaptable to the particularities of the event, and a plan for the medium to long-term recovery of the full activities of your business. Since it is people who will enact the plan, make sure all the key parties are represented. And bear in mind that there are four distinct phases involved: reviewing hazards and assessing risks and their potential impact on the organisation and business; developing, maintaining, auditing and testing your contingency plans; managing the incidents and coordinating the implementation of plans during an incident and its immediate aftermath; and making the recovery to normal business operation.

References

Gregory, W (1994) Halt? Is your security system secure? *HR Focus* **71** (2) pp 9–11, European Database ASAP

Home Office (1996) *How Resilient is your Business to Disaster*? [Online] www.ukresilience.info/contingencies/business/resilient1.htm

Romano, C (1995) Is your business protected? *Management Review* **84** (8) pp 43–46, European Database ASAP

Further reading

Alexander, K (1995) Facilities Management, in *Managing the consequences of disasters*, Hughes, S, pp98–101

CreatE (1997) *Interpretative Document: Safety in Case of Fire* [Online] http://europa.eu.int

DOE (2001) *Building Regulations and Fire Safety: Procedural Guidance* [Online] www.safety.odpm.gov.uk/bregs/brpub/firesafety/index.htm

Field, M (1993) How to Relocate a Building Office at Short Notice, *Architect's Journal*, May 1993

Fournai, A (1998) *Business Continuity Planning*, Work Workplace 1998

Home Office (1994) *Bombs: protecting people and property: a handbook for managers* [Online] www.homeoffice.gov.uk/oicd/bombs.pdf

HSE (1996) *A Guide to Risk Assessment Requirements* [Online] www.hse.gov.uk/pubns/indg218.pdf

HSE (1998) *Five Steps to Risk Assessment* [Online] www.hse.gov.uk/pubns/indg163.pdf

Jackson, K (1994) Selling disasters recovery to the board in *Survive! The business continuity magazine*

Moore, P (1995) *Critical elements of disaster recovery and business service continuity plan*

Reynolds, S (1994) Survey of Risk Assessment: the Art of Planning for Disaster, in *Contingency Planning*, Financial Times

Risk World (1997) *Risk Assessment and Risk Management in Regulatory Decision-Making* [Online] www.riskworld.com

Testing Recovery Plans (1994) *Survive! The business continuity magazine*

Varcoe, B (1993) Not Us, Surely? Disaster Recovery Planning for Premises, *Property Management* **11** (11) pp11–16

Guidance on insurance and business interruption [Online] www.swissre. com, www.munichre.com

20

The Renewal Decision in IT Outsourcing

Claire Coleman
Denton Wilde Sapte

Organisations who entered into IT outsourcing contracts in the first wave of outsourcing are generally continuing with the outsourcing model when those first contracts come to an end. However, the decision in favour of outsourcing does not necessarily mean a decision to continue with the existing service provider and renew the existing contract. Any customer facing the renewal decision will be asking itself a number of important questions. This chapter looks at some of the legal and commercial issues that may influence the decision.

Changes to service requirements

Although outsourcing is very much on the increase, trends have changed. Customers are looking more closely at what IT functions are outsourced. There is a trend away from reliance on service providers to manage the customers' entire IT operation. In many cases, the outsourcing arrangement is a contract vehicle for buying in additional services such as consulting, solutions design and applications development. In Europe more than 52 per cent of IT Services purchases now occur via an outsourcing contract.[1]

---

[1] Gartner Group Survey December 2000

Customers and their advisors involved in the renewal decision will want to look at these changes in outsourcing trends and consider what lessons should be learned, both from those trends and the customer's own experience. A common failing of early outsourcing arrangements was that they lacked flexibility and were not designed to adapt to the changing needs of the customer. Another problem was cultural incompatibility between the service provider and the customer which put a strain on the relationship. Second time around customers are more aware of the dangers of reliance on outsourcing service providers to manage their entire IT operation and to support business goals. Particularly because of the growing alignment of IT and business strategy that we have seen in recent years with the growth of the Internet, the customer will want to re-examine its own role and ensure that it remains in touch and in control.

The service required under a new agreement will also be influenced by changes to the customers business strategy and technology over the term of the current agreement. It is likely that since the last outsourcing the customer has embraced the Internet, with resulting changes to the way it does business and its technology. This will give rise to new service requirements and the need to buy in more expertise. The Internet has also, of course, created shared environment possibilities which means that options that were not available last time around will need to be considered.

Many companies who have outsourced their applications development and support will be considering the Applications Service Provider (ASP) option when the existing agreement comes to an end.[2] As this is a relatively new business model, many customers are so far reluctant to go this route until the capabilities of ASPs have been proven. Nevertheless, the Gartner Group has predicted that by 2010 most companies will use ASPs. At the moment smaller businesses seem more prepared to experiment with ASPs. However, considering the possibility will be part of any forward-looking decision about renewal of an existing outsourcing agreement covering applications development and support.

---

[2] An ASP is essentially a service provider that provides application functionality and associated services across a network to multiple customers on a 'pay as you go' payment model

Assessing past performance and market testing

Once the customer decides what its current service requirements are it will then need to consider whether its current service provider is best placed to provide them. Assuming that the current service provider is, in theory, a suitable candidate, part of the renewal decision will involve looking at the past performance of the incumbent and how its service compares to what is available on the market. The key success criteria are probably the quality of service and the quality of the relationship between the contract management teams. It may be that the current service provider has not achieved the agreed service levels, or has otherwise failed to deliver in accordance with the terms of the contract. If the contract did not include technology refresh obligations and provision for regular reviews of service levels it may be that, although the contract has been complied with, the service provided is no longer competitive or attractive compared with what is available in the market place.

If the existing contract has requirements for adjustment of price and service based on the results of regular benchmarking, the current service provider should still compare favourably with the rest of the market. In any event, a thorough benchmarking exercise will clearly need to be carried out as part of the renewal decision. The benchmarking should measure and compare service levels, pricing, customer satisfaction and user satisfaction with the relevant peer groups.

Whether the customer is content with the incumbent or not, it will usually go through a competitive tender process to further assess the interest and competitiveness of other potential service providers. If the value of the contract exceeds certain thresholds, public bodies and private sector organisations in the utilities sector must go through a competitive tender process and comply with relevant procurement regulations. These regulations are designed to ensure that the contract is awarded on the basis of non-discriminatory selection rules. Keeping an element of competition in the process is also likely to produce a better deal with the existing service provider, if the ultimate decision is to award the contract to the same company for a second term. The invitation to tender should describe the service required in as much detail as possible and include a set of specially tailored contract terms so that it is possible to compare like with like. The customer should be careful to avoid making the selection without sufficient prior agreement on contract terms. If this happens, the customer may later find that the incoming service provider is unwilling to accept certain risks, which has the effect of changing the commercial deal.

A successful tender process will also of course require co-operation and openness on the part of the current service provider. If the current service provider is tendering and has a reasonable prospect of being awarded the contract there is not likely to be a problem. However, if the relationship has deteriorated, the customer may find itself relying on contractual obligations to ensure that the service provider provides the information needed to re-tender the services and generally co-operates in the re-letting of the contract.

Effective exit provisions

In taking the renewal decision the customer will also need to consider whether any aspect of the current arrangements might jeopardise a smooth hand-over to a new service provider. In the worst case, the customer may find itself so heavily dependent on the incumbent that it is effectively in a 'lock-in' situation. If this happens, a move to a new service provider could be very costly and disruptive to the customer's business. The customer could find that the price to be paid for exiting the current arrangements outweighs the advantages of moving to a new supplier who provides a better service. These situations are very foreseeable and any well-drafted contract should contain provisions which ensure that a smooth hand over can take place. At the contract negotiation stage the parties will be seeking to ensure that the business relationship gets off to a good start and may be reluctant to get into detailed discussions about unravelling it. However it is essential to do so. The cost of not giving adequate attention to hand-over issues can be great and can significantly limit the options available to the customer when the contract comes to an end.

The contract should include an obligation on the service provider to prepare an exit plan in the initial stages of the contract and to update it regularly to take account of changes throughout the term. Broad parameters of the hand-over plan should also be included in the contract. The question of who bears the costs of hand-over should also be addressed. It may be that this is related to the cause of termination. For example the contract may state that the service provider will bear the costs of hand-over if the agreement is terminated for the service provider's default, and that the customer will bear the costs if the agreement is terminated for any other reason or expires. The following are some of the service provider obligations which an outsourcing agreement should include to ensure that a smooth hand-over to a new service provider is possible:

Cooperation and information

The contract should include a general obligation to co-operate and provide all information required by the new service provider during the hand-over period. The service provider should be obliged to provide full details of hardware and software used to provide the services. Contracts that place limits on the information the service provider will be obliged to provide to a competitor can be a barrier to smooth hand-over. By definition, the new service provider will be a competitor and withholding of information about how the services are provided will cause difficulties. Rights for the new service provider to access the premises from which the services are being run and access to the service provider's staff will also be important. If no such rights are included in the contract, the task of the incoming service provider during hand-over will be more difficult and the hand-over is likely to be more costly. The customer or new service provider may need assistance after the end of the hand-over period. A contract that gives the customer the option to require the outgoing service provider to provide technical advice or other information or support to the new service provider for a period after the hand-over has been completed will be of assistance, provided that the contract also specifies the charging basis for this support.

Rights to continued use of software

If the service provider has developed new software to provide the services and has not assigned intellectual property rights in it to the customer, the licence of that software should allow continued use by the customer or any new service provider after termination. The same applies where the service provider has used pre-existing proprietary software which is customised for services and licensed. In addition, if third party software that is not commercially available is used it will be important that the service provider is contractually obliged to secure post-termination rights of use for the customer and a new service provider. These licenses should be royalty free, except that this may not be possible in the case of third party software. Ensuring that post-term licenses are in place will avoid the cost and disruption of changing essential software used in providing the services if the customer moves to a new service provider.

Rights in data

The existing contract should make clear that all data processed or generated by the service provider on behalf of the customer will be owned by the customer and must be returned free of charge. It should also specify the manner and format in which the data is to be handed back. Failure of the current contract to adequately deal with hand-over of data could be troublesome and costly.

Rights in materials

Under the current contract, the customer should have either retained rights in or secured a sufficiently broad licence of specifications, documentation and materials produced by the service provider in connection with the services. The documentation prepared by the service provider will include vital information about the technology used and how the services are run. If the contract includes obligations to update documentation on a regular basis throughout the term, the customer will be able to insist on hand-over of documentation that reflects the existing technology and how the services are currently run. The contract should also include a specific obligation to provide copies of all documentation and material at the service provider's cost. In the absence of sufficient obligations on the service provider to hand over documentation and material and rights for a new service provider to use them, the ability of the incoming service provider to properly assess and provide the services will be impaired.

Right to purchase computer equipment

It may significantly assist a smooth hand-over if the existing contract includes an option to purchase hardware at book value or at an agreed price. Similarly an option to have any hardware leases assigned to the customer or a new service provider may be useful.

Third party contracts

The hand-over process may be significantly easier if the customer has a right to have assigned to it or a new service provider, free of charge, any third party contracts such as maintenance and support agreements entered into by the service provider in connection with providing the services.

Employees

People issues need to be carefully considered and could play a significant part in the renewal decision. The agreement should include a right for the customer or the new service provider to approach and recruit the service provider employees engaged in the provision of the services. The customer will also want to consider the potential application of TUPE[3] on termination or expiry of the existing agreement, giving rise to a so-called 'second generation' transfer. The intentions of potential new service providers as to the employees they will take on should be established, and the possible application of TUPE should be discussed. Because of the uncertainty of the law in this area it is possible that the outgoing service provider could claim that TUPE applied but the incoming service provider could claim that it did not. This could give rise to a situation where the existing service provider refuses to make the employees redundant, and the incoming service provider claims that it has no obligation to employ the individuals in question. The prospect of employees being left in limbo may be not only disruptive but also ultimately very costly to the customer, if it is found that TUPE does apply but the new service provider will only enter into the contract if it is indemnified against the application of TUPE by the customer. The customer will want to get agreement from potential service providers candidates at an early stage that any risk of TUPE applying on termination lies with the incoming service provider. Clearly, the potential problems should be examined at an early stage and form part of the overall decision as to who should be awarded the contract.

---

[3] Transfer of Undertakings (Protection of Employment) Regulations 1981

Conclusion

IT outsourcing is certainly here to stay. However, those customers and advisors looking at whether to renew an existing IT outsourcing agreement may find that the outsourcing deal needed today is very different from that entered into five or more years ago. There are lessons to be learned from the outsourcing experience so far. Before entering into a new agreement the customer should assess the successes and failures of its arrangements with the current service provider as well as the experience of customers for outsourced IT Services generally. It is likely that over the term of the existing agreement there have been changes to the customer's business strategies and service requirements, in particular because of the growth of the internet. These changes will influence the shape of the new contract and the selection of the appropriate service provider. A detailed review of hand-over arrangements and contract provisions dealing with hand over issues should form part of any renewal decision. If the current outsourcing contract makes adequate provision, a smooth hand-over to a new service provider will be achievable. If it does not, the customer may find that a move to a new service provider will be costly and disruptive.

21

Monitoring Client/ Consumer Feedback

Peter Roberts and Jonathan Reuvid

The present programme of monitoring feedback from consumers of services provided by Sodexho – clients, their customers and staff – was initiated at the end of the 1990s and driven by a desire to develop benchmarks of consumer satisfaction. The prelude to the programme was a research project carried out by Taylor Nelson on Sodexho's behalf, using telephone interviews to measure levels of client commitment. The same mechanism was adopted in the Business and Industry division of Sodexho with its major client contracts.

Early research identified the different factors, in order of importance, which determine a client's long-term commitment to Sodexho as its service provider from the bidding process through contract management. The findings of that survey in respect of client behaviour may be summarised simply as 'buy on price; retain on quality'.

The experience of the first survey helped Sodexho to see that there was value in being seen to research client reactions and that the 'consumers' of Sodexho's services are both the client's own staff and, in some cases, its customers. It is also understood that a high level of correlation between levels of approval by client management and consumer satisfaction is not an inevitable outcome.

The Sodexho customer feedback programme

The pilot programme carried out by the Business and Industry division in 2001 with 23 high-value clients for Sodexho catering services was designed to satisfy seven clear objectives:

- meet client expectation;
- aid client retention;
- demonstrate Sodexho customer management skills;
- provide a minimum standard for customer research;
- identify regional customer preferences;
- develop a cost effective, easy to use operational tool;
- provide a mechanism to calculate customer satisfaction index scores.

Conduct of the pilot project

Planning and preparation

In planning the pilot research, early preparation consisted of:

- devising, testing and modifying the questionnaire;
- establishing feedback programme principles;
- devising and manufacturing customer feedback boards;
- producing guidelines, questionnaires and collateral material;
- appointing and training feedback coordinators;
- the establishment of a central processing facility.

Internal preparation also included:

- presentations to divisional teams;
- issuing guidelines for district and unit managers;
- developing a 'results package' of:
  - analysis data and charts
  - framework for client presentation
  - charts for customer feedback;
  - use of coordinators to help operators with interpretation;
  - client presentation and call for action.

Processes

The feedback programme was introduced with extreme care, preceded by a six-month questionnaire and package test before implementation. The research was piloted among Sodexho consumers and non-consumers alike. In the course of the pilot, the questionnaire was proven to be applicable across a majority of sites and the research team developed a capability to create client-specific questionnaires when required. Regional feedback coordinators, while reporting on activity, were able to:

- share best practice;
- support operators and retention champions;
- ensure that the research timetable was met.

The eight key stages in the conduct of the feedback pilot are summarised in Figure 21.1 and extend from the initial request for

CUSTOMER FEEDBACK – The process

Request	Planning	Distribution	Research		Data Prep	Analysis & Presentation	Client Meeting

Week No. 0 1 2 3 4 5 6 7 8

DM approaches client / Client approaches us / Sales request

Client/prospect meeting & discussion

Questionnaire distribution / Incentive & promotions / Advance publicity

Customers complete & return questionnaires

Central receipt and data process / Calculate satisfaction / Index

Data return to division for analysis & interpretation / Presentation preparation / Board clients & message preparation

Client & Customer feedback at unit

Sodexho Customer Feedback

Figure 21.1 Customer feedback

participation (either from divisional management to the client, from the client to Sodexho or otherwise) up to the final client meeting to discuss findings and action fall-out.

Client meetings

At initial client meetings the objectives and benefits of the research are explained and the timescales and method of capturing consumer responses (the data) – on hard copy forms or electronically – are agreed. Questionnaire distribution and incentivisation for questionnaire return and client support are discussed, the feedback method is explained and the questionnaire is shown to the client.

The focus of final client meetings is the presentation of findings which will include report back on the following areas:

- respondent profile, overall opinion, value for money;
- daily spend;
- dining area, food quality, food service;
- what do customers want?
- comparison of customer satisfaction within the region;
- recommendations for action/discussion;
- summary.

All of these cover areas of significant interest to the food service customer. Thus recommendations to clients for development of their operations are based upon informed opinions.

Performance

Sodexho operators and coordinators are considered to have performed effectively during the pilot programme. Presentations to clients were judged to be smart and comprehensive, and the continuity of style and professional look received favourable comment. The feedback mechanism for customers was found to have worked well, although the levels of response in each unit varied widely among the 23 participating clients from 10 per cent to 65 per cent. However, the average response rate of 33 per cent from client staff was judged to be satisfactory.

The Sodexho central processing facility achieved a rapid turnaround in data analysis, providing charts and findings to divisions within two to three days and establishing an in-house resource capable of expansion for future surveys. The overall cost of materials and processing was assessed at £100 per unit, although this estimate does not reflect the cost of management time in administering the programme.

Feedback programme findings

The main part of the questionnaire invites respondents to comment on identified features of the catering services and their use of facilities, with quality assessed on five-point scales. The overall response from the 12 structured questions is summarised in Figure 21.2. The final question identifies the gender and age groups of respondents. Interestingly, approximately two-thirds of respondents were male and more than 70 per cent were in the 21 to 30 age group with only 2.4 per cent each under 20 or over 40.

Analysis of structured questionnaire

By cross-analysing responses to individual questions, Sodexho's operational management are able to draw conclusions about the behaviour of groups of respondents of the total universe both regionally and nationally. These conclusions are displayed in reader-friendly bar charts for internal discussion by Sodexho managers and subsequently by operations management with their clients. For example, the relative strength of customers' various reasons for using catering facilities can be analysed by factor according to a five-point scale. The value for money rating of catering services is analysed by customers' daily spend on food and drink. Even variations in the importance of price as a decision factor according to the amount spent are analysed and displayed in bar chart format.

When combining findings from Sodexho's individual regions, in order to develop a national summary, it is important to take account of regional variations in customer attitudes, so the central computer weights the regional results according to separate research conducted to identify the relative importance of issues for the consumer. The regional weighting factors are calculated on the basis of a national weighting survey that Sodexho carries out annually. Figure 21.3 shows the current weighting survey rankings for Sodexho catering services in each region.

Please place a cross in the appropriate box for your response

Q1 On how many days in the week do you eat in the restaurant at work?

Daily	4 days	3 days	1 day	Never
40.9%	15.4%	16.3%	19.1%	5.5%

Q2 Is the catering service open during your normal working hours?

Yes	No
93.8%	3.7%

Q3 What times of day do you normally use the restaurant?

Morning	Lunch time	Afternoon	Evening	Night time	Never
25.2%	85.5%	16.9%	11.1%	4.0%	2.5%

Q4 What is your overall opinion of the catering service at work?

Excellent	Good	Satisfactory	Poor	Unacceptable
1.8%	27.4%	41.5%	21.5%	4.0%

Q5 How do you rate the catering service at work represent value for money?

Excellent	Good	Satisfactory	Poor	Unacceptable
2.5%	22.8%	39.7%	29.5%	4.0%

Q6 Thinking of the dining area, what is your opinion about:

	Excellent	Good	Satisfactory	Poor	Unacceptable
Design & decoration	4.3%	27.1%	55.1%	12.3%	0.3%
Room cleanliness	2.5%	32.3%	47.4%	14.8%	1.5%
Comfort/ambience					
Noise levels					
Room layout					

Q7 Thinking about the meals available, how do you rank:

	Excellent	Good	Satisfactory	Poor	Unacceptable
Daily food choice					
Menu variety					
Flavour of food					
Food freshness & quality					
Food temperature					
Portion sizes					
Attractiveness of food					

Q8 Normally, how much do you spend daily on food and drink at work? (pounds and pence)

Q9 Particularly considering the service of food, what is your opinion about:

	Excellent	Good	Satisfactory	Poor	Unacceptable
Decor & atmosphere					
Cleanliness of area					
Cleanliness of cutlery & crockery					
Speed of service					
Staff attentiveness					
Staff friendliness					
Complaint handling					
Speed at cash desk					
Menu & tariff display					

Q10 How important are these reasons in choosing whether to use the catering facility or not?

	Very Important	Quite Important	Not Important	Not at all Important
Quality of food				
Price				
Speed of service				
Convenience				
Social aspects				
Habit				
Environment				

Q11 If you choose NOT to use the catering facility, what other arrangements do you make, if any?

- Have food delivered to my desk
- Bring in a packed lunch
- Go home
- Buy from sandwich shop
- Buy from pub/restaurant
- Buy from fast food outlet
- Prefer to go shopping
- Other

Q12 To assist us in analysing your responses please provide the following information about yourself:

Gender: Male | Female

Age Group: Under 20 | 21 to 30 | 31 to 40 | 41 to 50 | 50+

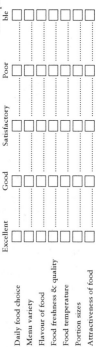
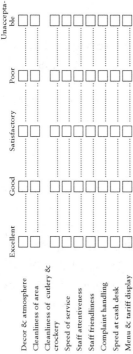

Figure 21.2 Twelve structured questions

Weighting Research

Importance: Weighting Survey Rankings

	Sample Size (Units)	1	4	2	8	20	31	4	6	6	1	1	1	85
		North Eastern	Scotland	North Western	W & C	Northern Ireland	R.O.I.	South Eastern	Eastern	Education	Citation London	Citation South	S& SW	Average
Q1	Value for Money	8.50	7.41	6.86	8.19	7.72	7.47	8.01	7.87	8.74	7.86	8.35	7.05	7.84
Dining Area														
Q2A	Design & Decoration	6.70	6.01	5.94	5.48	6.28	6.10	6.25	6.32	6.36	4.73	6.35	8.52	6.25
Q2B	Room Cleanliness	9.90	8.17	7.21	7.46	8.19	8.49	7.80	8.10	7.96	6.78	6.85	8.26	7.93
Q2C	Comfort/Ambience	8.60	7.44	6.34	5.93	7.02	7.06	7.09	6.82	7.03	5.21	7.05	6.57	6.85
Q2D	Noise Levels	7.70	5.84	7.13	6.00	6.92	6.21	6.45	6.70	6.27	5.66	6.40	4.94	6.35
Q2E	Room Layout	6.60	4.92	6.37	5.81	6.27	6.09	6.33	6.53	6.24	4.86	6.40	6.00	6.04
Meals Available														
Q3A	Daily Food Choice	8.60	7.82	6.04	6.25	7.64	7.62	7.47	6.62	7.05	8.00	7.82	7.63	7.38
Q3B	Menu Variety	8.40	8.52	6.14	6.62	7.67	7.62	6.52	6.70	7.17	7.93	5.68	7.63	7.22
Q3C	Flavour of Food	9.30	8.59	6.73	6.96	8.11	8.17	7.33	7.19	7.65	8.71	6.61	8.21	7.80
Q3D	Food freshness and quality	9.90	8.71	7.00	7.38	8.47	8.66	7.81	7.70	7.92	8.26	7.33	8.73	8.16
Q3E	Food Temperature	9.70	8.41	7.42	7.48	8.18	8.19	7.60	7.92	7.72	8.20	7.33	8.26	8.03
Q3F	Portion Sizes	9.10	7.76	7.69	6.62	7.65	7.53	7.25	7.00	7.87	7.20	6.66	7.31	7.47
Q3G	Attractiveness of Food	8.80	7.74	7.57	7.10	7.91	7.56	7.00	6.96	7.30	7.20	6.55	7.52	7.43
Food Service Area														
Q4A	Décor & Atmosphere	7.60	7.07	6.18	5.75	6.86	6.71	6.73	6.58	6.39	5.93	6.66	6.89	6.61
Q4B	Cleanliness of Area	9.60	8.70	6.57	7.17	8.36	8.74	7.46	8.05	7.60	7.40	7.38	8.73	7.98
Q4C	Cleanliness of Cutlery & Crockery	9.40	9.12	7.34	7.35	8.39	8.81	7.47	7.68	7.72	7.40	7.44	9.05	8.10
Q4D	Speed of Service	9.30	7.89	7.41	7.15	7.79	7.82	6.81	7.43	7.44	7.46	6.82	7.84	7.60
Q4E	Staff Attentiveness	9.00	7.37	7.73	7.40	8.10	8.13	6.66	7.64	7.84	7.60	7.33	8.00	7.73
Q4F	Staff Friendliness	9.20	8.17	7.67	7.79	8.24	8.19	7.22	7.97	8.01	8.06	8.11	8.52	8.10
Q4G	Complaint Handling	9.10	8.03	7.72	7.21	7.82	7.86	6.66	7.01	7.75	7.86	6.70	7.64	7.61
Q4H	Speed at Cash Desk	9.10	7.52	7.65	7.23	7.84	7.80	6.80	7.60	7.78	7.73	7.11	7.63	7.65
Q4I	Menu & Tariff display	8.70	7.95	6.27	6.70	7.69	7.22	6.26	7.22	7.56	7.80	6.94	7.36	7.31

Sodexho Customer Feedback

We identify which elements are important to customers in unit and the division

Example of table and questionnaire in pack

Figure 21.3 Weighting research

Verbatim response

On the back page of the questionnaire, respondents are invited to 'add any other views you have or suggestions you would like to make as to how we can improve our service to you' and these unprompted responses add flesh to the structured answers. The following is just a sample of actual comments received:

- 'what about a Pizza Hut, McDonald's, Burger King or KFC?';
- 'is it possible to have, say, three different types of food bars?';
- 'the variety of sandwiches is very limited for vegetarians';
- 'how about selling papers like they do in our sister site in the next town';
- 'the shop is an excellent idea but there needs to be a lot more choice'.

Main findings from the 2001 survey

At the conclusion of the research and after discussions of the findings with clients Sodexho circulates to all client staff on site the key findings and actions to be taken in response to the survey.

Sodhexo presents findings to their clients in close meetings where the implications and issues are discussed in the context of the specific site and circumstances concerned. Whether the research has been done to inform decision-making or, indeed, to give an informed evaluation of Sodexho's performance to date, the process is very valuable to all.

The surveys are designed in such a way that they can be used in conjunction with customer profiling (a specific evolution from social group typology) and other techniques such as mystery shopping and focus research amongst consumers.

Further developments

Building on the experience of the early research results, Sodexho is now determined to identify the key success factors which have generated favourable responses, and to refine questionnaires and best practice methods for conducting future research. This whole process has now been implemented in other business sectors and for other food services.

Similar feedback programmes are planned for the soft services – other than catering – which Sodexho provides to clients, such as:

- switchboard;
- reception;
- helpdesk;
- mailroom;
- reprographics;
- cleaning.

The research is planned on a fully inclusive basis to cover all these services irrespective of whether they are operated as individual activities or whether run under a multi-skilled, multi-tasked approach.

Since visitors, as well as staff, are the 'consumers' of some of these services, they will be included as respondents in these programmes where appropriate. Pilot activity has already started to conduct these using hand-held computers (PDAs) to gather the data.

Customer profiling is another tool that supplements feedback monitoring and is being employed by Sodexho in its quest to strengthen customer relations. The group's experience in customer profiling is discussed separately in Chapter 22.

make your
local authority
smile

By offering a range of services from catering and cleaning to grounds maintenance, Sodexho is improving the daily quality of life in the workplace. This can increase productivity, cut staff turnover and enhance your reputation in the community – which means not only more contented staff and local stakeholders but a happier, healthier look to your finances. **Call 0800 169 49 59.**

Sodexho
Catering and Support Services

turning a cost into a value

22

Customer Profiling and Improving the Quality of Daily Life at Work

Peter Cardwell

Sodexho has an exclusive method of understanding people's service preferences called Customer Profiling. The basis of Customer Profiling is a focus on customer needs; this matching the Sodexho services, food brands and promotions to the profile of the site population enables us to predict and influence what customers buy.

We all know that sites are different from one another. Customer Profiling gives us a systematic approach, enabling us to make comparisons against a national benchmark so that we can understand how one site differs from another and optimise service offer development for each site.

Historically, Customer Profiling was championed by Sodexho Business & Industry and was used exclusively for assisting with determining the food offer. But in the past 18 months, its use has been broadened to extend across Sodexho's market segments and now includes customer preferences across many support services.

By applying the latest consumer marketing techniques, such as profiling customers' lifestyle needs and applying this to workplace service provision, Sodexho has developed Customer Profiling in association with FirstPerson Consulting. It enables Sodexho clients to achieve their objectives through increased patronage, higher spend and greater satisfaction levels in the pursuit of reduced or zero subsidy.

The drive to reduce costs and improve quality of life at work

It is Sodexho's clear strategy to provide services in the workplace that improve employee efficiency and loyalty by making the client workplace more efficient, convenient and enjoyable – in other words, by improving the quality of daily life at work. The idea of quality of life is one we see increasingly applied to the workplace. But should senior managers, focused on the drive to reduce costs, actually care about it?

As our research has shown, there are commercially sound reasons to be concerned about the quality of daily life at work, not least because it impacts on the company's reputation as an 'employer of first choice' and companies who ignore its importance face losing the battle for talent. With today's busy lifestyles and the blurring of the line between work and home, a company is rated by the number and quality of services it offers which make employees' lives easier and more efficient – at work and home.

Quality of life at work – support services improve productivity

In mid-1999 Sodexho set itself the task of finding out:

- the incidence of support services in the workplace, split by manufacturing and service companies;

- the impact provision of support services had on productivity, efficiency and loyalty, from the employee's perspective;

- how support services affected the employees' view of quality of life at work;

- how employees felt about being treated as 'consumers in the workplace'.

This involved two large-scale, nationally representative surveys conducted by FirstPerson on behalf of Sodexho, through which employees were interviewed in their place of work. In total, over 7,000 people were interviewed between December 1999 and September 2000, and since then we have conducted ongoing research involving over 10,000 employees.

When employees were asked if they would like to see more services in the future, more manufacturing industry employees (62 per cent) than service industry employees (57 per cent) strongly agreed.

From the employee perspective, there is a perceived link between the provision of key support services and their productivity and loyalty. When asked whether support services – such as staff restaurant, help desk, childcare, on-site shop, vending or gym – made them more productive and efficient, 80 per cent of employees and 90 per cent of senior managers agreed, and one in three agreed that services made them a great deal more productive and efficient.

More men (81 per cent) than women (76 per cent) believe that services make them more efficient and productive and there is a 'straight line' relationship with hours worked; the longer employees work, the more services are seen to contribute to efficiency and productivity. This is especially important in the UK, where employees work the longest hours in Europe.

Support services and loyalty

Loyalty is a concept that is out of fashion in a workplace subject to constant change. But when we asked employees whether they thought that services made them more loyal, one in three said that services made them 'a great deal more loyal', with women rating the loyalty effect of services higher than men – 38 per cent of women as opposed to 28 per cent of men agreeing that services make them a great deal more loyal.

As can be seen from Figure 22.1, this is in direct contrast to the productivity and efficiency effect of services, which are rated more highly by men.

Q: How much more loyal do these services make you as an employee?

- 1 in 3 people say that the provision of services in the workplace 'makes me a great deal more loyal'
- There is a gender bias with women rating the loyalty effect higher than men
- The longer people work, the more critical services become to efficiency and productivity

---

Figure 22.1 The gender differences in the loyalty effect of services

The employee as 'consumer in the workplace'

High on the agenda of many organisations are the twin objectives of reducing costs associated with support services on the one hand and increasing both the range of services and the quality of service delivery on the other – two seemingly conflicting objectives. In order to do this, many organisations are passing an increasing proportion of the cost of services, such as staff restaurant, retail shop, health clubs etc, on to the employee. Our research shows that there is a willingness among some employees to be treated as a 'consumer in the workplace'.

Employees are demanding more services and some are prepared to pay for them. There are many reasons for this, not least of which is the blurring of the line between work and home. In a report, the Industrial Society expressed the opinion that 'work is becoming more like home' in the sense that many facilities and services associated with life outside work are being provided by an increasing number of organisations in the workplace.

Our research confirms that in larger organisations (employing over 500 people) we can identify segments of employees who are prepared to pay higher prices for services already accepted in the workplace – such as a staff restaurant – and also for new, innovative services not yet associated with the workplace but which improve quality of life at work, such as those listed in Figure 22.2.

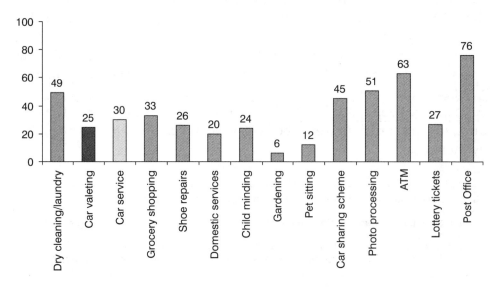

Figure 22.2 Services that could improve quality of life at work

Q: Do you think that these services could help improve your quality of life at work?

Q: If provided would you be prepared to pay for some of these services?

MALE

FEMALE

Figure 22.3 and **Figure 22.4** Responses to questions about services to improve quality of life

These services are those that blur the line between work and home; services not yet generally associated with the workplace. They can be as wide ranging as car valeting and maintenance in the staff car park, grocery shopping via a workplace internet café for delivery to the boot of the freshly valeted car, or hairdressing/beauty treatments/manicures and personal training in the company fitness suite. There are gender differences in the willingness to pay for some of these services, as is shown in Figure 22.4.

Key to providing these services is outsourcing the 'softer' people services to a partner organisation that understands the changing nature of the employee in the workplace – a partner organisation that can be trusted to help deliver services that enhance the reputation of the client company through the proactive provision of support services at the level of quality and service delivery demanded by discerning employees. After all, employees don't stop being consumers once they are at their place of work.

Understanding service preferences: typology comparison against a benchmark

Nearly all consumer markets consist of segments: groups of consumers tied by common characteristics. An understanding of these characteristics can help companies begin to predict service preferences. But to understand consumers fully, a technique is needed which gives insight into their underlying motivations and beliefs, and how these manifest themselves as lifestyles and workstyles which are linked to service preferences in the workplace.

Once we can understand and satisfy these needs by providing the range and quality of services that 'the customer in the workplace' values, we have a virtuous cycle of increased patronage, spend per head, satisfaction and improved perception of quality of daily life at work.

Different people, different preferences

Through this research, conducted over a number of years, we have identified six different and distinct service preference groups, each exhibiting very different preferences when it comes to service choice, service style, and being treated as a 'consumer in the workplace'.

Different people have different preferences, and understanding which groups are present in which numbers on each site will enable the optimisation of services – whether food or support services – to the site population.

For example, when it comes to services, **Innovators** (17 per cent of the UK working population) have a positive attitude to a range of services, are willing to be treated as a consumer in the workplace, but expect high standards of service delivery and good branding. When it comes to food, Innovators prefer ethnic, spicy foods and will try anything served to them. They see food as a pleasure, not a necessity.

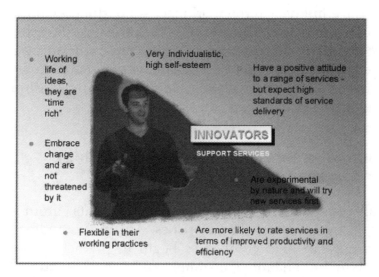

Figure 22.5 Innovators

Activators (8 per cent) are very action-oriented and 'time poor' in their own minds, so they expect service delivery to be quick and efficient and will complain if it is not. They are the group most likely to use the company gym. They require food on demand, anywhere and at any time, so are very convenience-oriented. They are the core market for 'grab and go'.

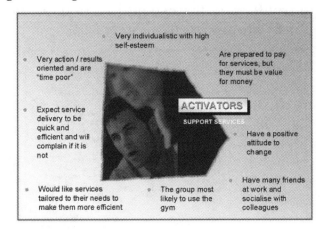

Figure 22.6 Activators

Aspirers (7 per cent) will pay for services, but these must be well presented and appeal to their 'consumer power' attitude to life. They are ardent consumers of 'badge brands' and services in the workplace should be equally well branded. They have a traditional bias towards food and like the ritual of mealtimes. They follow Innovators and – to a certain extent – Activators when it comes to new food trends.

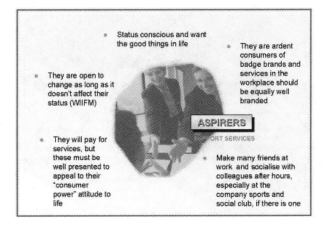

Figure 22.7 Aspirers

Supporters (13 per cent) are a group over-represented by women. While they are willing to be treated as a consumer in the workplace, they have a keen sense of value when it comes to food. They are also the group most likely to rate the importance of a staff restaurant very highly. Being over-represented by women, they are also most likely to rate the type of services offered in Figure 22.2 as those that they would be prepared to pay for and that would have a direct impact on the quality of their daily life at work (see Figure 22.4).

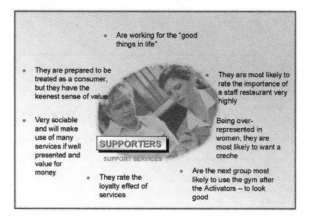

Figure 22.8 Supporters

Acceptors (26 per cent) are wary about being treated as a consumer in the workplace and so need to be 'marketed' to more than the other groups. They are price conscious and not as open to change as other groups. When it comes to food, they are true traditionalists, preferring quantity over quality.

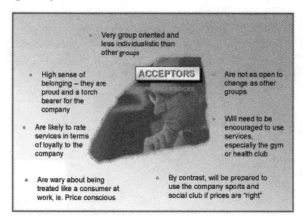

Figure 22.9 Acceptors

Defenders (29%) are more associated with older manufacturing industries. They actively resist being treated as a consumer in the workplace. For them, company subsidy is still an important part of the employee benefit package. Their food preference is for simple dishes and they are uninterested in ingredients or preparation.

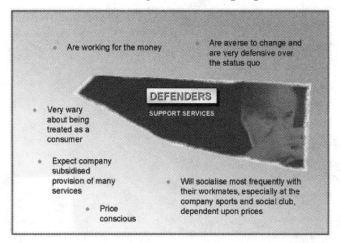

Figure 22.10 Defenders

We have been tracking food and meal preferences over time and our research shows that new food trends start among the more experimental and risk-taking groups – the Innovators and Activators – and then move from left to right, through Supporters and Aspirers to Acceptors and Defenders, who pick up the new trends last.

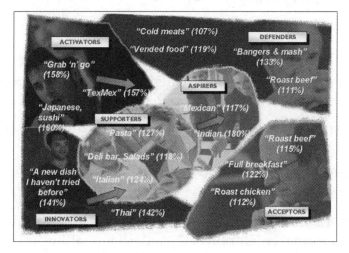

Figure 22.11 Food preferences by group

The appeal of 'softer' support services to employees has also been tracked, as Figure 22.12 shows. Some services are more appealing than others and the numbers indicate how much more than the average they are rated by the six service preference groups.

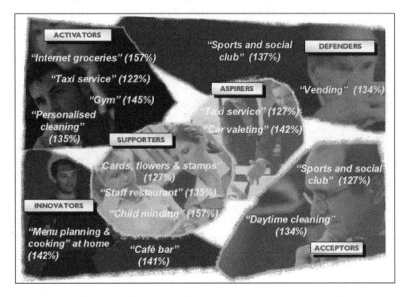

Figure 22.12 Servicing preferences by group

How can this help with company service provision?

Customer Profiling helps by identifying:

- The mix and balance of different people on site;

- Why they have the needs that they do;

- How the current service mix (catering and other support service) satisfies their needs;

- What changes are required to improve patronage, spend and customer satisfaction;

- The potential to introduce new services, which may be paid for by the employee.

The results of the Customer Profiling survey identify the different groups and uncover employees' underlying attitudes to support services, identifying opportunities in the pursuit of zero subsidy.

Part 5

Case Studies

1
Universal Sodexho and Shell Exploration and Production Alliance: a Business Partnership Development

Background

The business partnership alliance between Shell Exploration and Production ('Shell Expro') and Sodexho is built on a longstanding relationship stretching back 20 years. Prior to the alliance Sodexho were operating seven independent contracts with Shell Expro, involving over 40 services offers with similar scopes of work but with seven different contracts and reward structures. Shell Expro saw little benefit in returning to competitive tender – a mechanism which it perceived as slow to respond to marketplace changes. Nevertheless, the pre-alliance contract was market driven rather than cost and business improvement driven.

The North Sea Alliance Relationship

Key points of the contract

The single contract between Universal Sodexho and Shell Exploration and Production takes the form of a long-term strategic partnering arrangement to provide eight generic service lines which offer over 40 distinct services to 20 Shell Expro units, both onshore and offshore. It replaced the previous variety of disparate FM/multi-service contracts, involves 535 Universal Sodexho employees and supports 4370 client employees.

The following are the main terms of the contract:

- The contract commenced on 1 February 2000 and is for seven years with annual extension options to the end of the asset/field life;

- Contract value is circa £113 million based on an annual turnover of £18.1 million, with a commitment to drive out £13.5 million of direct costs over 5 years, representing 16.5 per cent of the total cost base of £82 million;

- There is a further commitment to drive out £4.2 million of indirect costs over the same 5-year period through aiming for 'fit-for-purpose service quality'.

- The return Universal Sodexho earns from the contract is performance-based against the following criteria:

  - net cost of work;
  - performance against a scorecard consisting of weighted elements of financial control, service quality, contract leadership and customer satisfaction;
  - performance against health, safety and environment scorecard.

- Reducing costs while increasing quality and customer satisfaction results in additional return being earned. Conversely, higher costs, unsatisfactory quality and low customer satisfaction entail a reduced return with no lower limit.

- Sodexho invoices Shell Expro monthly for the services and costs incurred. The contract provides for a single invoice per month covering all locations with back-up providing the breakdown to location level.

The definition and measurement of 'fit for purpose'

How the 'fit for purpose' service quality level is initially set up and then refined is a key issue in the operation of the contract. An FM Scorecard is established, which is intended to reflect joint learning, and is used at every location to assess performance within the following agreed definition:

> *The vision of the FM Scorecard is to provide value for money FM services to Shell Expro which are delivered safely and are continuously improving. The 'added value' of this contract must come from reflecting the business needs of each principal stakeholder using the contracted service scope.*

FM Scorecard assessments are made using various formats: judgmental (25 per cent weight); focus groups; observations and statistical information (25 per cent each).

- Performance Management is focused on *HSE (Health, Safety & Environment) Performance; Financial Management; Business Integrity (Service Quality); Contract Leadership;* and *Customer Satisfaction.* These are weighted according to priority (HSE not weighted): *Financial Management (50 per cent); Business Integrity (Service Quality) (20 per cent); Contract Leadership (15 per cent)* and *Customer Satisfaction (15 per cent).*

- Service Level Agreements (SLAs) are used to establish the level of return to Universal Sodexho and savings to Shell Expro. SLAs ensure that both the customer and Universal Sodexho are certain of each other's expectations and obligations. SLAs are established for each distinct work activity within the contract, and each SLA addresses:
  - the objective of the service;
  - the general capability required;
  - detailed service delivery activities;
  - key stakeholders;
  - key reference documents.

- The SLA will also provide consistent application and quality control across all locations. Exceptionally, SLAs may be altered locally, so individual customer requirements can be catered for.

- The Universal Sodexho performance for the first two quarters of 2001 were: *HSE Performance* – Very Good; *Financial Management* – Very Good; *Business Integrity (Service Quality)* – Outstanding; *Contract Leadership* – Good; and *Customer Satisfaction* – Outstanding.

- The SLAs aim to achieve lateral learning and continuous improvement across all service elements.

Objectives and organisation of the North Sea Alliance

Objectives

The objectives of the alliance are to bring: breakthroughs in health, safety and environment (HS&E) performance; a long-term approach to continuous improvement; excellent management of Shell Expro's cost and profit; quality services and satisfied customers.

Among the 40 distinct service offers, comprising a combination of direct and subcontracted service lines, are service elements such as :

- *Hygiene* (within which the service lines include waste management, pest control and feminine hygiene);

- *Office Environment* (of which service lines include management, hire and repair, reconfiguration, signage, space planning, furniture & equipment;

- *Distribution* (franking, couriers, porterage, mail distribution);

- *Property Management* (housing, office and facilities management);

- *Catering* (meals, vending, shop, bonded retail);

- *Building and Maintenance* (utilities supplies, plant and equipment, fabrics maintenance, ground maintenance, planned maintenance);

- *Health, Safety and Security Services* (guarding, security equipment, fire safety equipment, medical); and

- *Support Services* (technical administration, conference, helpdesk, reception, photocopier services, transport, stationery, welfare, communications).

Organisation of the Alliance

The 20 Shell Expro units involved include onshore HQ at Aberdeen (two offices), an office base at Lowestoft, gas plants at St Fergus and in Fife; and 15 offshore platforms.

The stated benefits of the contract structure are considered to be:

- Shared risk;

- Coherent strategy for procurement of FM services across divisions;

- Return based entirely on performance;

- Development of jointly owned and improved efficiencies;
- Focusing attention on service delivery, quality and integrity;
- Guaranteed cost savings.

Universal Sodexho and Shell Expro use annual Best Practice workshops to review progress and discuss priorities for the forthcoming year. They note that cooperation, trust, respect, discussion, joint management and feedback between Shell Expro and Universal Sodexho personnel are key ingredients for providing a successful relationship with benefits to all. They have identified the following core values of that relationship:

- Safety is top priority;
- The relationship is an alliance contract to deliver a vast portfolio of multi-services;
- The shared ownership of FM business works towards win/win solutions;
- All costs are visible and transparent – return is based entirely on performance;
- Parties have equal status in the management of the business;
- Financial targets and plans and business plans are shared.

The contract operates through a two-tier management structure involving a management board and a leadership team.

The management board has the following roles:

- Approve strategy and annual business plan;
- Review performance (operational and HSE);
- Approve major changes to contract;
- Approve exceptional changes to target costs;
- Liaise with key stakeholders;
- Provide guidance and advice to the leadership team;
- Endorse Universal Sodexho's earned annual return;
- Endorse extraordinary return payments.

The leadership team has the following roles:

- Establish contract strategies;
- Develop and deliver the business plan;
- Review target costs;
- Monitor performance;
- Visibly lead contract development and performance;
- Deliver HSE plans.

Cornerstones for success

The Alliance has identified the following 'big rules', which must be applied to make the contract work:

- Target costs will be jointly managed by Shell Expro and Universal Sodexho representatives for each location;
- Costs cannot be swapped between service lines;
- No changes to the quality of service without leadership team approval;
- Non-planned items/costs must be clearly identified;
- A target cost is set for each location, comprising the following elements:
  - management fee;
  - overhead fee;
  - net cost of SLAs;
  - net costs of projects.

The 2001 Annual Report of the joint Facility Management Alliance recorded some excellent results for the Alliance in its first year, particularly in terms of both safety and cost management. Asset safety representatives reviewed the Alliance safety effort twice during the year. At both times the Alliance approach was rated as 'very good' with some additional development targets identified.

Universal Sodexho received a commendation from the British Safety Council for the second year running with a 'Special Achievement in Safety' award from the IADC and, subsequently the Safety Excellence Award as a part of the Scottish Offshore Achievement Awards. In addition, Universal Sodexho employees were recognised at the Shell Expro HS&E conference.

In cost management, although activity levels increased, causing the revision of target costs at some locations, the total of sustainable savings achieved during the year was £1.4 million with an additional £0.3 million saved through deferred projects. Excluding the deferred works, the original savings target of £1.1 million was therefore comfortably exceeded.

11

Full Circle – the Return Transfer from Outsourced to In-house Management

Trevor Payne
Oxford Radcliffe Hospitals NHS Trust

This chapter will focus on the option to insource facilities services (creating or re-creating directly employed, in-house service delivery teams) following on from an earlier exercise to outsource those services. The decision to insource may be driven by a number of factors such as:

- poor contract performance;

- poor contract management (client or contractor);

- outdated service delivery/specification;

- technical obsolescence;

- a Best Value service review;

- contractor leverage (lack of competition);

- a mixture of internal or external pressures.

Many management tools, trends and theories become slaves to economic or organisational 'fashion trends' (examples such as downsizing, rightsizing, de-layering, etc, spring to mind). The core principles or key benefits of such initiatives are sometimes forgotten, or perhaps not fully considered, in the rush to follow the new or latest fashion. Many organisations are keen to gain competitive advantage and be seen as innovators, implementing strategies that offer quick wins but only provide short-term solutions. Some have an agenda which may in part be achieved by adopting one of these strategies, such as reducing headcount or cost. As a result, implementation can offer short-term benefit but result in long-term issues regarding service delivery and performance. Management often mirrors fashion in that styles and trends often come in and out of fashion in a cyclical manner. How often are staff heard to say 'we have now come full circle – this is the way we used to do it'? The benefit of hindsight, experience and organisational change often results in the reinvention of the wheel or the regurgitation of the most successful components of previous processes and procedures. Organisations that follow the principles of business process re-engineering should constantly be looking inward at their operations and service delivery and asking themselves:

- 'Why do we do the things that we do?'

- 'How do we do the things that we do?'

- 'Do we still need to do them?'

- 'If we do, could we improve upon them?'

At the macro level, the reinvention cycle may be driven by technological change, external market influences (the economy, etc), internal influences (merger/acquisition, change in strategic direction) or, perhaps, the need to regain competitive advantage.

At the micro level, the reinvention cycle may be driven by contract renewal dates, new technology or service review in order to ensure a best value approach with respect to service delivery.

This cycle of reinvention must be considered when developing business strategy – any strategy must identify and attempt to deal with all of the known issues at that point in time, whilst retaining flexibility to cope with any unknowns that may take effect – in order to accommodate emergent strategy. Reinvention offers opportunity; this chapter will focus on the factors that may influence the decision to insource, along with some of the key points to consider relating to the insourcing decision.

However, putting the outsourcing theory into practise presents a number of problems and challenges, and there are several key stages in the process (both pre- and post- the decision to outsource) that will influence the degree of outsourcing success. Insourcing may be considered as an option when it is felt that the initial decision to outsource services may have been wrong, ill-informed, poorly managed/monitored or has now become inappropriate.

Outsourcing – where did it all go wrong?

If outsourcing has failed to deliver, for whatever reason, it is important to revisit and dissect the circumstances and reasoning behind the original decision to outsource and to establish exactly why the process didn't work before making a 'knee jerk' decision to insource or revisit the market. Establish the current position before launching into a potential solution. It is essential that the way forward dovetails into both the facilities and the host organisation's strategy.

Factors to consider when analysing the original decision are:

- in-house vs outsourced supply – (re-visiting the original decision to outsource);

- core or non-core activity;

- service specification and contract;

- benefits perceived and benefits received;

- contract management and performance monitoring;

- organisational change (people, process, workplace);

- contract relationship – power and leverage.

In-house vs outsourced supply

The decision to outsource elements of an organisation's facilities activity or support service delivery is a major strategic decision. The ultimate decision must be based on confidence that the service provider can deliver a consistent, affordable, high quality service in accordance with the specification, whilst demonstrating synergy (a desire to explore and develop shared values) with the future strategic directions of the host organisation. The decision will be based upon a key set of circumstances usually focused around cost, quality and service delivery – unique in each instance and for each organisation, often with each factor weighted to reflect impact and importance. One size does not fit all with respect to service delivery. Also, for example, with facilities management (FM) there are no 'off-the-shelf solutions'; the bundling of service packages/functions designed to attract economies of scale must be carefully considered. Outsourcing packaged service bundles (catering, security, maintenance and cleaning as part of one contract for example) can be an effective way of adding value and maximising flexibility. However, many total FM firms evolved from companies with expertise in one particular professional field and have gone on to buy in additional expertise and knowledge relating to other service functions: this can often result in variable service delivery performance across the contract bundle.

Charles Handy (1994: 26) wrote:

> *Organisations are responding to the challenge of efficiency by exporting unproductive work and people as fast as they can.*

It is true to say that some of the early outsourcing decisions were made for all of the wrong reasons. Rather than tackling or managing issues relating to lack of flexibility, generic working methods or rigid demarcation boundaries, many organisations outsourced what they considered to be inflexible and unco-operative departments and service functions. In doing so, unruly management and supervision were transferred to the outsourced provider for them to manage and control. For many organisations, outsourcing was initially seen as an opportunity to clear the dead wood and reduce headcount, fuelled by the trend or fashion to downsize. The decision to outsource may also have been influenced by focus on the complexity of the day-to-day service issues, without perhaps considering some of the longer-term issues.

What did the organisation originally gain from outsourcing? The decision to outsource (or insource) must be thoroughly considered and evaluated before a decision is made. Outsourcing (or insourcing) can have a demoralising impact on staff groups and result in a reduction of output and productivity in the short-term. If the original decision to outsource was wrong, then this may lead an organisation to consider bringing the service back in-house; but often by the time this point has been reached a considerable pool of labour, expertise, loyalty and knowledge has been lost as a result of the initial transition, and this will make insourcing more difficult. More difficult does not mean impossible, but there will undoubtedly be a time lag whilst the service re-establishes itself and expertise is developed. In addition, an upfront hump of costs associated with setting up HR, payroll, management and supervisory structures, etc, will be incurred as systems are put back into place. There could also be costs associated with TUPE (transfer of undertakings protection of employment regulations, 1981) if staff are transferred from the contractor into the in-house team. These issues must be recognised as part of the cost of transition/mobilisation.

Facilities management – core or non-core activity?

The traditional view of FM has been that of a non-core or pure support function which is often seen to be at an arm's length to the organisation. Certainly in the early days of FM much emphasis was placed upon facilities taking control of and managing all of the non-critical or non-core functions, which would in turn enable the organisation to focus on the main business agenda and the core issues that it might be facing. There are clear benefits relating to cost, staffing and management overheads to be gained from combining the management of support functions under one facilities umbrella. These service functions could be provided by an outsourced supplier or an in-house team. Additional benefit is achieved by breaking down traditional demarcation boundaries and combining service functions in an innovative manner, cutting out duplication and wasteful practices.

If the operational function of most organisations was mapped out in the form of a supply chain (each link representing a key service delivery task), then a number of the processes and sub-processes or key links in the supply chain would be provided and managed by the facilities function. In its best operational mode, the facilities function could be described as the 'glue' that holds the organisation together and enables it to produce its output in a seamless manner. The range and complexity of the support that facilities offer to the organisation touches on and impacts upon all levels of hierarchy (from the top to the bottom) of the organisation. Facilities services could equally be viewed as vital enabling functions or 'business enablers'. In most forward-looking organisations there is an appreciation at a senior management level of the contribution that a well-managed and effective FM service provision can bring, ensuring that a 100 per cent focus is placed upon the support of the business activities of the organisation.

The core vs non-core discussion should have been considered in the outsourcing context in order to scope the services that the organisation retains or manages in-house. Careful consideration needs to be given to identifying those services that are best managed directly by the organisation. For example, in the past, computer producers have outsourced elements of service that they considered to be non-core, such as software development. Those outsourced software companies have now grown to be more powerful and more profitable than the host computer organisation, which demonstrates the importance of scoping core and non-core activity.

A strategic view must be established regarding the importance of each service element concerning risk and business continuity. It is important to identify where the knowledge sits in each service area, and to establish the value of that knowledge and gauge how difficult it would be to replicate each function. It is therefore vital that the functional linkages and service boundaries that exist inter-department and inter-directorate are identified and mapped before any contract bundle or service package is assembled in order to be outsourced.

In most organisations, there are often casual arrangements in place between departments (e.g. discussion of minor problems, etc, over lunch). This interaction may not be carried on within the contract scenario as it happens on an informal but regular basis and was never captured and detailed in the service specification; as a result it becomes a variation to contract. Some companies have found out too late that they have mistakenly outsourced core services. In the facilities context there are potential problems with outsourcing services which bring the contractor face to face with the customers of these services. Kotler and Bloom (1999: 147) define service as:

> A service is any activity of benefit that one party can offer to another that is essentially intangible and does not result in ownership of anything. Its production may or may not be tied to a physical product.

Services are performances not objects, and staff therefore need to be trained to give the correct performance to a variety of audiences. Contract staff need to be proficient in customer care and sufficiently empowered so as to handle difficult situations as and when they arise.

Service specification and contract

Many early attempts at outsourcing failed due to poor specification. Often specifications were badly prepared and incomplete, resulting in post-contract variations and escalating costs; alternatively, specifications were so detailed and complicated that they scared off contractors. There has been a shift away from detailed input specifications (which are said to limit or stifle innovation) towards output specifications (which are not so prescriptive and focus on the required service output).

In simple terms:

- *Input specifications* – focus on the **how,** e.g. how it should be done, how many staff should do it, how much material/product is required, etc.

- *Output specifications* – focus on the **what**, e.g. what needs to be carried out.

There are pros and cons associated with both types of specification and it is up to each organisation to consider which approach is more suitable for them to adopt. One thing is certain: the specification only represents the starting point for a contract or service level agreement. It is also possible to consider a hybrid approach to specification which seeks to gain the middle ground between input and output specifications – that is, which effectively procures the clarity and control of an input specification but which has the potential for the innovation of an output specification. The success of outsourcing can be directly related to the quality and content of the specification. The specification represents the blueprint for the contract (the route map to effective service delivery).

The dynamic nature of many organisations means that specifications can quickly become outdated. When it is developed, the specification represents a 'snapshot' of a moment in time and is a reflection of the service requirements existing at that period. In some organisations, service contracts have been 'rolled over' for a second or third term and often the specification is not reviewed at the time of rollover. This results in a specification that is out-of-step with the service delivery – a scenario which makes it very difficult to monitor performance against the specification. In effect, the contractor knows more about the service delivery requirements than the client.

This cultivates an environment which leads to service variation and adversarial contracting. Specifications are best developed in collaboration with, or with input from, the users of the service in order to capture the needs/values and priorities of the customer. The need to review service delivery and to update service specifications could act as a driving force to consider insourcing the services or conducting a best value review.

Benefits perceived and benefits received?

Many of the perceived cost benefits resulting from outsourcing were never realised in many instances, particularly those relating to corporate overhead reduction associated with HR, payroll, etc. Often the stated savings remained on paper and did not materialise – the freed-up resource or staff capacity in departments like payroll, HR and finance was often being redeployed to manage other internal pressures. Decisions to outsource based upon reducing headcount, exporting inefficient staff groups and work practises out of the organisation only provided short-term benefits.

So why outsource? For some it was access to flexible working methods, new technology, training and innovation. For others it was short-term revenue savings or access to scarce pots of capital for enhancing facilities such as kitchens or restaurants (a bypass or short cut to bidding for capital against other departments or functions in the organisation). In the NHS it has been stated that, in some Trusts, revenue savings of up to 15 per cent have been made from outsourced FM budgets as a result of participating in two or more consecutive waves of market testing. There is growing evidence to suggest that stripping out the costs and reducing the headcount have had a delayed but pronounced effect on reducing the quality of service delivery for key enabling services such as catering, cleaning, portering, etc. There are also indicators to support the view that repeated visits to the market (re-tendering) produces only marginal cost improvements. Since innovative and flexible working methods have previously been adopted, the innovation promised at the start of the contract does not always get delivered.

Cost savings have had a direct and adverse impact upon the quality of service delivery in many organisations, particularly in the public sector. As the potential for generating savings from market testing services at regular intervals are limited, there is little to be gained from routinely going back out to tender – particularly as a number of recent mergers and acquisitions have resulted in a limited pool of able and competitive FM service providers. This presents a concern, as outsourcing into a limited supply market can be very risky. As a result, a number of large NHS Trusts and private sector companies are exploring options associated with in sourcing and Best Value service reviews. A Best Value review of a service function will focus on the Four Cs which:

- **challenge** the fundamental basis of service delivery;
- **consult** on the views of all relevant stakeholders;
- **compare** the service(s) against local and national standards; and
- ensure the provision of **competitive** services.

Contract management and performance monitoring

Contracts that have been outsourced but not properly monitored or managed will result in poor performance, poor customer satisfaction and poor value for money. A clear specification and a realistic expectation of service delivery are vital in order to manage and monitor the contract effectively. Ideally, monitoring should be considered whilst developing the specification in order to ensure that monitoring is timely, relevant and invokes penalty for instances of repeated poor performance. Monitoring is a vital process and an effective tool for checking performance and quality of service delivery. Regular, structured monitoring enables the informed client or contract manager to keep a close eye on the quality and performance of service delivery, whilst ensuring that the service provider remains focused on performing to specification (it is often said that 'what gets measured gets done'). Contracts need to be effectively and proactively managed. Services that are outsourced, and then left to deliver unchecked, are doomed to failure. There needs to be expertise in evidence on both parties to the contract (the informed client or contract manager and the service provider). Poor performance due to ineffective contract management or contract monitoring may be a driver to consider insourcing the services in question; however, the in-house team will still need to be monitored and managed effectively. Insourcing may offer the opportunity to consider restructuring or changing the management team to ensure that managers and monitors are competent.

Organisational change

Organisations are constantly changing. Consider the following three elements of the organisation: the built environment (workplace), the work processes and the personnel. A change in any one of these elements will have an impact upon the other two. For example, if a multi-site manufacturing company consolidated its activities on to one new, large site, the processes and workflow activities would change as new technology and new layout have an effect. This move may result in the need to utilise a smaller, more efficient workforce. People, place and process interact with each other and outsourcing will impact upon this relationship. When one of these elements changes significantly it may be a good time to review service provision and, if outsourced, perhaps consider insourcing.

Contract relationship – power and leverage

Often organisations have found out too late that they have exported valuable knowledge and expertise (which was difficult to value and even more difficult to replace once it had been lost). That expertise and knowledge will represent power and now it sits with the contract provider. This shift of power is often exploited in the contract scenario in order to add leverage to decisions relating to, for example, extensions to contracts. The contractor will assess the competence of the informed client or the contracts manager during the mobilisation stage of the contract, and if it transpires that the contractor knows more about the outsourced service than the informed client, and if the knowledge and expertise has been transferred to the contractor as a result of outsourcing, then the contractor is placed in a very powerful position. This power shift may in itself be a spur to in-source the service and develop expertise, particularly if it is considered to be in an area of core activity. A decision to insource based on this scenario will often be difficult, time consuming and have high switching costs – but it is not impossible to achieve. Supplier leverage can be demonstrated in a number of ways, such as:

- price hike;
- withholding access to new technology;
- a reduction in the quality of work produced.

Lonsdale and Cox (1998) summarise the factors which lead to supplier leverage as follows:

- *Poor contracting* – issues that are known within the firm are omitted from the contract, inappropriate personnel are assigned to the task of closing the deal or the personnel concerned have inappropriate priorities;

- *Limited supply market options* – the firm chooses to outsource although there are a limited number of supply options available to it;

- *High asset specificity* – because of the highly specific nature of the investment a firm makes in an outsourcing relationship (ie there are high switching costs), there is an effective absence of competition at the end of the contract period;

- *Uncertainty* – in situations where the firm has made highly specific investments, it will be even more vulnerable to supplier leverage if the nature of the transaction between the buyer and the supplier is characterised by uncertainty. Uncertainty will lead to an incomplete contract, which will in time give the supplier the opportunity to charge excess fees.

The decision to insource

If outsourcing hasn't worked out, for whatever reason, then insourcing may be one of the options open to consideration. As stated earlier in this chapter, it is vital that the main drivers that led to outsourcing the services in the first place are revisited, and the reasons why outsourcing hasn't worked fully identified. The decision to insource needs to complement the strategic direction of the organisation. The service will need to be reviewed in order to ensure that the facilities input matches and complements the required organisational output. This is difficult to achieve as there are many customer layers in any organisation – each with their own set of expectations, and if the insourced service is to be responsive, pro-active and flexible, then all of the customer layers will need to be consulted regarding their individual service requirements. Having thoroughly analysed the original decision to outsource services and identified the reasoning behind the desire to insource those services now, there will be a number of issues to consider such as:

Switching costs associated with bringing the service back in-house

These will include staffing set-up (internal management and supervisory structure, monitoring team), TUPE issues, payroll set-up costs, training/corporate induction, sickness cover, HR support and equipment purchase. IT systems may need to be changed, as may signage, stationery, telephone directories uniforms and badges/access control systems.

Mobilisation period

A coordinated handover of staff and operational control will need to take place. There will be a time lag before full productivity and efficiency will be achieved. Effective communication at all levels of the organisation will need to be in place and a service recovery strategy or contingency plan (perhaps including a rapid response team) will need to be organised to deal swiftly with early service failure. If knowledge was transferred out of the organisation at the time of outsourcing, and that knowledge is not insourced via TUPE or re-employment of former employees, a time lag will be experienced whilst that knowledge is built up or procured. It may be prudent to procure some of the skills and knowledge to work alongside the insourced service providers, which will have an associated cost. There could also be costs incurred at handover due to duplication and continued contractor involvement during the early stages of mobilisation.

Contract termination

There may be buy-out or termination costs incurred – depending on the type of contract that is in place and the situation that has led to termination of contract. It is advisable to study carefully the terms, conditions and the implications of the contract before terminating it.

Technology

If new technology is to be introduced at the point of contract handover then cost associated with removal/disposal of old equipment/systems along with installation costs, training and familiarisation will need to be considered.

Summary

Careful consideration must be taken prior to insourcing in order to ensure that the decision is right for the organisation. There will be pressure to go for the quick fix, or the option that involves the least pain or takes the least time (perhaps a 'knee jerk' reaction to go straight back out to the market) to which contractors will be alerted through market intelligence. As a result, one problem may be solved but a number of others created as the organisation is put over yet another barrel.

Before any decision is taken, an analysis of the circumstances relating to the outsourced services will need to be undertaken. There are several stages to go through when considering insourcing and, on the whole, the steps will mirror those that need to be considered when outsourcing services are in the first instance. It is important to recognise that the change management process associated with insourcing services will need to be carefully managed – this point cannot be stressed enough. Insourcing will require management of the outgoing contractor, the in-house team and the customers during the mobilisation phase. A facilities strategy that is aligned to the organisation's strategic direction – sharing core values and goals alongside a good specification – is essential. To ensure services are delivered as specified, a robust and effective monitoring system will need to be developed and put into operation. Just as all organisations are different, the drivers influencing the insourcing decision will be different – with factors relevant to the host organisation. If insourcing has been thoroughly and carefully considered, there is absolutely no reason why it should not be effective (as long as it is specified, resourced, managed and monitored in an appropriate manner). Insourcing is now being considered as a viable alternative to outsourcing, as a vehicle to add value, a sense of corporacy and team spirit to the organisation.

References

1. Handy, C. (1994) *The Empty Raincoat* Hutchinson
2. Kotler, P. and Bloom, P.M. (1999) *Marketing Professional Services* Free Press
3. Lonsdale, C. and Cox, A. (1998) *Outsourcing: A Business Guide to Risk Management Tools and Techniques* Boston, Earlsgate
4. Payne, T. (2000) *Facilities Management – A Strategy for Success* Chandos Publishing

III

Some Sodexho Contracts Summarised

Client/Partner	Relationship	Functions and Achievements
MoD Aldershot Garrison	Contract for 5 years + 2 year optional extension.	Accommodation services; stores management; administrative transport; kitchen deep cleaning; vehicle maintenance; typing & word processing; clerical support; PAs and secretaries; footwear repair; environmental health monitoring; domestic assistance; catering and mess management; office cleaning; POL point operation; window cleaning; chimney sweeping; laundry; dry cleaning; reproduction/ photocopying; tailoring; pest control; swill and kitchen waste; toxic waste; conservancy; road sweeping; grass cutting; primary medical care; grounds maintenance; caretaking; snow clearance; gardening; sports ground management; sanitary waste; clinical waste; general labouring.
	Monthly Contract Review, Resources and Finance Committee meetings.	
	Mechanism to incorporate PFI for longer term high investment projects.	
	Share of gains in general efficiencies above fixed profits level 60/40 in favour of MoD.	
	High level Steering Group (HSG) Quarterly review.	After 3 years, savings of 24% being delivered.
		Private Venture Gainshare generated during first four years of contract.

Client/Partner	Relationship	Functions and Achievements
Hasbro (European market leader in toys and games) (Stockley Park, UK and European HQ)	Strategic partnership outsourcing range of support services. Cleaning at Stockley Park based on output Specifications.	Reception; switchboard; help desk; staff and hospitality catering; vending; post room; goods in; photocopying; document archiving; meeting room management; cleaning; window cleaning; building services; security; portering. Staff restaurant serves each of 350 Hasbro staff at least once a day. Multi-skill training introduced following TUPE transfer of 15 staff. During HQ refurbishment catering provided to up to 150 contractors.
Hereford Hospital	A £65 million PFI development project; 30 year contract (from mid-1999) Consortium partners with Sodexho: – Alfred McAlpine, Charterhouse, W S Atkins Sodexho met weekly With the design team during planning and construction period. Phased occupation of wards and departments from November 2001 with final completion April 2003	Patient, staff and visitor catering; domestic/'hotel' service; linen and laundry; sterile services department (SSD); window cleaning; car park management; pest control. More than 300 staff transferred from Hereford NHS Trust under TUPE. ISO 9002 accreditation achieved almost a year ahead of contractual deadline. MDA registration achieved at first submission. High quality chilled meals, supplied by Sodexho's Tillery Valley Foods (TVF) are regenerated on the ward. New 'Spires' staff restaurant has capacity for 115,000 meals p.a. Sodexho operates a 100m2 'Just Trading' retail outlet and 'Caffe Toscana' for visitors.

Client/Partner	Relationship	Functions and Achievements
British American Tobacco (Glebe House headquarters)	Catering and support services partner.	Staff and hospitality catering; reception; help desk; CAD administration; waste management and recycling; vending; housekeeping; facilities administration; porterage.
(Cannon Street, London)	Support services contract.	Reception; catering for hospitality functions; vending; housekeeping.
(Rothmans Aylesbury)	FM contract.	Landlord services to other tenants in building.
CIBA Speciality Chemicals (Bradford)	Support services contract (January 2000).	Staff and hospitality catering; vending; office and laboratory cleaning; switchboard and helpline.
	Joint investment in new building works, fixtures and fittings to upgrade and develop restaurant facilities.	Most catering and cleaning staff transferred to Sodexho under TUPE. Improved terms and conditions.
	Improvement targets for performance levels in each service subject to regular joint reviews.	Increased job flexibility and multi-skilling in more positive working atmosphere.
Thales Optronics (Glasgow, St. Asaph, Staines)	Support services contract in three locations (extension to 2007).	Multi-lingual reception; translations; cleaning/window cleaning; Clean Room cleaning; hospitality; corporate entertainment mobile phone administration; heavy plant/electrical services;
	Monthly client meetings.	Clean Room laundry; hygiene services; pest control; airport transport; catering; security; gardening/interior plants; carpet cleaning; provision of uniforms; office administration assistance; vending; VIP tours; pool car administration; PAT testing; janitorial supplies; road gritting.
		Introduction of multi-skilling has delivered improved efficiency and greater flexibility. Marked improvements in service quality and cost savings on cleaning at Glasgow.

Client/Partner	Relationship	Functions and Achievements
University of Huddersfield (Storthes Hall Park)	Fixed price contract for soft facilities services (from 1995 and extended to 2002).	Security; mail distribution; planned preventative services; linen and laundry services; café bar; vending; special events; reception; retail; portering; key control and access; catering; bars; housekeeping; conferencing;
(Ashenhurst)	Contract to manage second site awarded (2000).	accommodation bookings; help-desk facility; waste management.
	Self-monitoring; student questionnaires.	ISO 9002 standard achieved. (December 2000).
	Regular meetings with client, senior residents and staff committees. Bi-monthly newsletter.	First ISO award among universities. Staff involved in NVQs, BIC Assessments, NEBS, IOSH and RIPHH certificates.
Epsom College	Catering consultancy (1982); full catering contract (1984); now three-year guaranteed contract.	Integrated telephone system; monthly billing, management and collection of payphones; full catering services, including college and private functions; holiday lettings and all commercial business; reprographics
	Facilities manager appointed through Sodexho (1997).	department and purchasing of paper; reception services; housekeeping for boarding houses and teacher accommodation; window
	Contract monitored by Bursar.	cleaning; vehicle procurement and maintenance; college laundry service; vending services; office
	Deputy facilites manager appointed (August 2000).	cleaning; school security; general labouring and portering services; stationery supply; school and office furniture supply; sanitaryware and dustmats throughout campus.
	Profit share on commercial business.	Turnover raised from £50,000 in 1998 to £250,000 in 2000.
		All college catering employees transferred to Sodexho under TUPE in 2000.

IV
Contributors' Contact Details

AMA Alexi Marmot Associates Ltd
Linton House C2
39–51 Highgate Road
London NW5 1RS
Tel: 020 7284 5888
Fax: 020 7284 5889
Email: mail@aleximarmot.com
Website: www.aleximarmot.com

Cap Gemini Ernst & Young
130 Shaftesbury Avenue
London W1D 5EU
Tel: 0870 905 3260/ 700 3260
Email: elias.mazzawi@cgey.com

Denton Wilde Sapte
5, Chancery Lane
Clifford's Inn
London EC4A 1BU
Tel: 020 7242 1212
Fax: 020 7404 0087

EC Harris
Lynton House
7–12 Tavistock Square
London WC1H 9LX
Tel: 020 7391 2744
Fax: 020 7388 6335
Email: weng.lee@echarris.com

FirstPerson Consulting
Medina Chambers
Town Quay
Southampton SO14 2AQ
Tel: 023 8023 1600
Fax: 023 8023 5300
Email: prcardwell@firstpersongroup.com

Fox Williams
City Gate House
39–45 Finsbury Square
London EC2A 1UU
Tel: 020 7628 2000
Fax: 020 7628 2100
Email: rmbaron@foxwilliams.com
Website: www.foxwilliams.com

Glasgow Caledonian University
Dept of Building & Surveying
Glasgow Caledonian University
City Campus
Glasgow G4 0BA
Tel: 0141 331 8631
Fax: 0141 331 3696
Email: J.R.Kelly@gcal.ac.uk

Heriot-Watt University
Dept of Building, Engineering and Surveying
Heriot-Watt University
Riccarton EH14 4AS
Tel: 0131 449 5111
Fax: 0131 451 3161

Hertfordshire County Council
County Hall
Hertford SG13 8DQ
Tel: 01992 556 216
Fax: 01992 556 206
Email: phil@pennant.demon.co.uk
Website: www.hertsdirect.gov.uk

International Centre for Facilities
440 Laurier Avenue West u200
Ottawa
Ontario
Canada K1R 7X6
Tel: 001 613 727 1788
Fax: 001 613 723 9167
Email: info@icf-cebe.com
Website: www.icf-cebe.com

Jonathan Reuvid
Little Manor
Wroxton St. Mary
Banbury
Oxfordshire OX15 6QE
Tel: 01295 738 070
Fax: 01295 738 090
Email: jr.wroxton@ndirect.co.uk

KLR Consulting
Suite 200
4170 Still Creek Drive
Burnaby
British Columbia
Canada V5C 6C6
Tel: 001 604 294 2292
Fax: 001 604 294 2694
Email: ken.robertson@klr.com
Website: www.klr.com

London Borough of Hillingdon
4S.01, Civic Centre
High Street
Uxbridge
Middlesex UB8 1UW
Tel: 01895 277 177
Fax: 01895 250 290
Email: pcordy@hillingdon.gov.uk
Website: www.hillingdon.gov.uk

Oxford Radcliffe Hospitals
The Churchill
Old Road
Headington
Oxford OX3 7LJ
Tel: 01865 225 427
Fax: 01865 225 396
Email: trevor.payne@orh.nhs.uk

Queensland University of Technology
Gardens Point Campus
2 George Street
GPO Box 2434
Brisbane Q4001
Australia
Tel: 0061 7 3864 1733
Fax: 0061 7 3864 1170
Email: d.then@qut.edu.au

Sodexho
Mandora
Louise Margaret Road
Aldershot
Hants GU11 2PW
Tel: 01252 352 000
Fax: 01252 352 029
Website: www.sodexho.co.uk

The Centre for Advanced Built Environment (CABER)
Tel: 0141 331 6038
Email: J.Hinks@caber.org.uk

Index of Advertisers